PRENTICE HALL LITERATURE

PENGUIN EDITION

Teaching Resources

Unit 4
Poetry

Grade Eight

PEARSON

Prentice Hall

Upper Saddle River, New Jersey
Boston, Massachusetts

ISBN 0-13-165368-7

1 2 3 4 5 6 7 8 9 10   09 08 07 06 05

Contents

Part 1 Context Clues

The Poetry of Jacqueline Woodson
Vocabulary and Reading Warm-ups 1
Listening and Viewing 5
Learning About Poetry 6
Model Selection: Poetry 7
Selection Test A 8
Selection Test B 11

Part 1 Concept Map 14

Diagnostic Test 7 15

Poetry Collection: Eleanor Farjeon, Walter de la Mare, Georgia Douglas Johnson
Vocabulary and Reading Warm-ups 18
Reading: Previewing to Determine Meanings from Context. 22
Literary Analysis: Sound Devices 23
Vocabulary Builder 24
Support for Writing an Introduction for a Poetry Reading 25
Support for Extend Your Learning. 26
Enrichment: Phases of the Moon 27
Selection Test A 28
Selection Test B 31

Poetry Collection: Eve Merriam; Nikki Giovanni; Alfred, Lord Tennyson
Vocabulary and Reading Warm-ups 34
Reading: Previewing to Determine Meanings from Context. 38
Literary Analysis: Sound Devices 39
Vocabulary Builder 40
Support for Writing an Introduction for a Poetry Reading 41
Support for Extend Your Learning. 42
Enrichment: Fingerprints 43
Build Language Skills: Vocabulary 44
Build Language Skills: Grammar 45
Selection Test A 46
Selection Test B 49

Poetry Collection: Patricia Hubbell, Richard García, Langston Hughes

Vocabulary and Reading Warm-ups 52
Reading: Rereading and Reading Ahead to Determine Meanings from Context 56
Literary Analysis: Figurative Language 57
Vocabulary Builder 58
Support for Writing a Study for a Poem 59
Support for Extend Your Learning 60
Enrichment: Concrete 61
Selection Test A 62
Selection Test B 65

Poetry Collection: Pablo Neruda, Elizabeth Bishop, Emily Dickinson

Vocabulary and Reading Warm-ups 68
Reading: Rereading and Reading Ahead to Determine Meanings from Context 72
Literary Analysis: Figurative Language 73
Vocabulary Builder 74
Support for Writing a Study for a Poem 75
Support for Extend Your Learning 76
Enrichment: Wind Force 77
Build Language Skills: Vocabulary 78
Build Language Skills: Grammar 79
Selection Test A 80
Selection Test B 83

Poetry by May Swenson, Billy Collins, and Dorothy Parker

Vocabulary and Reading Warm-ups 86
Literary Analysis: Comparing Humorous Imagery 90
Vocabulary Builder 91
Support for Writing to Compare Humorous Imagery 92
Selection Test A 93
Selection Test B 96

Writing Workshop: Writing for Assessment 99

Writing Workshop: Integrating Grammar Skills 100

Benchmark Test 7 101

Part 2 Paraphrase

Part 2 Concept Map. 107

Diagnostic Test 8 108

Poetry Collection: Robert Hayden, William Shakespeare, Ricardo Sánchez

Vocabulary and Reading Warm-ups 111
Reading: Rereading to Paraphrase. 115
Literary Analysis: Lyric and Narrative Poetry. 116
Vocabulary Builder. 117
Support for Writing 118
Support for Extend Your Learning. 119
Enrichment: Old Age and Harriet Tubman 120
Selection Test A 121
Selection Test B 124

Poetry Collection: Emma Lazarus, Henry Wadsworth Longfellow, Paul Laurence Dunbar

Vocabulary and Reading Warm-ups 127
Reading: Rereading to Paraphrase. 131
Literary Analysis: Lyric and Narrative Poetry. 132
Vocabulary Builder. 133
Support for Writing 134
Support for Extend Your Learning. 135
Enrichment: American Heroes 136
Build Language Skills: Vocabulary 137
Build Language Skills: Grammar 138
Selection Test A 139
Selection Test B 142

Poetry Collection: John Updike, N. Scott Momaday, Alice Walker

Vocabulary and Reading Warm-ups 145
Reading: Reading According to Punctuation to Paraphrase 149
Literary Analysis: Imagery. 150
Vocabulary Builder. 151
Support for Writing 152
Support for Extend Your Learning. 153
Enrichment: The Pulitzer Prize 154
Selection Test A 155
Selection Test B 158

Poetry Collection: Amy Ling, Wendy Rose, E. E. Cummings

Vocabulary and Reading Warm-ups 161
Reading: Reading According to Punctuation to Paraphrase 165
Literary Analysis: Imagery 166
Vocabulary Builder 167
Support for Writing 168
Support for Extend Your Learning 169
Enrichment: The Telegraph and the Telephone 170
Build Language Skills: Vocabulary 171
Build Language Skills: Grammar 172
Selection Test A 173
Selection Test B 176

Poetry by Robert Frost and Walt Whitman

Vocabulary and Reading Warm-ups 179
Literary Analysis: Comparing Types of Description 183
Vocabulary Builder 184
Support for Writing to Compare Description in Literary Works 185
Selection Test A 186
Selection Test B 189

Writing Workshop: Comparison-and-Contrast Essays 192

Writing Workshop: Integrating Grammar Skills 193

Spelling Workshop Support: Words with Prefixes and Suffixes 194

Communications Workshop: Evaluating Media Messages 195

For Further Reading 196

Benchmark Test 8 197

Answers 203

Vocabulary Warm-up Word Lists

Study these words from the poetry of Jacqueline Woodson. Then, apply your knowledge to the activities that follow.

Word List A

awhile [uh WYL] *adv.* for a short time
   I stayed <u>awhile</u> at the library, reading the newspapers.

dabbing [DAB ing] *n.* gently touching something, usually with a cloth
   Dad kept <u>dabbing</u> his chin where he cut himself shaving.

grins [GRINZ] *v.* smiles with a very big smile
   The toddler next door always <u>grins</u> and waves when she sees me.

regular [REG yuh luhr] *adj.* usual; not different or special
   On a <u>regular</u> school day, not during exams, I have about two hours of homework to do.

squints [SKWINTS] *v.* looks at something with eyes partly closed
   The boat captain <u>squints</u> into the sun as he steers us toward the dock.

upstate [UHP stayt] *adv.* in or toward the northern part of a state
   The winter weather is quite cold <u>upstate</u>, but the summers are balmy.

Word List B

lava [LAH vuh] *n.* hot melted rock
   In the pictures I have seen, <u>lava</u> looks like a boiling, red river.

maple [MAY puhl] *n.* a hardwood tree in northern areas that has sweet sap
   Every year we get sap from the <u>maple</u> in our yard and make syrup.

moment [MOH muhnt] *n.* a particular point in time
   My sixteenth birthday was an important <u>moment</u> in my life.

preacher [PREECH er] *n.* Minister; one who speaks about religion
   A <u>preacher</u> prepares a sermon for the weekly service.

superheroes [SOO puhr heer ohz] *n.* fictional characters with super powers
   As a child, I liked the <u>superheroes</u> who could fly through the air.

volcano [vahl KAY noh] *n.* a mountain that can erupt lava, rocks, gas, and ash
   Some scientists get very close to a <u>volcano</u> even when it is active.

Name _____ Date _____

Poetry by Jacqueline Woodson
Vocabulary Warm-up Exercises

Exercise A *Fill in each blank in the paragraph below with an appropriate word from Word List A. Use each word only once.*

My grandmother lives [1] _____, alone on a big farm. Last year,
I got to ride the bus up there by myself. It was a long trip! I would read
[2] _____, then sleep, then listen to music. A few times I looked around
at the other passengers. One man seemed sad, and he kept [3] _____
his eyes with a tissue. I spotted plenty of young people and older folks, too. A few riders
were dressed in strange outfits, but most of them wore [4] _____
clothes. Have you ever noticed how sometimes a person our parents' age
[5] _____ while reading? Does closing your eyes part way really help you
to see better? Anyway, my grandmother always [6] _____ when she sees
me. When I finally got off that bus, I don't know whose smile was bigger!

Exercise B *Revise the sentences so the underlined vocabulary words are used in logical ways. Be sure to keep each vocabulary word in your revisions.*

1. When <u>lava</u> and ash shoot out of a <u>volcano</u>, tourists are urged to get very close to take good pictures of the unusual sight.

   _____

2. Planting a <u>maple</u> in the front yard of a house in south Florida is a wise choice.

   _____

3. The <u>preacher</u> addresses his congregation each Sunday to talk about fire prevention.

   _____

4. When creating <u>superheroes</u>, the artists try to make them seem just like ordinary people.

   _____

5. The most amazing <u>moment</u> of the year was the month of July when I went to camp.

   _____

Name _____ Date _____

Poetry by Jacqueline Woodson
Reading Warm-up A

Read the following passage. Pay special attention to the underlined words. Then, read it again, and complete the activities. Use a separate sheet of paper for your written answers.

When life gets too hectic, it is soothing simply to enjoy nature. This is true for young people and adults alike. We all have many stresses during our <u>regular</u>, everyday lives. School, work, relationships, and responsibilities can sometimes weigh heavily on all of us. Taking <u>awhile</u> away from it all and, for a brief time, enjoying the beauty of nature can be very helpful.

Whether you are <u>upstate</u> among the lakes and mountains of the northern country, or farther south, or closer to a city, natural wonders are everywhere. Even a small park in the middle of town can be home to many plants and animals. If you are nowhere near a park of any kind, just look up at the sky! Clouds and their endless shapes are fun to watch during the day. Stars are lovely to see twinkling at night. In between are the amazing "light shows" of sunrise and sunset! Imagine how an artist <u>squints</u> at his painting, peering as he reaches for the perfect shading; the morning and evening skies seem to achieve this harmony with no effort at all.

Many people find that shifting their focus away from their worries and on to something bigger—like the natural world—can help to turn frowns into smiles, and even <u>grins</u>, This can happen more quickly than they might expect. Someone who might have been sadly <u>dabbing</u> a tear away might suddenly feel peaceful. Sometimes it is good to remind ourselves that we are only a very small part of a big world.

A hike on a shady woodland trail can be inspirational. The view of the nighttime sky from a city rooftop can be awe-inspiring. Even the sights right outside our windows can surprise us sometimes. Nature's gifts are everywhere.

1. Circle the word that means the same as <u>regular</u>. What is your *regular* morning routine?

2. Underline the words that describe what <u>awhile</u> is. Tell about something that you did *awhile* today or yesterday.

3. Circle the words that describe the opposite of <u>upstate</u>. Tell what *upstate* means.

4. Circle the word that is the opposite of <u>grins</u>. Then, underline the word that means the same as *grins*.

5. Underline the words naming what someone might be <u>dabbing</u>. What else might someone be *dabbing*?

6. Underline the word that tells what <u>squints</u> means. When someone *squints*, what are they doing?

Name _____ Date _____

Poetry by Jacqueline Woodson
Reading Warm-up B

Read the following passage. Pay special attention to the underlined words. Then, read it again, and complete the activities. Use a separate sheet of paper for your written answers.

When Tonya heard her family was moving to Hawaii, it was the most confusing day of her life. On one hand, she thought about how incredible it would be to live on a beach in one of the most beautiful places on earth. On the other hand, she could hardly stand to leave her friends in Chicago. That would the most horrible <u>moment</u> of her life. She blinked back the tears as she stared into the only backyard she had ever known. Her favorite climbing tree, the <u>maple</u>, was like an old friend, too. You could not climb a palm tree, could you?

Tonya's little brothers did not have mixed feelings because for them moving to Hawaii was an exciting new adventure. Her ten-year-old brother sounded like the family <u>preacher</u> when he said, over and over, "It is gonna be paradise!" Tonya's eight-year-old brother, who was currently very interested in seeing a real <u>volcano</u>, could not believe his good luck in going to an island where he might actually see <u>lava</u> flowing.

In the face of so much confidence about the move, Tonya fled to her room with her seesawing emotions. She wished she were eight or ten years old instead of thirteen. Back then, she still believed in <u>superheroes</u>, fairy-tale endings, and the ease of change. Now, practically a grown-up, she knew a move across the ocean to a strange place would not be magically easy. How would she make friends when she could not even surf? Wasn't that a requirement in Hawaii?

Tonya felt like throwing herself on the bed and crying. Then, she remembered that she was thirteen, practically a grown-up, and she should choose a more mature course of action. She took a deep breath, picked up the phone, and called her best friend Julia to discuss the news.

1. According to the passage, what would be the most horrible <u>moment</u> for Tonya? Explain what a *moment* is.

2. Underline the words giving more information about the <u>maple</u>. Then, describe a *maple* in your own words.

3. Circle the words identifying the person who sounded like a <u>preacher</u>. Then, explain why a *preacher* might talk about paradise.

4. Underline the words in the sentence that name the place where a <u>volcano</u> and <u>lava</u> can be seen. Then, write a sentence that explains the meanings of both *volcano* and *lava*.

5. Circle the words naming two other things Tonya believed in besides <u>superheroes</u>. Then, write a description of one of your favorite *superheroes*.

Jacqueline Woodson
Listening and Viewing

Segment 1: Meet Jacqueline Woodson
- How did Jacqueline Woodson's fascination with the "power of words" spark her interest in writing? Jacqueline Woodson tries to keep her writing "real and honest." What do you think that phrase means, and why is "real and honest" important?

_____
_____
_____
_____

Segment 2: Poetry
- Why does Jacqueline Woodson believe that the white space surrounding a poem on its page is important? How do you think poetry can give readers "room for free space" in their lives?

_____
_____
_____
_____

Segment 3: The Writing Process
- Why does Jacqueline Woodson call her writing "character driven"? Which one of Jacqueline Woodson's writing strategies would you use and why?

_____
_____
_____
_____

Segment 4: The Rewards of Writing
- In what way is writing rewarding to Jacqueline Woodson? Jacqueline Woodson thinks a writer must be brave and should welcome any reaction to his or her work. Do you agree or disagree with her? Why?

_____
_____
_____
_____

Learning About Poetry

Poets put words together to create a musical quality and highly charged meaning. A poem combines verbal music and meaning to create a fresh outlook on a subject.

Figurative language is imaginative writing or speech that is not meant to be taken literally. Here are some common figures of speech:

- A **simile** uses a word such as *like* or *as* to compare two apparently unlike things: *Her eyes were like beacons of light.*
- A **metaphor** compares two apparently unlike things but does not use *like* or *as*: *The grass was a carpet of green.*
- **Personification** gives human qualities to nonhuman or inanimate things: *The waves danced in glee.*

Poets use **images**—descriptive, sensory language appealing to the senses: sight, sound, touch, taste, and smell. Poets also use various sound devices:

- **Rhyme** is the repetition of sounds at the ends of words.
- **Meter** is the rhythmical pattern—or the arrangement and number of stressed and unstressed syllables—in a poem.
- **Alliteration** is the repetition of consonant sounds in the beginning of words, as in *fearsome foe.*
- **Assonance** is the repetition of similar vowel sounds in stressed syllables that end in different consonant sounds, as in *made* and *rail.*
- **Consonance** is the repetition of final consonant sounds after different vowel sounds in stressed syllables, as in *lend* and *hand.*
- **Onomatopoeia** is the use of words that imitate sounds, as in *rap, swish,* and *flutter.*
- **Repetition** is the use of any element of language—a sound, word, phrase, clause, or sentence—more than once.

DIRECTIONS: *Circle the letter of the answer that best matches each numbered item.*

1. comparison using *like* or *as*
   A. metaphor   B. personification   C. simile
2. pair of rhyming lines
   A. assonance   B. couplet   C. limerick
3. sensory language
   A. consonance   B. imagery   C. alliteration
4. pattern of stressed and unstressed syllables
   A. free verse   B. meter   C. consonance
5. a line of poetry that says, "Their words are trumpet blasts."
   A. simile   B. metaphor   C. personification
6. *buzz, clink, toll, hiss*
   A. personification   B. assonance   C. onomatopoeia

Name _____ Date _____

The Poetry of Jacqueline Woodson
Model Selection: Poetry

Two basic elements of poetry are sound and meaning. Poets use **sound devices**—such as rhyme, meter, alliteration, assonance, and onomatopoeia—to create musical effects with words. Poets use **figurative language**—such as simile, metaphor, and personification—to go beyond the ordinary meanings of words to express ideas or feelings in a striking way. Meaning also becomes vivid and memorable when it is conveyed through **imagery,** or words appealing to the senses: sight, sound, smell, taste, and touch.

DIRECTIONS: *Read the following passages from "Describe Somebody" and "Almost a Summer Sky." Then, use the space below each passage to answer the questions.*

I wrote, Ms. Marcus is tall and a little bit skinny. (from "Describe Somebody")

1. Name two sound effects in the preceding line. Which words are involved in each sound effect?

_____

Eric's voice was like something
that didn't seem like it should belong
to Eric.
Seemed like it should be coming out of an angel. (from "Describe Somebody")

2. What figure of speech do the preceding lines contain? What is being compared with what?

_____

_____

You know what I love about trees, Rodney says.
It's like . . . It's like their leaves are hands reaching
out to you. Saying Come on over here, Brother.
Let me just . . . Let me just . . .
Rodney looks down at me and grins.
Let me just give you some shade for a while. (from "Almost a Summer Sky")

3. What figure of speech is most prominent in the preceding passage?

_____

4. In the second line from "Almost a Summer Sky," which two words create the sound effect called assonance? Which words create alliteration?

_____

The Poetry of Jacqueline Woodson
Selection Test A

Learning About Poetry *Identify the letter of the choice that best answers the question.*

____ 1. Which word or phrase best explains what an *image* in poetry is?
    A. sensory language
    B. musical sound effect
    C. repetition
    D. simile

____ 2. Which of the following types of poetry tells a story?
    A. lyric
    B. haiku
    C. couplet
    D. narrative

____ 3. What is the name for poetry with no regular meter, no intentional rhyme, and no fixed line length?
    A. lyric
    B. ballad
    C. free verse
    D. haiku

____ 4. What is the general term for the words *popped, crackled, clanged,* and *murmured?*
    A. alliteration
    B. assonance
    C. consonance
    D. onomatopoeia

____ 5. What is the term for a figure of speech that uses *like* or *as* to compare two apparently unlike things?
    A. metaphor
    B. personification
    C. couplet
    D. simile

Critical Reading

____ 6. Who is Ms. Marcus in "Describe Somebody"?
    A. the speaker's foster mother
    B. Eric's mother
    C. Angel's sister
    D. the teacher

___ 7. Who has talent in science, according to the speaker in "Describe Somebody"?

A. Eric

B. Lamont

C. Angel

D. Miss Edna

___ 8. What can you conclude about Eric from the speaker's description of him in "Describe Somebody"?

A. Eric's singing had very little impact on the listeners.

B. Eric had chosen a piece that was too difficult for him.

C. Eric fears being teased for singing in a church choir.

D. Eric was preparing to resign from the choir.

___ 9. In the final lines of "Describe Somebody," why does the speaker say, "Now I gotta write a whole new poem"?

A. His first draft doesn't rhyme, but it should.

B. He knows that Ms. Marcus will not like his first draft.

C. He knows not to tell classmates about Eric's singing and choir robe.

D. He feels he hasn't praised Eric enough.

___ 10. In "Describe Somebody," what makes Miss Edna dab at her eyes during Eric's solo?

A. She is upset that he is ruining a favorite song of hers.

B. She is emotionally moved by the beauty of his voice.

C. She wishes Lonnie had gotten the solo part.

D. She is reacting to the preacher's earlier sermon.

___ 11. In "Almost a Summer Sky," what detail about life upstate made the biggest impression on Rodney?

A. the constant rain

B. the farm animals

C. the trees

D. the late-night whistle of a train

___ 12. Which of the following describes the relationship between Rodney and Lonnie in "Almost a Summer Sky"?

A. foster brothers

B. classmates

C. distant acquaintances

D. uncle and nephew

____ 13. Name the figure of speech in the following lines from "Almost a Summer Sky."

> No, upstate they got maple and catalpa and scotch pine,
> all kinds of trees just standing.
> Hundred-year-old trees big as three men.

What figure of speech do these lines contain?
   A. metaphor
   B. simile
   C. personification
   D. alliteration

____ 14. In "Almost a Summer Sky," what does the speaker say he "can't even imagine"?
   A. how big the trees are upstate
   B. why Rodney keeps talking about the trees
   C. moving away and living anywhere else but home
   D. why Ms. Marcus told him he had a poet's heart

____ 15. The *tone* of a poem is the author's attitude toward the characters, the subject matter, or the audience. Which of the following best describes the tone in "Almost a Summer Sky"?
   A. hostile
   B. sad
   C. affectionate
   D. indifferent

Essay

16. In both "Describe Somebody" and "Almost a Summer Sky," the speaker is Lonnie C. Motion. In an essay, first describe Lonnie in your own words. Then state whether you would like to know him personally, and explain why or why not.

17. The *theme* of a literary work is its central insight or overall message about human life or behavior. Authors sometimes state the theme of their works directly. More often, however, they invite readers to find clues in the work in order to figure out the theme themselves. In an essay, state what you think is the overall message of either "Describe Somebody" or "Almost a Summer Sky." Then, support your conclusion about the theme by mentioning specific details from the poem.

Name _____ Date _____

Selection Test B

Learning About Poetry *Identify the letter of the choice that best completes the statement or answers the question.*

____ 1. Which of the following poetic devices describes one thing as if it were something else but does not use *like* or *as*?
    A. simile
    B. metaphor
    C. onomatopoeia
    D. assonance

____ 2. In a poem, the rhythmical pattern, or the arrangement and number of stressed and unstressed syllables, is known as
    A. consonance.
    B. personification.
    C. symbolism.
    D. meter.

____ 3. Sensory language in a poem creates
    A. repetitions.
    B. rhymes.
    C. images.
    D. lyrics.

____ 4. The words *sizzle, hiss,* and *clink* are examples of
    A. alliteration.
    B. assonance.
    C. onomatopoeia.
    D. consonance.

____ 5. The type of poetry that expresses the thoughts and feelings of a single speaker in musical verse is called
    A. narrative.
    B. dramatic.
    C. ballad.
    D. lyric.

____ 6. How many lines does a haiku contain?
    A. 3
    B. 5
    C. 7
    D. 17

____ 7. Humorous five-line poems with a specific rhythmical pattern and rhyme scheme are called
    A. lyrics.
    B. sonnets.
    C. ballads.
    D. limericks.

Critical Reading

____ 8. In "Describe Somebody," what is it about Ms. Marcus that makes the speaker "feel all good inside"?
A. her pretty clothes
B. her smile
C. her promptness
D. the high grades she gives the speaker

____ 9. In "Describe Somebody," Angel and Lamont are good at
A. reading and math
B. science and drawing
C. history and civics
D. music and art

____ 10. In "Describe Somebody," the speaker has an unexpected insight about Eric
A. on the football field.
B. at a concert.
C. in a church.
D. at a meeting of the debate club.

____ 11. What figure of speech does the poet use in the following lines from "Describe Somebody"?

> Eric's voice was like something
> that didn't seem like it should belong
> to Eric.
> Seemed like it should be coming out of an angel.

A. simile
B. metaphor
C. personification
D. onomatopoeia

____ 12. Which of the following words or phrases best expresses the speaker's attitude toward Eric in "Describe Somebody"?
A. admiring but a little fearful
B. mocking
C. indifferent
D. critical but compassionate

____ 13. Based on the portrayal of Eric in "Describe Somebody," why do you think Eric gives the speaker a "mean look"?
A. Eric has always disliked the speaker.
B. Eric will be embarrassed if the speaker tells the class that Eric sings in the choir.
C. Eric is coming down with the flu and feels uncomfortable.
D. Eric feels that the speaker is making fun of him.

Name _____ Date _____

_____ 14. In "Almost a Summer Sky," where are Rodney and the speaker going?
    A. to the grocery store
    B. to the movies
    C. to a park
    D. upstate

_____ 15. Based on his words in "Almost a Summer Sky," what can you conclude about Rodney?
    A. He is bored living in the city.
    B. He has a deep love and appreciation for nature.
    C. He is not doing well in school.
    D. He often becomes impatient with Lonnie, the poem's speaker.

_____ 16. What poetic device appears in the following lines from "Almost a Summer Sky"?
    You know what I love about trees, Rodney says.
    It's like . . . It's like their leaves are hands reaching
    out for you. Saying Come on over here, Brother.
    A. rhyme
    B. personification
    C. consonance
    D. all the above

_____ 17. In "Almost a Summer Sky," why does the speaker mention Miss Edna's Sunday cooking and Lily's pretty dresses and great big smile?
    A. to show that he is a keen observer
    B. to stress how happy he is at home with his foster family
    C. to suggest that Rodney was wrong to live upstate
    D. to prove to Ms. Marcus that he has the heart of a poet

_____ 18. Which statement about "Describe Someone" and "Almost a Summer Sky" is true?
    A. They have the same speaker.
    B. They are both written in free verse.
    C. Ms. Marcus is a character in both poems.
    D. all the above

Essay

19. In "Describe Somebody" and "Almost a Summer Sky," Jacqueline Woodson uses many details to create a vivid picture of Lonnie and his surroundings. In an essay, select one of the poems, and identify three details that you think are especially important in that poem. Then, tell what kind of atmosphere, or mood, those details contribute to. Finally, discuss how the details and the atmosphere suggest the theme of the poem, or its central insight or message.

20. Select one of the poems—"Describe Somebody" or "Almost a Summer Sky"—and tell why it can be described as a lyric poem. Then, for the poem you have selected, go on to give an example of its figurative language, images, or repetition.

Name _____   Starting Date _____   Ending Date _____

Unit 4: Poetry
Part 1 Concept Map

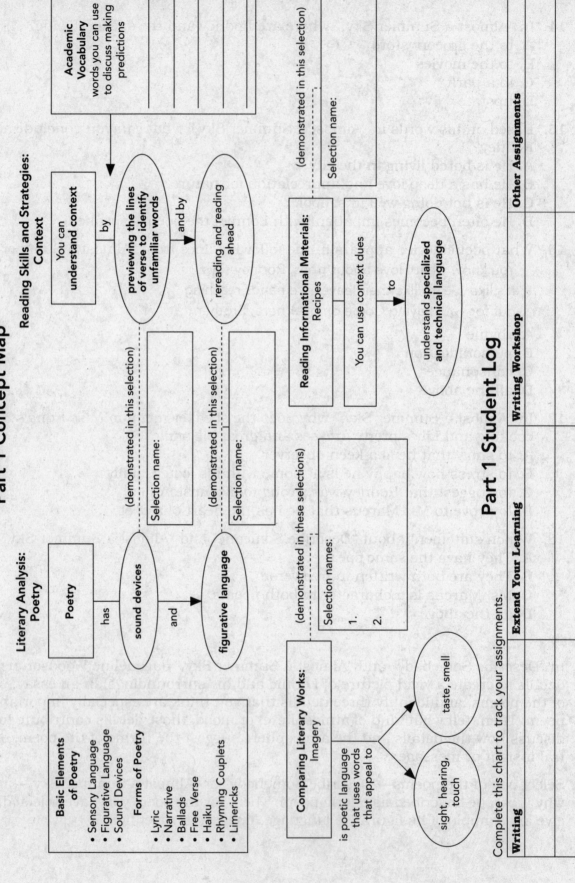

Reading Skills and Strategies: Context

You can understand context

by

previewing the lines of verse to identify unfamiliar words

and by

rereading and reading ahead

Academic Vocabulary words you can use to discuss making predictions

Literary Analysis: Poetry

Poetry

has

sound devices

and

figurative language

(demonstrated in this selection)

Selection name:

(demonstrated in this selection)

Selection name:

Basic Elements of Poetry
- Sensory Language
- Figurative Language
- Sound Devices

Forms of Poetry
- Lyric
- Narrative
- Ballads
- Free Verse
- Haiku
- Rhyming Couplets
- Limericks

Reading Informational Materials: Recipes

You can use context clues

to

understand specialized and technical language

(demonstrated in this selection)

Selection name:

Comparing Literary Works: Imagery

is poetic language that uses words that appeal to

taste, smell

sight, hearing, touch

(demonstrated in these selections)

Selection names:
1.
2.

Part 1 Student Log

Complete this chart to track your assignments.

Writing	Extend Your Learning	Writing Workshop	Other Assignments

14

Name _____ Date _____

MULTIPLE CHOICE

Read the selection. Then, answer the questions that follow.

International Space Station Alpha is a cooperative effort of the U.S. along with other countries, including Russia, Canada, and Japan. The science facility has been inhabited by astronauts continually since November 2000.

Due to the Earth's circular orbit, the space station orbits the Earth sixteen times a day. It is the job of Alpha astronauts to study changing conditions on the planet. They make careful observation using expert data from scientific equipment. They then add their own informal field notes from their observations.

Alpha crews describe the heart-pounding sensations that come from getting a stars-eye look at Earth. They also worry about troubling developments. Astronaut Frank Culbertson piloted shuttle missions in the early 1990s. He took command of ISS Alpha in 2001. An immediate surprise was the change in what he could observe of Earth's face. Pollution now creates a far more cloudy view than in the decade before. "There is smoke and dust in wider-spread areas than we have seen before. . . ," he explained in an interview. He also recalled the magnificent light shows on Earth's surface at night. "It's quite amazing to see how many people actually live down there . . . ," he marveled.

1. How many times per day does ISS Alpha orbit around Earth?
   A. 1
   B. 6
   C. 16
   D. 26

2. According to the information in the selection, what is the main purpose of ISS Alpha?
   A. to study the Earth and help us to understand our world better
   B. to see how long people can live and work in space
   C. to find out if people from different countries can work together
   D. to develop advanced weapons systems that will work in space

3. According to the selection, what is one troubling development that concerns ISS Alpha crews?
   A. night-time light shows from Earth's huge population
   B. conflicts between crew members from different countries
   C. faulty equipment on the space station giving incorrect data
   D. increasing smoke and dust from pollution in Earth's atmosphere

4. How does Frank Culbertson know that pollution is wider-spread now than it was a decade ago?
   A. He sees how many people live on the planet and realizes they must be spreading pollution.
   B. He was a shuttle pilot in the 1990s and saw less pollution from space then.
   C. He is simply drawing a logical conclusion that pollution must have spread during that time.
   D. He was told by others that pollution has spread over the last ten years.

5. Why do the night-time light shows on Earth's surface amaze Frank Culbertson?

A. They look like tiny, twinkling holiday lights.

B. They completely cover the face of the planet.

C. There are not as many lights as he would have thought.

D. They are evidence of how many people live on the planet.

6. Why do you think this selection was written?

A. to inform readers about ISS Alpha

B. to entertain readers with stories about life on ISS Alpha

C. to persuade readers to fight pollution

D. to make readers feel proud of the U.S. role in ISS Alpha

7. Which of the following choices best describes Frank Culbertson's reaction to his first view of Earth from ISS Alpha?

A. fear and regret

B. thrill and wonder

C. joy and confusion

D. amazement and concern

Read the selection. Then, answer the questions.

Like modern scientists, ancient astronomers learned a great deal from observing the stars. However, because they did not have the sophisticated instruments of modern astronomers, the ancients made a very important, but incorrect, assumption. For thousands of years, these astronomers believed that the Earth was at the center of the universe.

It was not until 1543 that Nicolaus Copernicus of Poland proposed a strange and intriguing theory: the Earth revolved around the sun. Many found it impossible to accept this sudden, abrupt turnabout from a long-held belief. Earth, as the center of the universe, placed humans in the central role. Copernicus's theories were rejected as false.

In the early 1600s, a crude telescope was invented. In Italy, Galileo Galilei refined the design to make it twenty times stronger than the human eye. Upon first using it, he immediately found undiscovered stars. He also located four moons revolving around Jupiter. He made other discoveries that similarly supported Copernicus's idea that the Earth, infact, does revolve around the sun. However, it wasn't until the late 1600s that the English scientist Sir Isaac Newton had new evidence that finally convinced people that Galileo and Copernicus were correct. "If I have seen further it is by standing upon the shoulders of giants," Newton wrote. Modern astronauts would surely agree.

8. What is the main focus of this selection?

A. the ancient idea that the universe revolves around the Earth

B. the lives of astronomers Copernicus, Galileo, and Newton

C. how astronomers proved that the Earth revolves around the sun

D. how modern scientists are more intelligent than ancient astronomers

9. The selection states that ancient astronomers learned about the stars and planets by simple observation. What was the main problem with relying on what could be seen with the naked eye?

A. They made incorrect assumptions.

B. They could not see anything useful.

C. They did not share their findings.

D. Each person saw somethign different.

10. What was the main reason why people rejected Copernicus's idea that the Earth revolves around the sun?

    A. because the first crude telescopes showed them that the sun was revolving around Earth

    B. because they thought Copernicus misunderstood his data

    C. because they did not want to think that humans were not at the center of the universe

    D. because their observations clearly told them that the opposite was true

11. What effect did the invention of the telescope have on the controversy about whether or not the Earth revolves around the Sun?

    A. It had no effect because Galileo was unable to find anything to support or disprove Copernicus's theory.

    B. Galileo was able to find some evidence that supported Copernicus's theory.

    C. It distracted most astronomers from the controversy, so the theory was forgetten for some time.

    D. Galileo was able to prove Copernicus's theory once and for all.

12. How did Galileo's discovery of new stars and of moons orbiting Jupiter effect Copernicus's theory?

    A. It was logical to assume from this discovery that the Earth, like Pluto, orbits the sun.

    B. It showed that Jupiter is a larger planet than Earth, so Earth must not be the center of the universe.

    C. He saw that some stars orbit Jupiter, so the entire universe must not be orbiting around Earth.

    D. He still assumed that the new stars and Jupiter were revolving around Earth, the center of the universe.

13. How long did it take to prove Copernicus's theory?

    A. almost 50 years

    B. a little less than 100 years

    C. about 150 years

    D. more than 200 years

14. Whose evidence convinced people that Earth revolves around the sun?

    A. Galileo Galilei

    B. Nicolaus Copernicus

    C. modern scientists

    D. Sir Isaac Newton

15. Why would modern astronauts agree with Newton's statement about "standing upon the shoulders of giants"?

    A. because stars and planets look like giants from space

    B. because they know that early astronomers Copernicus and Galileo were right about Earth revolving around the sun

    C. because all astronauts admire Sir Isaac Newton and his discoveries

    D. because they would not be able to go into space without the discoveries and inventions of those who came before them

Vocabulary Warm-up Word Lists

Study these words from the poetry collection. Then, complete the activities that follow.

Word List A

gleam [GLEEM] *v.* shine
   I liked how the wood floors would <u>gleam</u> after we cleaned them.

horizon [huh RY zuhn] *n.* where the land or water seems to meet the sky
   Watching the sun sink beneath the <u>horizon</u> is a wondrous sight.

peers [PEERZ] *v.* looks hard at something as if to see it more clearly
   Jerry <u>peers</u> down the country road, waiting for a car to come.

scampering [SKAM per ing] *n.* running with short, quick steps
   I saw the puppy <u>scampering</u> away with my shoe in its mouth.

scatter [SKAT er] *v.* to toss around here and there
   The strong wind will surely <u>scatter</u> the leaves that I raked into a pile.

throbbed [THRAHBD] *v.* beat quickly; pulsed
   My heart <u>throbbed</u> with excitement before my first plane ride.

Word List B

battered [BAT erd] *v.* hit something over and over
   Ancient warriors <u>battered</u> castle gates with huge logs to get through them.

casements [KAYS muhnts] *n.* window frames built so the windows swing outward
   We opened the <u>casements</u> wide, so a breeze could come in the windows.

immensity [i MEN si tee] *n.* hugeness or vastness
   I was shocked at the <u>immensity</u> of the trees in the redwood forest.

slithery [SLITH er ee] *adj.* slippery
   Misty loved watching the <u>slithery</u> eels in the huge tank.

thatch [THACH] *n.* dried straw used to make roofs
   I would guess that insects live in the <u>thatch</u> on those old houses.

uttermost [UH ter mohst] *adj.* farthest away; outermost
   I wonder how old the stars are at the <u>uttermost</u> parts of our galaxy.

Name _____ Date _____

Vocabulary Warm-up Exercises

Exercise A *Fill in each blank in the paragraph below with an appropriate word from Word List A. Use each word only once.*

I stand at the front of the boat, watching the sun [1] _____ and

sparkle on the waves. As far as I can see, all the way to the [2] _____,

there is nothing but the sea. Standing beside me, my little brother

[3] _____ into the water. He wants to see a dolphin. I remember

when I was his age and saw a whale emerge from the ocean. My whole body had

[4] _____ with excitement. My yells of joy had sent everyone

[5] _____ as fast as they could up the deck toward me. Now, years later,

I hope my brother can see a whale, too. Suddenly, just ahead, a giant form seems to

[6] _____ the waves everywhere as it shoots up toward the sky. "A

whale!" my brother and I scream.

Exercise B *Answer the questions with complete explanations.*

1. How do <u>casements</u> make windows different from those that move up and down?

   _____

2. Would you rather sleep on a mattress of <u>thatch</u> or one of cotton?

   _____

3. In which state, besides Hawaii, might you find a U.S. city at the <u>uttermost</u> point
   from a city in Alaska?

   _____

4. What would be happening if the ocean <u>battered</u> the rocky areas along the coast?

   _____

5. What do you think a small child might see as having <u>immensity</u>?

   _____

6. What, besides an animal, would you describe as <u>slithery</u>?

   _____

Poetry Collection: Eleanor Farjeon, Walter de la Mare, Georgia Douglas Johnson
Reading Warm-up A

Read the following passage. Pay special attention to the underlined words. Then, read it again, and complete the activities. Use a separate sheet of paper for your written answers.

As the sun sinks slowly over the <u>horizon</u> each evening, darkness creeps across the land. For many animals, this hour is the time to wake up and become active. As you prepare for bed, these nighttime are just awakening.

In a forest setting, as a person <u>peers</u> into the growing gloom and hustles home before nightfall, small animals like the raccoon begin <u>scampering</u> around. These animals are starting their nightly search for food. Red foxes, mule deer, and badgers join the raccoons on the prowl. However, all are as silent as possible. Some do not want to be heard by those they hunt. Others are quiet to protect themselves from animals that hunt them.

The peacefulness of the night is rarely disturbed by loud animal sounds. If forest animals do make noise, they usually are raising an alarm. Perhaps an enemy or a fire has been sighted.

Up in the sky, the moon begins to <u>gleam</u>. Then, you can spot other creatures of the night. Bats whir along, black as death. A barn owl swoops gracefully through the night air, its white face shining. Its dive toward the ground will <u>scatter</u> all small animals aware of the owl's presence. They are afraid of becoming the mighty bird's evening meal.

If you are lucky, you might also catch sight of a flying squirrel one night. Its cousin, the tree squirrel, whose body <u>throbbed</u> with activity and excitement all day, peacefully sleeps the night away in a snug nest. The flying squirrel, on the other hand, soars through the trees until morning. Always on the go, it watches the action above and below its path.

So, as you drift off into the land of dreams tonight, imagine creatures large and small roaming the night. If you listen very carefully, maybe you'll hear the quiet whoosh of a squirrel or the soft patter of a fox.

1. Underline the words that tell what happens at the <u>horizon</u> each evening. Then, explain what the *horizon* is.

2. Circle the words naming where a person in the forest <u>peers</u>. Then, explain why the word *peers* is a good word to use in describing this action.

3. Underline the words that tell what a person does while the small animals begin <u>scampering</u>. Then, explain what *scampering* means.

4. Circle the word naming what begins to <u>gleam</u>. Then, describe something else that might *gleam* at night.

5. Underline the sentence telling why the owl will <u>scatter</u> small animals. Then, explain what *scatter* means.

6. Circle the words telling with what the tree squirrel's body <u>throbbed</u> all day. Then, explain what *throbbed* means.

Name _____   Date _____

Poetry Collection: Eleanor Farjeon, Walter de la Mare, Georgia Douglas Johnson
Reading Warm-up B

Read the following passage. Pay special attention to the underlined words. Then, read it again, and complete the activities. Use a separate sheet of paper for your written answers.

Since the earliest times, long before <u>thatch</u> covered the tops of makeshift shelters, people have looked at the sky and dreamed of soaring above the world. Every night across our planet, <u>casements</u> are thrown open so people can lean out and look up at the heavens. As we wish upon stars, we wonder if we might ever reach them.

Each year, a few highly trained people get to move beyond these dreams to soar through the skies. Unafraid of the <u>immensity</u> of the universe, these people explore space. The first person to travel in space was the Soviet cosmonaut Yuri Gagarin. On April 12, 1961, his rocket shot into space. It traveled once around the Earth and then returned home. On July 20, 1969, American astronaut Neil Armstrong became the first person to stand on ground in a place other than Earth. On that day, he walked on the moon. Since then, many astronauts have traveled to space and back aboard space shuttles. Others have lived in space for months in a space station.

Space flight is not always a comfortable experience. Astronauts have to learn to move around in a weightless state. They hold onto lines, using twisting movements to avoid each other and all of the equipment. The bottoms of their shoes and the floor of the space vehicle are made of fabric that sticks together, which also helps the astronauts move around. <u>Slithery</u> surfaces would be a disaster for these space travelers.

Many astronauts suffer from space sickness during the first few days of flight. Whether the trip is smooth or the vehicle is <u>battered</u> by forces in space, astronauts might experience headaches, nausea, and heavy sweating.

Despite these and other uncomfortable parts of space flight, each trip is unforgettable. Astronauts describe the beauty of space and the amazing views of Earth from far away. As humans continue to explore the <u>uttermost</u> limits of our universe, people will always want to be part of the great adventure.

1. Underline the words describing where <u>thatch</u> was found. Then, explain what *thatch* is.

2. Circle the words naming the action that is taken with <u>casements</u>. Then, without using the word *casements*, rewrite the sentence in your own words.

3. Underline the name of something that has <u>immensity</u>. Then, explain why some people might be afraid of this *immensity*.

4. Circle the words in the previous sentence that are the opposite of <u>slithery</u>. Then, explain why *slithery* surfaces would be a disaster.

5. Circle the word that describes the opposite of a <u>battered</u> flight. Then, name some forces in space that might have *battered* space vehicles or stations.

6. Circle the word that tells what has <u>uttermost</u> limits. Explain why humans want to explore the *uttermost* limits.

Poetry Collection: Eleanor Farjeon, Walter de la Mare, Georgia Douglas Johnson
Reading: Preview to Determine Meanings From Context

Poetry often contains unusual words with which you may not be familiar. When you read a poem, it is a good idea to **preview** it, or examine it in advance, to identify any unfamiliar words. Then, as you read the poem more closely, look for clues in the **context** that can help you determine the meanings of these words. The **context** is the other words and phrases that surround a particular word. The following chart shows common types of context clues and an example of each. In the examples, the possibly unfamiliar words are underlined, and the context clues are in italics.

Clue	**Synonym/Definition:** words that mean the same as the unfamiliar word
Example	Knowing the importance of *exercise*, she does calisthenics every day.
Clue	**Antonym/Contrast:** words that mean the opposite of the unfamiliar word
Example	She does calisthenics every day, *but her brother is a couch potato*.
Clue	**Explanation:** words that give more information about the unfamiliar word
Example	Calisthenics *can improve your muscle tone and breathing*.
Clue	**Example:** a word or words that illustrate the unfamiliar word
Example	Calisthenics include *pushups and situps*.
Clue	**Sentence Role:** structural clue that indicates the unfamiliar word's part of speech
Example	Joanna *does* calisthenics every morning. [clearly a noun; seems to be an activity]

DIRECTIONS: *Answer these questions about words in the three poems in this collection.*

1. What synonym later in the poem shows the meaning of *git* in line 11 of "Cat!"? __

_____

2. A. In lines 26–27 of "Cat!" what does the context suggest that a *sycamore* is?

_____

   B. What other word is a clue to the meaning of *sycamore*? _____

_____

3. In line 3 of "Silver," what synonym shows the meaning of *peers*? _____

_____

4. In lines 5–6 of "Your World," what words give an explanation of *horizon*? _____

_____

5. A. Looking at the role of *reaches* in line 11, what part of speech is it? _____

_____

   B. From the context, what do you think *reaches* means here? _____

_____

Name _____ Date _____

Poetry Collection: Eleanor Farjeon, Walter de la Mare, Georgia Douglas Johnson
Literary Analysis: Sound Devices

Poets often use **sound devices** to make their poems more musical and memorable. Four of the most popular sound devices are rhythm, rhyme, alliteration, and onomatopoeia.

- **Rhythm** is the pattern of strong and weak beats, as in TWINkle TWINkle LITtle STAR.
- **Rhyme** is the repetition of sounds at the ends of words, as in *star* and *far.*
- **Alliteration** is the repetition of consonant sounds at the beginnings of nearby words, as in *twinkle* and *twist.*
- **Onomatopoeia** is the use of words that imitate sounds, such as *bang* and *sizzle.*

DIRECTIONS: *As you read the three poems in this collection, record on this chart examples of rhythm, rhyme, alliteration, and onomatopoeia.*

Poem	Rhythm	Rhyme	Alliteration	Onomatopoeia
"Cat!"				
"Silver"				
"Your World"				

Unit 4 Resources: Poetry

Poetry Collection: Eleanor Farjeon, Walter de la Mare, Georgia Douglas Johnson
Vocabulary Builder

Word List

kennel	flatterer	rapture

A. DIRECTIONS: *Using your knowledge of the underlined Word List words, circle* T *if the statement is true or* F *if the statement is false.*

T / F   1. Someone experiencing <u>rapture</u> is probably frowning.

T / F   2. A <u>flatterer</u> always tells the truth.

T / F   3. Dogs may be housed in a <u>kennel</u>.

B. DIRECTIONS: *Answer each question with a sentence that uses one of the Word List words. Use a different Word List word in each of your answers.*

1. What sort of person lavishly praises someone else?

_____

_____

2. Where might you keep your pet?

_____

_____

3. How might a person who is feeling absolutely wonderful describe his or her state?

_____

_____

C. DIRECTIONS: *For each related pair of words in CAPITAL LETTERS, circle the letter of the pair that best expresses a similar relationship.*

1. KENNEL : DOG : :
   A. ostrich : bird   C. book : library
   B. aquarium : fish   D. kitten : cat

2. FLATTERER : COMPLIMENT : :
   A. critic : insult   C. singer : dancer
   B. chatterer : praise   D. response : answer

3. HAPPINESS : RAPTURE : :
   A. sun : brightness   C. sorrow : tear
   B. love : like   D. anger : fury

Name _____ Date _____

Poetry Collection: Eleanor Farjeon, Walter de la Mare, Georgia Douglas Johnson

Support for Writing an Introduction for a Poetry Reading

Use this chart to jot down your ideas about what to include in your introduction to the poetry reading.

Title	
Author	
Subject	
New or Unusual Ideas	
Sound Devices	
Concluding Tips	

Name _____ Date _____

Support for Extend Your Learning

Research and Technology

Record the authors' dates and world events on this timeline. One listing has been done as an example.

1850	1875	1900	1925	1950	1975

•------------------------------Farjeon's lifetime-----------------------------•

1881   1965

Listening and Speaking

Use this chart to record details about the sound devices and the mood they create.

Poem Title and Author	
Mood of Poem	
Rhyme	
Rhythm	
Alliteration	
Onomatopoeia	

Name _____   Date _____

Poetry Collection: Eleanor Farjeon, Walter de la Mare, Georgia Douglas Johnson
Enrichment: Phases of the Moon

The light of the moon seen from Earth is the reflected light of the sun. The amount of light depends on the moon's position in relation to the sun and Earth. The different stages in the moon's appearance are called the **phases** of the moon. The moon goes through its phases every 29.5 days, or in just about one month.

The phases start with a **new moon,** when the moon is between the sun and Earth. The side facing Earth is completely dark. As the moon moves in its orbit, a thin curve becomes visible, called a **crescent moon.** When the moon reaches the point where it is at right angles to Earth and the sun, people call it a **half moon** because half the surface we think of as the moon is visible. As the moon grows bigger, it is called a **gibbous moon.** Finally, halfway through its cycle, it reaches the phase called the **full moon,** when Earth is between the moon and the sun, and the entire side of the moon facing Earth is lighted. The phases then move in reverse. During the period when the moon seems to become larger, it is said to be **waxing.** During the period when it seems to become smaller, it is said to be **waning.**

	First Quarter Moon	
Waxing Gibbous Moon	(Waxing Half Moon)	Waxing Crescent Moon
Full Moon		New Moon
Waning Gibbous Moon		Waning Crescent Moon
	Last Quarter Moon	
	(Waning Half Moon)	

DIRECTIONS: *Answer these questions based on what you have read.*

1. The word *month* has the same origins as the word *moon.* Explain the relationship.
   _____

2. Before the use of electricity, why do you think people preferred to travel during a full moon? _____
   _____

3. Before the use of electricity, during what phase of the moon did criminals most often commit their nighttime crimes? Why? _____
   _____

4. The verbs *wax* and *wane* can describe situations not related to the moon. Explain what they mean. Then, use *wane* in a sentence that is not about the moon. _____
   _____

Name _____ Date _____

Poetry Collection: Eleanor Farjeon, Walter de la Mare, Georgia Douglas Johnson
Selection Test A

Critical Reading *Identify the letter of the choice that best answers the question.*

____ 1. What seems to be happening in the poem "Cat!"?
   A. The speaker is chasing a cat.
   B. The speaker is feeding a cat.
   C. The speaker is petting a cat.
   D. The speaker is looking for a lost cat.

____ 2. Which of these words from "Cat!" is an example of onomatopoeia?
   A. ark
   B. wuff
   C. cat
   D. green

____ 3. Which statement best expresses the speaker's feelings about the cat in "Cat!"?
   A. The speaker loves it.
   B. The speaker admires its beauty.
   C. The speaker dislikes it and wants to drive it off.
   D. The speaker is afraid of it and does not like to go near it.

____ 4. What does the word *git* mean in the context of these lines from "Cat!"?
   > Git her, git her,
   > Whiskery spitter!
   > Catch her, catch her,
   > Green-eyed scratcher!

   A. catch
   B. scram
   C. scratch
   D. a small insect

____ 5. What does the poem "Silver" describe?
   A. the many stars in the nighttime sky
   B. a dark evening in a city
   C. an eerie, dead landscape
   D. a scene slowly lit up by moonlight

____ 6. Which words in this line from "Silver" are an example of alliteration?

This way, and that, she peers, and sees

A. *this* and *way*

B. *this* and *that*

C. *peers* and *sees*

D. none of the words

____ 7. In these lines from "Silver," what synonym for *peers* points to the word's meaning?

This way, and that, she peers, and sees
Silver fruit upon silver trees.

A. way

B. sees

C. silver

D. trees

____ 8. Which word does the poet repeat most often in "Silver"?

A. slowly

B. silently

C. silver

D. moon

____ 9. What does the speaker in "Your World" compare herself to?

A. a world

B. a bird

C. a rope

D. a song

____ 10. According to the speaker in "Your World," how big is a person's world?

A. as big as he or she makes it

B. not as big as he or she thinks

C. as big as time will allow

D. as big as a star

____ 11. What does the word *horizon* mean in the context of these lines from "Your World"?

But I sighted the distant horizon
Where the sky-line encircled the sea

A. a ship

B. the imaginary circle around the center of Earth

C. the line where the sky seems to meet the land or sea

D. the sound of ringing bells

Unit 4 Resources: Poetry
29

___ 12. Of "Cat!" "Silver," and "Your World," which poems use a regular pattern of rhyme at the ends of lines?
A. "Cat!" and "Silver"
B. "Silver" and "Your World"
C. "Your World" and "Cat!"
D. all three poems

___ 13. Which phrase from "Your World" best illustrates alliteration?
A. narrowest nest
B. close to my side
C. distant horizon
D. this immensity

Vocabulary and Grammar

___ 14. What kind of subject complement is used in this sentence?
That cat is a green-eyed little monster.

A. predicate noun
B. predicate pronoun
C. predicate adjective
D. There is no subject complement.

___ 15. Which word is most nearly *opposite* in meaning to the word *rapture*?
A. joy
B. opening
C. silence
D. depression

Essay

16. Write a short essay in which you explain what is happening in "Cat!" Tell what the speaker and the cat are doing and how the speaker feels about the cat.

17. Which of the three poems—"Cat!" "Silver," or "Your World"—do you think is the most musical? State your opinion in a short essay. Then, support your opinion with at least two examples of the poem's sound devices, such as rhythm, rhyme, onomatopoeia, and alliteration.

Poetry Collection: Eleanor Farjeon, Walter de la Mare, Georgia Douglas Johnson
Selection Test B

Critical Reading *Identify the letter of the choice that best completes the statement or answers the question.*

____ 1. In "Cat!" how does the speaker seem to feel about the cat?
   A. pleased
   B. annoyed
   C. affectionate
   D. sad

____ 2. Which word best describes the cat in "Cat!"?
   A. lazy
   B. cuddly
   C. spooky
   D. fast

____ 3. In these lines from "Cat!" what sound does the made-up onomatopoeic word *scritching* try to imitate?
   Scritching the bark
   Of the sycamore tree,
   A. the sound of scratching
   B. the sound of barking
   C. the sound of chewing
   D. the sound of weeping

____ 4. Which statement best describes the rhythm in "Cat!"?
   A. The short rhythmic lines capture the sound of the running animals.
   B. The even-numbered lines all have fewer beats than the odd-numbered lines.
   C. Every line opens with a stressed syllable followed by an unstressed syllable.
   D. all of the above

____ 5. Which phrase best describes the mood of the scene in "Silver"?
   A. magical and peaceful
   B. tense and scary
   C. dark and depressing
   D. beautiful but sad

____ 6. Based on the context, what does *shoon* mean in these lines from "Silver"?
   Slowly, silently, now the moon
   Walks the night in her silver shoon.
   A. hat
   B. shoes
   C. moonlight
   D. night

____ 7. Which sound is repeated most often at the start of words in "Silver"?
   A. the *s* sound
   B. the *k* sound
   C. the *l* sound
   D. the *th* sound

____ 8. How many strong beats occur in the following line from "Silver"?
   Slowly, silently, now the moon

   A. one
   B. two
   C. three
   D. four

____ 9. What change in herself does the speaker in "Your World" describe?
   A. She was once bold and daring, but now she is less confident.
   B. She was once like a child, but now she is more mature.
   C. She once lived a narrow life, but in time she grew more adventurous.
   D. She once was more worldly, but now she has become more spiritual.

____ 10. What does the context suggest that *abide* means in these lines from "Your World"?
   I know, for I used to abide
   In the narrowest nest in a corner

   A. obey
   B. welcome
   C. conceal
   D. remain

____ 11. Based on the following line, how many strong beats are there in each line of "Your World"?
   Your world is as big as you make it

   A. one
   B. two
   C. three
   D. four

____ 12. Based on the following lines, which statement most accurately describes the rhyme pattern in "Your World"?
   1 Your world is as big as you make it
   2 I know, for I used to abide
   3 In the narrowest nest in a corner
   4 My wings pressing close to my side

   A. The last words in each pair of lines rhyme.
   B. The last words in lines 1 and 3 rhyme, as do the last words in lines 2 and 4.
   C. The last words in lines 2 and 4 rhyme, but the last words in lines 1 and 3 do not.
   D. There is no rhyme pattern in "Your World."

_____ 13. Which poem in this collection makes the most frequent use of onomatopoeia?
   A. "Cat!"
   B. "Silver"
   C. "Your World"
   D. none

Vocabulary and Grammar

_____ 14. Where would you most likely find a *kennel*?
   A. in a movie theater
   B. in a hospital
   C. in the attic of a house
   D. in someone's backyard

_____ 15. Which sentence uses the underlined vocabulary word correctly?
   A. The <u>rapture</u> sang several songs on his latest album.
   B. The gift boxes were covered in bright <u>rapture</u> and ribbons.
   C. Staying up all night studying for a test is <u>rapture.</u>
   D. The team was in <u>rapture</u> after winning the county finals.

_____ 16. Which sentence contains a predicate adjective as subject complement?
   A. The moon shone brightly.
   B. The moon becomes more lovely on a clear night.
   C. The moonlight is a beautiful beacon.
   D. all of the above

_____ 17. Which sentence correctly uses a subject pronoun as a subject complement?
   A. The winners were Nancy and I.
   B. The last visitors were Jack and me.
   C. She looks like my sister and I.
   D. Her older brother became her mentor.

Essay

18. Write an essay about the mood, or atmosphere, in the poem "Silver." Explain how the poem's details, including its sound devices, help create that mood.

19. Write an essay about the worldview expressed in "Your World." First, restate that view in your own words. Be sure to cite examples from the poem to support your general statement about it. Then, react to the worldview, telling whether or not you agree with the poem's observations, and why.

Vocabulary Warm-up Word Lists

Study these words from the poetry of Eve Merriam; Nikki Giovanni; and Alfred, Lord Tennyson. Then, complete the activities that follow.

Word List A

ancient [AYN shuhnt] *adj.* from times long ago
   The Olympic Games began in <u>ancient</u> Greece.

captured [KAP cherd] *v.* taken by force
   When enemy troops are <u>captured</u>, they must be treated decently.

foul [FOWL] *adj.* horrible
   Why do shoes always have such a <u>foul</u> smell when they get wet?

funeral [FYOO ner uhl] *adj.* having to do with a ceremony held after a person has died
   The <u>funeral</u> flowers brought beauty to a sad day.

interior [in TEER ee uhr] *adj.* inside; of a person's private self
   My diary told about the thoughts and feelings of my <u>interior</u> world.

triumph [TRY uhmf] *n.* a feeling of joy because of success
   Our <u>triumph</u> at finally winning the state spelling bee was huge.

Word List B

atom [AT uhm] *n.* the smallest part of a simple substance
   An <u>atom</u> is the building block of every element in nature.

imprint [im PRINT] *v.* to fix in the mind or memory for a long time
   I wish I could <u>imprint</u> that song in my brain forever.

mournful [MAWRN fuhl] *adj.* filled with deep sadness
   I will never forget the <u>mournful</u> cry of our cat when she lost her kitten.

signature [SIG nuh cher] *n.* how you sign your name
   The bank will double-check the <u>signature</u> on a large check.

slander [SLAN der] *n.* bad and untrue things said about someone
   People have taken others to court for <u>slander</u>.

whorls [HWURLZ] *n.* the circular ridges on the pads of your fingers
   When I saw my fingerprint next to yours, I could see the difference in the <u>whorls</u>.

Name _____ Date _____

Vocabulary Warm-up Exercises

Exercise A *Fill in each blank in the paragraph below with an appropriate word from Word List A. Use each word only once.*

Since [1] _____ times, people have had special ways to celebrate the lives of those who die. In addition to holding fancy [2] _____ services, people have built great structures to honor the dead. The best examples are the pyramids of Egypt. If a pharaoh [3] _____ enemies or gained great wealth, for example, paintings and statues tell the story. They show the [4] _____ the rulers felt after such victories. The Egyptians even figured out how to avoid the [5] _____ odor of a dead body. If only we could know the [6] _____ minds of these brilliant people! The way they preserved the bodies is amazing! Looking at the mummies, you almost believe that the world of the pharaohs is still alive.

Exercise B *Answer the questions with complete explanations.*

1. What do your <u>signature</u> and the <u>whorls</u> on your fingertips have in common?
   _____

2. What would be required to see an <u>atom</u>?
   _____

3. What important fact or understanding would you like to <u>imprint</u> on the mind of every human?
   _____

4. Why do people take others to court for <u>slander</u>?
   _____

5. What has happened in your life, or in the lives of others, that has made you feel <u>mournful</u>?
   _____

Poetry Collection: Eve Merriam, Nikki Giovanni, Alfred, Lord Tennyson
Reading Warm-up A

Read the following passage. Pay special attention to the underlined words. Then, read it again, and complete the activities. Use a separate sheet of paper for your written answers.

Dr. Martin Luther King, Jr., brought about many important changes in American life. His words and deeds have served as a model for creating change without violence or <u>foul</u> actions. At age thirty-five, King became the youngest person to receive the Nobel Peace Prize. By this time, he had helped many African Americans begin to feel the <u>triumph</u> of gaining equal rights.

How did he do it? King never chose the easy path. Instead, he encouraged peaceful protest. With thousands of followers, he staged boycotts and marches to speak out against injustices in America. King was <u>captured</u> and taken to jail again and again. Yet, despite being taken by force, he continued to encourage peaceful protests.

King traveled more than 6 million miles and spoke some 2,500 times. His words inspired people from all corners of the country to work for social change. This included changes in education and employment opportunities for the poor and the blacks in America. Few have spoken as well and as honestly about the need for equal treatment for all.

King was a brilliant man whose <u>interior</u> life must have been extraordinary. He graduated from high school at fifteen, and received many degrees and awards during his lifetime. King's speeches are among the most famous of modern times. Some have compared his ability to inspire others to that of the greatest speakers of <u>ancient</u> times.

Sadly, King was shot to death at age thirty-nine. This tragic event touched all Americans. Two <u>funeral</u> services were held: one at his home church in Atlanta; and the other, at his college. The President of the United States honored King's memory by ordering that all American flags fly at half-mast that day. The entire nation felt the terrible loss of Dr. Martin Luther King, Jr. Since then, each January, a national holiday reminds us of the importance of Dr. King's life.

1. Underline the word that is described by <u>foul</u>. Give an example of *foul* behavior prompted by violence.

2. Underline the words that tell what led people to feel <u>triumph</u>. Then, tell about a time when you have had a feeling of *triumph*.

3. Underline the sentence that tells what resulted in King being <u>captured</u> and taken to jail. Explain what *captured* means.

4. Circle the word describing naming King's <u>interior</u> life. Then, explain why a very smart person might have an interesting *interior* life.

5. Underline the word in the previous sentence that means the opposite of <u>ancient</u>. Give an example of an *ancient* time or civilization.

6. Circle the words that tell where the <u>funeral</u> services for King were held. Write a sentence describing one *funeral* service for King as you imagine it might have been.

Name _____ Date _____

Poetry Collection: Eve Merriam, Nikki Giovanni, Alfred, Lord Tennyson

Reading Warm-up B

Read the following passage. Pay special attention to the underlined words. Then, read it again, and complete the activities. Use a separate sheet of paper for your written answers.

Many scientists are working in a new field called biometrics. They are looking for reliable ways to identify individuals. In other words, they want you, and nobody but you, to be able to identify yourself.

The days of a person's <u>signature</u> being proof of identity are gone. Too many people are able to copy the handwriting of others.

More modern approaches to identification look at the human body and things that are unique to each person. These include the <u>whorls</u> on the pads of your fingers, the pattern in the colored part of your eyes, and the structure of your face and palms. Taking fingerprints and then scanning a person's fingers to check for a match is one new way to identify people. Researchers at Michigan State University have created "the ID mouse." It looks like a computer mouse but has a scanner built in to check a person's fingerprints.

Other researchers focus on photography that computers will recognize. Although people often <u>imprint</u> others' faces in their minds, mistaken identity can happen. One person might look a lot like another person. With this new method, a scan of a person's face, eye, or palm must match what is in a computer to prove identity.

Many people are <u>mournful</u> about these new developments. They fear the consequences of too much personal information residing in one place. A new card being tested with airport workers, for example, includes fingerprints, eye scans, palm geometry, and a digital photo. If someone steals and uses this information, the theft of a person's identity would be complete. Imagine accusing the true cardholder of a crime committed by the identity thief! That person could then sue you for <u>slander</u>. All this because of a stolen identity!

Scientists have figured out how to split an <u>atom</u>, but biometrics might be some of the trickiest research ever.

1. Underline the word in the next sentence that gives a clue about the meaning of <u>signature</u>. Then, explain what a *signature* is.

2. Underline the words telling where <u>whorls</u> are located. Then, write a sentence using *whorls*.

3. Circle the words naming what people can <u>imprint</u> in their minds. Then, tell about something you want to *imprint* on someone's mind.

4. Underline the words explaining what people are <u>mournful</u> about. Then, rewrite the sentence using a synonym for *mournful*.

5. Underline the sentence that tells why you might be sued for <u>slander</u>. In your own words, explain why this is *slander*.

6. Circle the word telling what scientists learned to do to an <u>atom</u>. Based on what you know about an *atom*, why would this be so difficult?

Poetry Collection: Eve Merriam; Nikki Giovanni; Alfred, Lord Tennyson
Reading: Preview to Determine Meanings From Context

Context is the words and phrases that surround a particular word. When you read a poem, first **preview** it, or examine it in advance, to identify any unfamiliar words. Then, as you read the poem more closely, look for clues in the **context** that can help you determine the meanings of those words. The following list shows common types of context clues and an example of each. In the examples, the possibly unfamiliar words are underlined, and the context clues are in italics.

- **Synonym or Definition:** words that mean the same as the unfamiliar word
  It will soon be time to commence the race, so please get ready to *start*.
  She shopped in a boutique, *a small specialty store*.

- **Antonym or Contrast:** words that mean the opposite of the unfamiliar word or tell what the unfamiliar word is *not*
  The race will commence at 6 o'clock and *end* three hours later.
  Did you buy that in a boutique or in *a large chain store?*

- **Explanation:** words that give more information about an unfamiliar word
  A feline is *any animal of the cat family*.

- **Example:** words that illustrate the unfamiliar word
  Felines include *lions, tigers, and leopards*.

- **Sentence Role:** structural clue that indicates the unfamiliar word's part of speech. For example, in the following sentence, a reader can figure out that a *boutique* is a noun and that it is not abstract, since it can be entered.
  The two friends *entered* the boutique.

DIRECTIONS: *The chart below lists three words from this collection's poems. You may not be certain of their meanings. Use context clues to help you understand the words, and on the chart, write the clues you use and your best guess about each word's meaning. Then, check a dictionary to see if you were right about the meaning.*

Word	*unique*	*kettles*	*slander*
Location	"Thumbprint," line 3	"The Drum," line 4	"Ring Out, Wild Bells," line 22
Context Clues			
Likely Meaning			
Dictionary Meaning			

Name _____ Date _____

Literary Analysis: Sound Devices

Poets often use **sound devices** to make their poems more musical and memorable. The chart below shows four of the most popular sound devices.

Sound Device	Definition	Example
rhythm	the pattern of strong and weak beats	*HICKory DICKory DOCK*
rhyme	the repetition of sounds at the ends of words	*dock* and *clock*
alliteration	the repetition of consonant sounds at the start of nearby words	*clock* and *close*
onomatopoeia	the use of words that imitate sounds	*fizz, bubble*

DIRECTIONS: *Answer these questions about the sound devices used in the poems in this collection. Include the line numbers of any examples you list.*

1. What are two examples of alliteration in "Thumbprint"? _____
   _____

2. List two examples of onomatopoeia in "The Drum." Also, explain what sound each example imitates. _____
   _____

3. List one example of alliteration and one example of onomatopoeia in "Ring Out, Wild Bells." Also, explain what the onomatopoeia imitates. _____
   _____

4. Of the three poems in this collection, which one follows a pattern of rhymes at the ends of lines? Describe that pattern. _____
   _____

5. Focus on the rhythm of "The Drum" as you say the lines to yourself. What rhythm is the poet trying to imitate? _____
   _____

6. Given the subject, why is it appropriate that "Ring Out, Wild Bells" is such a musical poem? _____
   _____

39

Name _____   Date _____

Vocabulary Builder

Word List

singularity	resounding	strife

A. DIRECTIONS: *Using your knowledge of the underlined Word List words, circle* T *if the statement is true or* F *if the statement is false.*

T / F   1. A person known for his or her <u>singularity</u> is just like everyone else.

T / F   2. When an echo is <u>resounding</u>, it bounces off the walls.

T / F   3. Most people look forward to a day of <u>strife</u>.

B. DIRECTIONS: *Answer each question with a sentence that uses one of the Word List words. Use a different Word List word in each of your answers.*

1. Was there a lot of misery in the world during the twentieth century?

    _____

    _____

2. What quality might an independent person display?

    _____

    _____

3. What sort of music might you hear at a loud concert?

    _____

    _____

C. DIRECTIONS: *For each related pair of words in CAPITAL LETTERS, circle the letter of the pair that best expresses a similar relationship.*

1. CYMBAL : RESOUNDING : :
    A. question : responding
    B. meal : fasting
    C. motor : humming
    D. whisper : screaming

2. STRIFE : JOY : :
    A. misery : woe
    B. war : peace
    C. memory : belief
    D. smile : happiness

3. UNIQUE : SINGULARITY : :
    A. lonely : isolation
    B. love : romance
    C. special : unusual
    D. lie : honesty

Poetry Collection: Eve Merriam; Nikki Giovanni; Alfred, Lord Tennyson
Support for Writing an Introduction for a Poetry Reading

Use this chart to jot down your ideas about what to include in your introduction to the poetry reading.

Title	
Author	
Subject	
New or Unusual Ideas	
Sound Devices	
Concluding Tips	

Name _____ Date _____

Poetry Collection: Eve Merriam; Nikki Giovanni; Alfred, Lord Tennyson
Support for Extend Your Learning

Research and Technology
Records the authors' dates and world events on this timeline. One listing has been done as an example.

1800   1850   1900   1950   2000   2050
_____

•-----Merriam's lifetime-----•
1916   1992

Listening and Speaking
Use this chart to record details about the sound devices and the mood they create.

Poem Title and Author	
Mood of Poem	
Rhyme	
Rhythm	
Alliteration	
Onomatopoeia	

Poetry Collection: Eve Merriam; Nikki Giovanni; Alfred, Lord Tennyson

Enrichment: Fingerprints

The skin on the tips of our fingers has small ridges that help us grasp and hold on to things. These ridges form a pattern. When we touch something, oils from our skin leave an impression of this pattern on the surface we touch. This impression is called a fingerprint.

"Thumbprint" recognizes something that was not widely known until the late nineteenth century: except for identical twins, no two people's fingerprints are exactly alike. William Herschel, a British official in India in the 1870s, was one of the first to understand this important quality of fingerprints. He collected fingerprints as a hobby and noticed that each person's was a unique pattern. Herschel ended up using fingerprints as a way to identify people.

Eventually, police organizations came to understand the importance of fingerprints in identifying criminals. In 1892, Argentina became the first nation in the world to use fingerprinting as standard police procedure. Soon police forces in Europe and North America began collecting prints left at crime scenes and using them to help identify criminals. Today, the FBI fingerprint file contains millions of prints. All the information is computerized and shared with state and local police agencies across the country. Police use not only fingerprints but also footprints, hairs, fibers, blood, and genetic evidence based on traces of DNA left behind at crime scenes.

A. DIRECTIONS: *Answer these questions based on the information you just read and your own knowledge.*

1. How can the FBI fingerprint file help tie crimes together?

   _____

2. What kinds of surfaces do you think would probably provide the clearest fingerprints?

   _____

3. What environmental factors might spoil fingerprints left at crime scenes?

   _____

4. How might a criminal avoid leaving his or her fingerprints at a crime scene?

   _____

5. For what purposes other than crime investigation might fingerprints be used?

   _____

B. DIRECTIONS *In the space below or on a separate sheet of paper, write a description of your own thumbprint or someone else's. Your description can be factual or more imaginative—telling what the pattern reminds you of, for example.*

_____

_____

_____

Poetry Collections: Eleanor Farjeon; Walter de la Mare; Georgia Douglas Johnson; Eve Merriam; Nikki Giovanni; Alfred, Lord Tennyson

Build Language Skills: Vocabulary

The Suffix -ous

The suffix -ous means "having" or "full of." It is often added to nouns to turn them into adjectives. For example, in the adjective *synonymous*, -ous has been added to the noun *synonym*. A *synonym* is a word with the same or nearly the same meaning as another word. The new adjective, *synonymous*, means "having the same or nearly the same meaning."

A. DIRECTIONS: *Write a sentence that uses the adjective form of each noun. Form your adjectives by using the suffix -ous. In number 5, make a spelling adjustment to the noun when you add -ous.*

Example: (synonym) *Pretty* and *beautiful* are nearly <u>synonymous</u>.

1. (poison) _____

_____

2. (humor) _____

_____

3. (marvel) _____

_____

4. (thunder) _____

_____

5. (glory) _____

_____

B. DIRECTIONS *Circle* T *if the statement is probably true or* F *if the statement is probably false. Your vocabulary should include the underlined words.*

T / F 1. *Give* and *take* are *synonymous* words.

T / F 2. A <u>restatement</u> always uses the same words as the original statement.

T / F 3. A person's intention may seem different if his or her words are taken out of <u>context</u>.

T / F 4. You might check an encyclopedia to <u>confirm</u> that your facts are accurate.

T / F 5. When you <u>clarify</u> an idea, you keep it a mystery.

Poetry Collections: Eleanor Farjeon; Walter de la Mare; Georgia Douglas Johnson; Eve Merriam; Nikki Giovanni; Alfred, Lord Tennyson

Build Language Skills: Grammar

Subject Complements

A **subject complement** is a word that follows a linking verb and tells something about the subject. One kind of subject complement is called a predicate adjective. It describes the subject. Other kinds of subject complements are called a predicate noun and a predicate pronoun. They further identify the subject. A predicate pronoun uses the subject, not object, form.

Predicate Adjective:	The visitor seems lost. [*Lost* describes the subject, *visitor.*]
Predicate Noun:	He was the best *player* on the team. [*Player* further identifies the subject, *He.*]
Predicate Pronoun:	The winner is *she.* [*She* further identifies the subject, *winner.*]

A. PRACTICE: *Circle the subject complement in each sentence that contains a subject complement. On the line before the sentence, write* PN *if the subject complement is a predicate noun,* PP *if it is a predicate pronoun, and* PA *if it is a predicate adjective. If the sentence does not contain a subject complement, write* none *on the line.*

____ 1. Poems are often very musical.

____ 2. That word is an example of onomatopoeia.

____ 3. The last speaker in the choral reading was I.

____ 4. The rhythm of the poem sounded familiar to me.

____ 5. The bell sounded at the end of English class.

B. Writing Application: *Add to each subject in the items below to build a sentence that includes a linking verb and subject complement. Include at least one predicate noun, one predicate pronoun, and one predicate adjective in your sentences.*

1. The cat _____

2. Martin Luther King, Jr., _____

3. The fingerprint _____

4. The bravest person _____

5. The bells _____

Poetry Collection: Eve Merriam; Nikki Giovanni; Alfred, Lord Tennyson
Selection Test A

Critical Reading *Identify the letter of the choice that best answers the question.*

___ 1. In "Thumbprint," what does the speaker stress most about her thumbprint?
   A. It is slim and beautiful.
   B. It is strong and thick.
   C. It is smooth and unlined.
   D. It is one of a kind.

___ 2. To what does the speaker in "Thumbprint" compare her thumbprint?
   A. a signature
   B. a gold mine
   C. an atom bomb
   D. a math problem

___ 3. Which word from "Thumbprint" is an example of onomatopoeia?
   A. whirls
   B. treasure
   C. universe
   D. atom

___ 4. What does the word *imprint* mean in the context of these lines from "Thumbprint"?
   Imprint my mark upon the world,
   Whatever I shall become.

   A. publish
   B. leave
   C. use block letters
   D. travel

___ 5. Which of these statements best sums up "The Drum"?
   A. It is about the achievements of Martin Luther King, Jr.
   B. It is about a drum that was made in Africa and brought to America.
   C. It is about the drums of war.
   D. It tells of some associations that the poet has with drums.

___ 6. What does "The Drum" tell us about Kunta Kinte?
   A. He beat a drum as he led the rats from town.
   B. He played a drum when he recited poetry.
   C. He said, "I was a Drum Major for peace."
   D. He was making a drum when he was captured.

___ 7. In "The Drum," what examples of onomatopoeia help capture the sound of a drum?

    A. *pa-Rum* and *rat-tat-tat*

    B. *oompah* and *rat-a-tat*

    C. *pa-dum* and *boom boom boom*

    D. *ba-da-da* and *boom*

___ 8. Why does the poet mention the Pied Piper, Kunta Kinte, Thoreau, and King in "The Drum"?

    A. They all played drums.

    B. They used or spoke about drums.

    C. They were each drummed out of town.

    D. They were drum majors.

___ 9. For what occasion are the bells ringing in "Ring Out, Wild Bells"?

    A. a wedding

    B. a funeral

    C. the new year

    D. Easter

___ 10. What does the speaker of Tennyson's poem mean by the expression "ring out" in the following line?

    Ring out the old, ring in the new,

    A. squeeze dry

    B. grow silent

    C. welcome

    D. send away

___ 11. What does the word *want* mean in the context of this line from "Ring Out, Wild Bells"?

    Ring out the want, the care, the sin,

    A. desire

    B. need

    C. value

    D. immorality

___ 12. Which word in "Ring Out, Wild Bells" is an example of onomatopoeia?

    A. ring

    B. wild

    C. grief

    D. rhymes

_____ 13. Which poem in this collection uses a regular pattern of rhyme at the ends of lines?
   A. "Thumbprint"
   B. "The Drum"
   C. "Ring Out, Wild Bells"
   D. none of the poems

Vocabulary and Grammar

_____ 14. Which word is most nearly *opposite* in meaning to the word *strife*?
   A. joy   C. silence
   B. opening   D. misery

_____ 15. What kind of subject complement is used in the following sentence?
   That drum seems louder.
   A. predicate noun   C. predicate adjective
   B. predicate pronoun   D. none

Essay

16. Write a short essay in which you explain how the speaker in "Thumbprint" feels about her thumbprint. Tell what the thumbprint means to her.

17. Which of the three poems—"Thumbprint," "The Drum," or "Ring Out, Wild Bells"— do you think is the most musical? State your opinion in a short essay. Then, support your opinion with examples of the poem's sound devices, such as alliteration, onomatopoeia, rhythm, and rhyme.

Poetry Collection: Eve Merriam; Nikki Giovanni; Alfred, Lord Tennyson
Selection Test B

Critical Reading *Identify the letter of the choice that best completes the statement or answers the question.*

____ 1. In discussing her thumbprint, what does the speaker in "Thumbprint" recognize about herself?
   A. She is a part of nature.
   B. She is a criminal.
   C. She is her mother's daughter.
   D. She is unique.

____ 2. Which of these lines from "Thumbprint" does *not* contain alliteration?
   A. In the heel of my thumb
   B. Are whorls, whirls, wheels
   C. Can ever contain the same
   D. all of the above

____ 3. Why does the speaker compare her thumbprint to her signature?
   A. Both are unique indications of her individuality.
   B. Both are made in blue ink and appear on the same sheet of paper.
   C. Both control her "interior weather."
   D. Both are made with her right hand.

____ 4. Which is the correct meaning of *impress* in these lines from "Thumbprint"?
   My universe key,
   My singularity.
   Impress, implant,

   A. to inspire admiration
   B. to leave a mark
   C. to force to join the navy
   D. to seize for public use

____ 5. Which word is an antonym clarifying the meaning of *base* in these lines from "Thumbprint"?
   No other, however grand or base,
   Can ever contain the same.

   A. other
   B. grand
   C. contain
   D. same

____ 6. Which two sound devices contribute most to the drumlike sound in "The Drum"?
   A. alliteration and rhyme
   B. rhyme and onomatopoeia
   C. onomatopoeia and rhythm
   D. rhythm and rhyme

____ 7. What does *kettles* mean in the context of this line from "The Drum"?

　　　The big bass drums . . . the kettles roar . . . the sound of animal flesh

　　　A. pots
　　　B. guitars
　　　C. lions
　　　D. types of drums

____ 8. In "The Drum," what is the meaning of the remark "I was a Drum Major for peace" by Martin Luther King, Jr.?
　　　A. I constantly tried to encourage peace.
　　　B. I eventually found an inner peace.
　　　C. I saw the need for war as well as peace.
　　　D. I tried to silence the cries for peace.

____ 9. What does "The Drum" seem to be saying about life in general?
　　　A. Life is made up of all sorts of experiences, both good and bad.
　　　B. The person who makes the most noise gets the most.
　　　C. War is sometimes an easier choice than peace.
　　　D. It is dangerous to disturb the rhythms of nature.

____ 10. What is the speaker's main purpose in "Ring Out, Wild Bells"?
　　　A. to describe the sound of the bells
　　　B. to encourage people to behave morally
　　　C. to celebrate an important occasion in someone's life
　　　D. to express a message of hope at the new year

____ 11. What does the speaker mean by the following line from "Ring Out, Wild Bells"?

　　　Ring out false pride in place and blood,

　　　A. Send away false pride in one's social position or birth.
　　　B. Send away pride, which is a false value that keeps us from forgiving loved ones.
　　　C. Send away false pride instead of true pride in one's family background.
　　　D. Send away false pride in wealth or skill at warfare.

____ 12. In "Ring Out, Wild Bells," what is the effect of the repetition of *ring out* and *ring in*?
　　　A. It captures the sound of the bells ringing over and over.
　　　B. It stresses how cold and wild the winter weather is.
　　　C. It emphasizes how exasperated and angry the speaker is.
　　　D. It communicates a playful and somewhat puzzling tone.

____ 13. Which statement most accurately describes the rhyme pattern in these lines from "Ring Out, Wild Bells"?

> 1 Ring out the grief that saps the mind,
> 2 For those that here we see no more;
> 3 Ring out the feud of rich and poor,
> 4 Ring in redress to all mankind.

    A. The last words in each pair of lines rhyme.
    B. The last words in lines 1 and 3 rhyme, and the last words in lines 2 and 4 rhyme.
    C. The last words in lines 2 and 4 rhyme, but the last words in lines 1 and 3 do not rhyme.
    D. The last words in lines 1 and 4 rhyme, and the last words in the middle two lines rhyme.

Vocabulary and Grammar

____ 14. Which choice is a good example of *strife*?
    A. war   C. spring
    B. peace   D. loud music

____ 15. Which choice means the opposite of *singularity*?
    A. charity   C. conformity
    B. duplicity   D. marriage

____ 16. Which sentence contains a predicate adjective as subject complement?
    A. The bells rang loudly.   C. The bells are a beautiful sound.
    B. The bells grow louder every year.   D. all of the above

____ 17. Which sentence correctly uses a predicate pronoun as a subject complement?
    A. The last arrivals were Joe and I.
    B. This year's soccer champions were Lana and me.
    C. The tribute deeply touched my brother and I.
    D. My boyfriend became my best friend.

Essay

18. Write a brief essay in which you explain how the sound devices in "The Drum" help make the poem more effective. Discuss at least two different kinds of sound devices, citing specific examples.

19. Write a brief essay about the central message of "Ring Out, Wild Bells." Explain how the poem's details, including its sound devices, help convey that message.

Vocabulary Warm-up Word Lists

Study these words from the poetry of Patricia Hubbell, Richard García, and Langston Hughes. Then, complete the activities that follow.

Word List A

bulging [BUHLJ ing] *adj.* swelling out in a round shape or lump
 The huge frog, with <u>bulging</u> eyes, jumped into the water.

dew [DOO] *n.* small drops of water that form overnight outdoors
 I got up early, before the sun had dried up the <u>dew</u> on the grass.

direct [di REKT] *v.* to aim something in a particular direction
 Would you <u>direct</u> the heat vents more to my side of the car?

hose [HOHZ] *v.* to wash or pour water on something with a hose
 <u>Hose</u> off your muddy shoes before you come inside!

muck [MUHK] *n.* a substance that is sticky, wet, and dirty; mud
 After the floodwaters dried, the town was covered in <u>muck</u>.

perch [PERCH] *v.* to sit on the edge or on top of something
 We like to <u>perch</u> on the very top of the mountain and watch the sunset.

Word List B

concrete [KAHN kreet] *n.* building material made of cement, small stones, sand, and water
 The new art museum has strong walls of <u>concrete</u> with tiny windows.

elevator [EL uh vay ter] *adj.* relating to a machine that carries people up and down in a building
 We pushed all the <u>elevator</u> buttons but still the doors would not close.

raising [RAYZ ing] *v.* building; helping to rise to a standing position
 The workers were <u>raising</u> the house quickly to finish before winter.

tenders [TEN derz] *n.* caretakers
 The mayor hired three <u>tenders</u> to keep an eye on the town bonfire.

trough [TRAWF] *n.* long, open container for holding or mixing something
 The workers mixed cement in a large <u>trough</u> near the building site.

urban [UHR buhn] *adj.* having to do with a city
 In an <u>urban</u> area, life is often more hectic than in the country.

Name _____ Date _____

Vocabulary Warm-up Exercises

Exercise A *Fill in each blank in the paragraph below with an appropriate word from Word List A. Use each word only once.*

My shoes got wet with morning [1] _____ as I crossed the lawn to get the

newspaper. The [2] _____ plastic bag indicated a free sample inside.

Sure enough, when I opened the bag, I found a pouch of moist dog food, and it was

leaking onto the paper. I headed back to the house, knowing that I could never

[3] _____ off the paper and still read it. Just then, a red-throated bird

flew in front of me to [4] _____ on a high branch of the cherry tree.

While I followed it with my gaze, I stepped in a hole of gooey [5] _____

in the middle of the dirt-and-gravel path. Now, the paper wasn't the only thing that

needed cleaning off. It was only seven o'clock, but I had to [6] _____

my attention to two sloppy jobs before breakfast.

Exercise B *Revise each sentence so that the underlined vocabulary word is used in a logical way. Be sure to keep the vocabulary word in your revision.*

1. The <u>elevator</u> doors opened and we began to move sideways, from the shoe department to sporting goods.

   _____

2. We mixed cement in the sink while the vegetables drained in the <u>trough</u>.

   _____

3. The coal <u>tenders</u> let the supply of fuel run out.

   _____

4. Some <u>urban</u> shopping centers are far away from big cities.

   _____

5. The farmer is <u>raising</u> a new barn all by himself in just one day.

   _____

6. A floor made of <u>concrete</u> is much more likely to catch fire than one made of wood.

   _____

Poetry Collection: Patricia Hubbell, Richard García, Langston Hughes
Reading Warm-up A

Read the following passage. Pay special attention to the underlined words. Then, read it again, and complete the activities. Use a separate sheet of paper for your written answers.

The <u>dew</u> is still heavy on the grass. I take my dog, Rex, for his morning walk. The sun has risen just enough for us to walk safely without a flashlight. A nervous squirrel runs across our path. Then, it scurries up a tree to <u>perch</u> on a high branch and scold us from afar.

As I turn the corner, I see I am not the only one awake this early on a summer weekend. Justin is standing in front of his house. Alongside him is his white terrier, Terry. The dog has managed to get brown <u>muck</u> all over his coat. The bucket, brush, and shampoo bottle on the grass tip me off to what is about to happen.

Rex and I watch from a polite distance. Justin pulls out a ten-foot length of garden hose and turns on the faucet at the side of the house. He attempts to <u>direct</u> the stream of water at Terry. Of course, by now the dog has gotten wise to what is going on and high-tails it around to the other side of the house. I begin to doubt that Justin will manage to <u>hose</u> down anything but the front lawn.

From experience, I could tell Justin that he must get Terry on the leash in order to wash him, but I am curious to see if he will figure that out himself. When Justin disappears from sight, I think that is exactly what he has gone to do. Instead, he comes running back—not with Terry on a leash but with one pocket <u>bulging</u> at the side.

The next thing I know, Terry comes charging after him. He snaps his muzzle right on Justin's swollen pocket. Whatever is in the pocket must smell so good that Terry has risked a bath to follow its odor. Justin picks up the garden hose. With Terry still hanging onto his pocket, Justin begins washing off the slimy dirt. Now, why had not I thought of that?

1. Circle the sentence in the paragraph that explains why the <u>dew</u> is still on the grass. In your own words, explain what *dew* is.

2. Underline the place where the squirrel goes to <u>perch</u>. Give an example of some place you like to *perch*.

3. Circle the three objects named in the next sentence that give a clue to what <u>muck</u> is. Write about a time that you or someone else got covered in *muck*.

4. Circle what Justin attempts to <u>direct</u> at Terry. Rewrite the sentence, using a different word or words for *direct*.

5. Circle the words in the paragraph that help to understand <u>hose</u>. Explain whether you should *hose* down things inside a house.

6. Underline the word that tells what was <u>bulging</u>. Describe what you think was causing it to be *bulging*.

Poetry Collection: Patricia Hubbell, Richard García, Langston Hughes
Reading Warm-up B

Read the following passage. Pay special attention to the underlined words. Then, read it again, and complete the activities. Use a separate sheet of paper for your written answers.

If you live in a big <u>urban</u> area, you may take for granted the tall buildings that reach many stories above the city streets. For only a little more than a hundred years have workers been <u>raising</u> such tall buildings. There are a number of reasons for this.

Materials had to be strong enough to hold up tall structures. In older buildings, the walls carried the load, or weight, of the upper stories. There was a limit to how many floors could be built.

Then, some new building materials appeared. With these, builders could shift the load from walls to columns and beams.

One of these materials was ready-made steel that came from factories. Another was <u>concrete</u> that could arrive at a building site already formed into blocks. Sometimes, however, workers would make this substance at the building site by mixing cement, water, and other things inside a big <u>trough</u>. Then, they would pour the substance into molds.

Machines, such as cranes, had to be invented that could lift these huge blocks and pieces of steel high into the sky. <u>Tenders</u> of such heavy equipment have an important job. Safety rests on the shoulders of these workers who watch over bulldozers, cement mixers, cranes, and other heavy machinery. These people must be sure that everyone working on the buildings as well as those who will work or live inside them will be safe.

The <u>elevator</u> car was a nineteenth-century invention. Still, it waited patiently to rise to new heights until architects and builders created taller buildings. Advances in electricity, plumbing, heating, and air conditioning also helped to make taller buildings possible. In addition, using aluminum and glass on the sides of new buildings allowed outer walls to be lighter and to let in more light.

Even with all the advances in high-rise buildings, some critics believe that construction is an industry of low technology. We will see what changes as the twenty-first century progresses.

1. Underline two words that give clues to the meaning of <u>urban</u>. Explain whether or not you live in an *urban* area.

2. Circle what workers have been <u>raising</u>. Name some types of buildings that workers are *raising* in your town or state.

3. Underline what <u>concrete</u> is made of. Then, name something other than a high-rise building that is made of *concrete.*

4. Circle the words that tell what the <u>trough</u> was used for. Describe what else a *trough* might be used for.

5. Underline the words in the next sentence that tell what <u>tenders</u> of heavy equipment do. Write about a time that you were a *tender.*

6. Underline the pun (play on words) that the writer makes about the <u>elevator</u> car in the next sentence. Describe a trip you have made in an *elevator* car.

Poetry Collection: Patricia Hubbell, Richard García, Langston Hughes
Reading: Reread and Read Ahead to Determine Meanings From Context

Poetry often contains unusual words with which you may not be familiar. Nevertheless, you can often understand these words if you examine the **context**—the words and phrases surrounding an unfamiliar word. When you find an unfamiliar word, **reread and read ahead** for context clues that will help you figure out the meaning. When you think you have come up with a possible meaning, insert the meaning in place of the unfamiliar word, and reread the sentence. If it does not make sense, look for more context clues, or consult a dictionary.

In "Concrete Mixers" by Patricia Hubbell, for example, the word *ponderous* may be unfamiliar, but the context provides clues to its meaning.

Tough gray-skinned monsters standing *ponderous*,

Elephant-bellied. . . .

If you reread the line with *ponderous* and focus on "monsters standing" and then read ahead to "elephant-bellied," you can figure out from these clues that *ponderous* probably means "big and heavy."

DIRECTIONS: *Reread the poem "Concrete Mixers," looking for clues to the meaning of the underlined word in each item below. On the lines provided, write your best guess about the meaning of the word, and write the clue, if any, that pointed you to that meaning. When you are done, you can check the meanings in a dictionary.*

1. Likely meaning of <u>hose</u> in line 2: _____

   Clue(s): _____

2. Likely meaning of <u>muck</u> in line 5: _____

   Clue(s): _____

3. Likely meaning of <u>perch</u> in line 7: _____

   Clue(s): _____

4. Likely meaning of <u>bellow</u> in line 14: _____

   Clue(s): _____

5. Likely meaning of <u>urban</u> in line 16: _____

   Clue(s): _____

Name _____ Date _____

Literary Analysis: Figurative Language

Poets often use imaginative **figures of speech,** or **figurative language,** to make their poems more musical and memorable. Figures of speech often compare unlike things. A **simile** directly states the comparison of two unlike things by using a word such as *like* or *as*. A **metaphor** suggests a comparison between two unlike things by saying that one *is* the other. **Personification** compares something nonhuman to a human being by giving it human characteristics.

Similes: Life is like a dance. The ocean is as moody as a child.

Metaphor: Life is a dance.

Personification: The ocean laughs and cries.

DIRECTIONS: *On the chart below, record the desired examples.*

	Line Number(s)	What Two Things Are Compared	Type of Figure of Speech
1. Simile in "Concrete Mixers"			
2. Metaphor in "Concrete Mixers"			
3. Personification in "Concrete Mixers"			
4. Personification in "The City Is So Big"			

Name _____   Date _____

Poetry Collection: Patricia Hubbell, Richard García, Langston Hughes
Vocabulary Builder

Word List

ponderous   roam

A. DIRECTIONS: *Using your knowledge of the underlined Word List words, circle* T *if the statement is true or* F *if the statement is false.*

T / F   1. A skillful ballet dancer usually takes <u>ponderous</u> steps across the stage.

T / F   2. Some people tie up their dogs so that the dogs cannot <u>roam</u> the neighborhood.

B. DIRECTIONS: *Answer each question with a sentence that uses one of the Word List words. Use a different Word List word in each of your answers.*

1. What might a suitcase with lots of travel labels show about its owner?

   _____

   _____

2. What kind of suitcase would be hard to carry?

   _____

   _____

C. DIRECTIONS: *Select the letter of the word that means the* opposite *of the word in* CAPITAL LETTERS.

1. PONDEROUS
   A. weighty   B. clumsy   C. light   D. thoughtful

2. ROAM
   A. transport   B. wander   C. stay   D. explore

Name _____ Date _____

Support for Writing a Study for a Poem

Use this chart to jot down ideas about the figurative language that you hope to include in your poem about a city setting.

Comparison to Make	Wording to Use	Type of Figurative Language

Name _____ Date _____

Poetry Collection: Patricia Hubbell, Richard García, Langston Hughes
Support for Extend Your Learning

Research and Technology

Use this form to record information about the poems you choose for your mini-anthology. Under "Ideas for My Introduction," jot down points to be made and details to be included.

POEM 1	
Title of Poem	Author
Subject of Poem	Source
Ideas for My Introduction	

POEM 2	
Title of Poem	Author
Subject of Poem	Source
Ideas for My Introduction	

POEM 3	
Title of Poem	Author
Subject of Poem	Source
Ideas for My Introduction	

Listening and Speaking

After choosing the poem for your poetry recitation, write it on a separate sheet of paper so you can mark how to read the poem. For example, use capital letters for any words you plan to say louder than normal and tiny letters for any words you plan to say more softly. Use a bracketed *P* where you plan to pause or *LP* for a long pause. Put other notes about tone in brackets. Here is an example of how you might map out the beginning of "The City Is So Big."

Poem: The City Is So Big
The city is so BIG [LP]
Its bridges [shakily] qu-qu-QUAKE with fear [LP]

Name _____ Date _____

Enrichment: Concrete

Concrete, like that discussed in Patricia Hubbell's poem, is made from a mixture of cement, water, and inert materials such as sand or gravel. The inert materials are called aggregate. In a chemical process known as hydration, the cement reacts with the water (and the air that gets into the mixture naturally) to form a kind of paste that gradually hardens and holds together the inert materials, which do not participate in the reaction.

The ancient Egyptians knew how to make concrete. So did the ancient Romans, who used it at the base of monuments. Over time, however, the process of making concrete was nearly lost. It was revived in 1824 when a new kind of cement, called portland cement, was developed. Today, concrete is the most widely used construction material in the world.

There are three important factors in mixing concrete. The type of aggregate is one factor. Depending on the job, concrete is generally made with either a fine aggregate, such as sand, or a coarse aggregate, such as gravel. Generally, jobs requiring extremely strong concrete, like dams, need the coarsest aggregate. The water/cement ratio—the amount of water compared with the amount of cement—is another factor in mixing concrete. The higher the water/cement ratio, the more easily the concrete will flow before it hardens; the lower the water/cement ratio, the stronger the concrete will be later. The final factor in the mixing process is heat: The temperature must be kept steady to avoid cracking problems later.

A. DIRECTIONS: *Based on the passage above, write the definitions of each term below. Use context clues to help you with the meanings. Then, check the meanings in a dictionary.*

1. concrete: _____
2. inert: _____
3. aggregate: _____
4. hydration: _____
5. water/concrete ratio: _____
6. portland cement: _____

B. DIRECTIONS: *Imagine that you are an engineer at a construction site. On the lines below, list three questions you need to ask before you mix the concrete.*

1. _____
2. _____
3. _____

Poetry Collection: Patricia Hubbell, Richard García, Langston Hughes
Selection Test A

Critical Reading *Identify the letter of the choice that best answers the question.*

____ 1. What does "Concrete Mixers" describe?
   A. a rural village in Africa
   B. a zoo in India
   C. a construction site in a modern city
   D. a large corporation

____ 2. To what or whom does "Concrete Mixers" compare the operators of the concrete mixers?
   A. elephants
   B. elephant drivers
   C. firefighters
   D. hoses

____ 3. To what or whom does "Concrete Mixers" compare the mixing machines?
   A. elephants
   B. elephant drivers
   C. fire trucks
   D. washing machines

____ 4. What does the word *perch* mean in the context of these lines from "Concrete Mixers"?
   Their drivers perch on their backs like mahouts,
   Sending the sprays of water up.
   A. water
   B. sneeze
   C. fish
   D. sit

____ 5. What is the speaker doing in "Harlem Night Song"?
   A. hoping to join a band
   B. asking someone to join him or her
   C. giving a tour
   D. worrying about the weather

___ 6. In "Harlem Night Song," whom does the speaker seem to be addressing?

    A. a young child

    B. an elderly parent

    C. a homeless person

    D. someone he or she loves

___ 7. What kind of figure of speech do these lines from "Harlem Night Song" contain?

    Stars are great drops
    Of golden dew.

    A. simile

    B. metaphor

    C. personification

    D. none

___ 8. In the context of these lines from "Harlem Night Song," which word tells you that *dew* is probably some kind of moisture?

    Moon is shining,
    Night sky is blue.
    Stars are great drops
    Of golden dew.

    A. shining

    B. blue

    C. drops

    D. golden

___ 9. What does "The City Is So Big" suggest about the city?

    A. It is boring.

    B. It is actually very small.

    C. It is old and creaky.

    D. It is frightening.

___ 10. According to "The City Is So Big," where do people in the city "disappear"?

    A. in elevators

    B. on bridges

    C. on trains

    D. on moving stairs

___ 11. What does the word *quake* probably mean in the context of this line from "The City Is So Big"?

> Its bridges quake with fear

A. accident

B. shake

C. smile

D. stretch

___ 12. Which lines from "The City Is So Big" contain a simile?

A. The city is so big / Its bridges quake with fear

B. The lights sliding from house to house / And trains pass with windows shining

C. And trains pass with windows shining / Like a smile full of teeth

D. I have seen machines eating houses / And stairways walk all by themselves

___ 13. Which of these words often signal a simile?

A. *like* and *as*

B. *so* and *and*

C. *for* and *like*

D. none of the above

Vocabulary and Grammar

___ 14. Which word is most nearly *opposite* in meaning to the word *ponderous*?

A. light   **C.** awkward

B. strong   **D.** thoughtful

___ 15. What is the indirect object in the following sentence?

> The supplier needs to give us more cement for the concrete.

A. supplier   **C.** cement

B. us   **D.** concrete

Essay

16. You have read three poems about cities—"Concrete Mixers" by Patricia Hubbell, "Harlem Night Song" by Langston Hughes, and "The City Is So Big" by Richard García. Now, write a letter from one of the poets to another one. What might the poet writing the letter say about the other poet's poem? For example, what might Langston Hughes say to Richard García about "The City Is So Big," or what might Richard García say to Patricia Hubbell about "Concrete Mixers"?

17. Which of the three poems—"Concrete Mixers," "Harlem Night Song," or "The City Is So Big"—do you like best? State your opinion in a short essay. Then, support your opinion with examples of what you like, including the figurative language.

Poetry Collection: Patricia Hubbell, Richard García, Langston Hughes
Selection Test B

Critical Reading *Identify the letter of the choice that best completes the statement or answers the question.*

____ 1. What basic comparison controls the figures of speech in "Concrete Mixers"?
  A. Concrete mixers are elephants, and their drivers are elephant tenders.
  B. Concrete mixers are elephants, and their drivers are lions.
  C. Concrete mixers are like elephants' trunks, and their drivers are like elephants.
  D. Concrete mixers are like elephants, and their trunks are like hoses.

____ 2. In "Concrete Mixers," what seems to be the speaker's feelings about the concrete mixers?
  A. She thinks they are an ugly eyesore in the city.
  B. She thinks they are interesting and impressive.
  C. She thinks they are mysterious and frightening.
  D. She thinks they are boring and repetitious.

____ 3. Which of these lines in "Concrete Mixers" contains a metaphor?
  > The drivers are washing the concrete mixers;
  > Like elephant tenders they hose them down.
  > Tough gray-skinned monsters standing ponderous,
  A. the first line
  B. the second line
  C. the third line
  D. none of the above

____ 4. In these lines from "Concrete Mixers," which context word provides a synonym for *urban*?
  > Concrete mixers are urban elephants,
  > Their trunks are raising a city.
  A. concrete
  B. elephants
  C. raising
  D. city

____ 5. From the context of these lines in "Concrete Mixers," what can you assume about the word *bellow*?
  > Move like elephants
  > Bellow like elephants
  > Spray like elephants
  A. *Bellow* is a verb.
  B. *Bellow* is something elephants do.
  C. *Bellow* probably does *not* mean "move."
  D. all of the above

___ 6. What sort of night is described in "Harlem Night Song"?
   A. cold and windy
   B. bright and pleasant
   C. quiet and eerie
   D. dangerous but exciting

___ 7. Based on the content, what can you assume the speaker in "Harlem Night Song" enjoys?
   A. literature
   B. movies
   C. music
   D. sports

___ 8. From the details in "Harlem Night Song," how do you think Langston Hughes felt about the New York City neighborhood known as Harlem?
   A. He enjoyed it and found it a vibrant place.
   B. He tolerated it.
   C. He found it dull and stifling.
   D. He found its people arty and snobbish.

___ 9. Which of these passages from "Harlem Night Song" uses figurative language?
   A. Come / Let us roam the night together
   B. Moon is shining.
   C. Night sky is blue.
   D. Stars are great drops / Of golden dew.

___ 10. Which word best describes the mood, or atmosphere, of "Harlem Night Song"?
   A. tragic
   B. angry
   C. suspenseful
   D. joyful

___ 11. In using the simile "like a smile full of teeth" to describe the passing train in "The City Is So Big," what is the speaker suggesting about the train?
   A. It is warm and welcoming.
   B. It is somewhat menacing.
   C. It is false and deceitful.
   D. It spits out passengers at every stop.

___ 12. What is the logical explanation of "machines eating houses" near the end of "The City Is So Big"?
   A. termites eating wood houses with machinelike speed
   B. cars entering garages in houses
   C. machinery knocking down old buildings to put up new ones
   D. a computer game in which houses are gobbled

____ 13. In what way do the people actually "disappear" in "The City Is So Big"?
   A. They cannot be seen once they go inside the buildings.
   B. They disappear behind closed elevator doors.
   C. They are murdered.
   D. They move to the suburbs.

____ 14. Which line from "The City Is So Big" is an example of personification?
   A. Its bridges quake with fear
   B. I have seen machines eating houses
   C. And stairways walk all by themselves
   D. all of the above

Vocabulary and Grammar

____ 15. Which of these things would you most likely describe as *ponderous*?
   A. an unabridged dictionary
   B. a bright green leaf
   C. a leather wallet
   D. a lace bedspread

____ 16. Which sentence contains an indirect object?
   A. The city is my favorite place.
   B. City life gave me wonderful experiences.
   C. Riding the subway makes me nervous.
   D. all of the above

____ 17. Which sentence correctly uses a pronoun as a direct object?
   A. The best runners were Pedro and me.
   B. My mom gave me a lift to school.
   C. My sister resembles my mother and I.
   D. Take me to the next bus stop, please.

Essay

18. Write a short essay in which you examine the figurative language in "Concrete Mixers." Explain what the concrete mixers are compared to, what the parts of the concrete mixers are compared to, and what the drivers of the concrete mixers are compared to. Then, show how all these comparisons are related.

19. Write an essay in which you compare and contrast the impressions of city life given in all three poems—"Concrete Mixers," "Harlem Night Song," and "The City Is So Big." Then, react to the impressions by giving your own opinion of city life and citing examples or other details to support it.

Vocabulary Warm-up Word Lists

Study these words from the poetry of Pablo Neruda, Elizabeth Bishop, and Emily Dickinson. Then, complete the activities that follow.

Word List A

cicada [si KAY duh] *n.* a large, winged insect, the males of which make a loud sound
   I heard my first <u>cicada</u> of the summer humming in the tree.

drifting [DRIFT ing] *adj.* moving slowly in the air or on water
   The wind loosened the leaf that I saw <u>drifting</u> toward the ground.

limp [LIMP] *adj.* not firm
   To keep the carrot strips from going <u>limp</u>, place them in water.

relieved [ri LEEVD] *adj.* glad because a worry or stress is gone
   We were <u>relieved</u> when the tornado finally passed our town.

rut [RUHT] *n.* a deep track in the ground made by a wheel
   We didn't see the <u>rut</u> in the road and drove over it bumpily.

sawing [SAW ing] *adj.* like the sound of a hand saw
   The <u>sawing</u> noise coming from the garage woke us up early.

Word List B

boulevard [BOOL uh vahrd] *n.* a wide street, often tree-lined
   The <u>boulevard</u>, twelve lanes wide, had a grassy center strip.

diadem [DY uh dem] *n.* a crown worn as a sign of royalty
   The queen wore a sparkling <u>diadem</u> on her head.

heron [HAIR uhn] *n.* a long-necked, long-legged bird that lives near water
   I saw a graceful white <u>heron</u> standing in the shallow water.

keys [keez] *n.* small, low islands near the shore
   During the hurricane, water washed over several <u>keys</u> in the bay.

latticework [LAT is wurk] *n.* a structure of crisscross strips
   The tree's branches formed a natural <u>latticework</u> that let in little light.

mangrove [MAN grohv] *adj.* relating to tropical tree that grows near water and has thick roots
   <u>Mangrove</u> trees grow in salty water along the shore.

68

Poetry Collection: Pablo Neruda, Elizabeth Bishop, Emily Dickinson
Vocabulary Warm-up Exercises

Exercise A *Fill in each blank in the paragraph below with an appropriate word from Word List A. Use each word only once.*

It was the kind of sunny, hot, muggy summer afternoon that made you feel tired
and [1] _____ right down to your bones. To add to my discomfort, one
[2] _____ after another was "serenading" me with its loud
[3] _____ noise. The sound, [4] _____ through the air
from trees far and near, had reached the level of annoyance that could drive a person
crazy. Just as I thought there was no chance of being [5] _____ of my
discomfort, I noticed a low band of clouds headed in my direction. The sky briefly dark-
ened, and a cool breath of fresh air ruffled the curtains. Rain suddenly burst from the
clouds, quickly filling the [6] _____ in the driveway with water. Just as
suddenly, the rain stopped and the sun beat down anew.

Exercise B *Decide whether each statement below is true or false. Circle T or F. Then, explain your answer.*

1. A <u>boulevard</u> is usually narrower than a country lane.
   T / F _____

2. It is unlikely that a poor farmer would own a <u>diadem</u>.
   T / F _____

3. The <u>mangrove</u> tree is one of the few types of trees that grow high on a mountain.
   T / F _____

4. <u>Keys</u> are large, mountainous islands such as Iceland and Greenland.
   T / F _____

5. In wooden <u>latticework</u>, all the strips of wood run in the same direction.
   T / F _____

6. The <u>heron</u> is one of the few birds that live in high rocky places.
   T / F _____

Name _____ Date _____

Read the following passage. Pay special attention to the underlined words. Then, read it again, and complete the activities. Use a separate sheet of paper for your written answers.

I was used to the fall lingering well into November, with roses still blooming as we sat eating Thanksgiving turkey. Here in the country, however, snow began dropping the first of November. Nearly a foot of the white stuff fell, <u>drifting</u> with the wind into mounds three feet high. That was only the beginning.

By the time the first crocus appeared during the last week of March, we had seen nearly a hundred inches of snow. The white blanket had been almost continuous for five months. The three-day thaw and rain in January had temporarily freed us from the snow, only to replace it with mudslides. Every <u>rut</u> in every road was filled with water or mud.

Spring took a while longer to arrive, and not without two more hefty snowstorms. Far from disappointing us, however, spring overwhelmed us. Hardly had the daffodils bloomed than tulips and irises followed. Before we knew it, wild roses and wisteria were spilling over the corral fence.

I had expected my first summer in the country to be a lot more bearable than in the city. It was true. The temperature and humidity were much lower. Also, we had gotten to the third week of July without so much as a sign—or sound—of a <u>cicada</u>. I didn't miss the loud <u>sawing</u> noise of that ugly insect all morning and afternoon.

Well, the cicadas did arrive, and the weather grew hot and muggy. I turned into the human counterpart of a wet, <u>limp</u> dishrag. It was not to last long, though. Fall arrived on a cool breeze in September, and my senses were <u>relieved</u>. Rain soon cleaned the air rather than making it stickier. I did not sneeze nonstop through September and October, as I usually did in the city.

When November rolled around again, I left the country, but it was not because of the weather. In fact, that year, with its dramatic seasons, would be one to remember forever.

1. Circle the cause of the <u>drifting</u> snow. Write a sentence that describes something else you might see *drifting*.

2. Underline the phrases that help you understand the meaning of <u>rut</u>. Tell about the damage a *rut* in a road can do.

3. Circle the words in the next sentence that tell what a <u>cicada</u> is and the sound it makes. Describe something else that makes a *sawing* noise.

4. Circle the words in the paragraph that tell why the writer felt like a wet, <u>limp</u> dishrag. Describe a *limp* handshake.

5. Underline what caused the writer's senses to be <u>relieved</u>. Tell about a time that you were *relieved* and explain what caused the change.

Name _____ Date _____

Read the following passage. Pay special attention to the underlined words. Then, read it again, and complete the activities. Use a separate sheet of paper for your written answers.

A <u>mangrove</u> tree is an unusual kind of tree. It grows along tropical shores, including the southern Gulf Coast of Florida. There are two reasons why mangrove trees can live in the muck and shallow water along the coast. First, unlike most other trees, they can survive in salty water. Second, their roots form a thick <u>latticework</u> that look like twisted stilts. Some of these roots take in air so that the tree can "breathe" in the mud.

These amazing trees grow in mangrove <u>keys</u>, or low-lying islands. The so-called Ten Thousand Islands are hundreds of tiny keys that stretch along the Gulf Coast of Florida north of the Everglades National Park. They play an important role in the area's ecosystem. They protect the shore from winds and floods. When mangrove leaves and branches fall into the water, they become the first link in important food chains for both land and sea creatures.

Tiny marine creatures hatch and feed among the mangrove roots. They become food for shrimp, other shellfish, and fish. Those, in turn, become food for birds and turtles. White-tailed deer eat their fill of plants. All of these creatures may wind up as food for crocodiles.

During a storm, the gulf may flood a key. An area between thick growths of trees then becomes a watery <u>boulevard</u> where wading birds stroll, foraging for food. An egret stirs up mangrove roots to find a fish, a frog, or insects. A <u>heron</u> dips its long beak into the water and comes up with dinner.

A huge nest atop a mangrove tree has survived the storm. The bird's nest looks like a strange <u>diadem</u>, or crown, for a giant. Soon, it will be a safe place for young osprey to hatch and grow.

You can see that a mangrove key is the site of much activity. In recent years, people have realized that they must help protect the balance of life there.

1. Underline the words that tell you what a <u>mangrove</u> tree is. Tell whether a *mangrove* tree could grow where you live.

2. Circle the words that help give you a picture of what <u>latticework</u> is. In a sentence, describe what a pie's *latticework* top crust would look like.

3. Underline the definition of <u>keys</u>. Write a sentence using this meaning of *keys*.

4. Underline the word that describes this <u>boulevard</u>. Describe a *boulevard* that you may have been on or heard of.

5. Circle the words in the paragraph that tell what kind of creature a <u>heron</u> is. Based on the description, what might be dinner for a *heron*?

6. Circle the synonym for <u>diadem</u>. Tell about someone you have seen wearing a *diadem*.

Name _____ Date _____

Poetry Collection: Pablo Neruda, Elizabeth Bishop, Emily Dickinson
Reading: Reread and Read Ahead to Determine Meanings From Context

Poetry often contains unusual words with which you may not be familiar. Nevertheless, you can often understand these words if you examine the **context**—the words and phrases surrounding an unfamiliar word. When you find an unfamiliar word, **reread and read ahead** for context clues that will help you figure out the meaning. When you think you have come up with a possible meaning, insert the meaning in place of the unfamiliar word, and reread the sentence. If it does not make sense, look for more context clues, or consult a dictionary.

DIRECTIONS: *The chart below lists three words from this collection's poems that you may not immediately be able to define. Use context clues to help you understand the words, and on the chart, write the clues you find and your best guess about each word's meaning. Then, check a dictionary to see if you were right about the meaning.*

Word	*latticework*	*heron*	*uninjured*
Location	"Ode to Enchanted Light," line 5	"Little Exercise," line 7	"Little Exercise," line 21
Context Clues			
Likely Meaning			
Dictionary Meaning			

Unit 4 Resources: Poetry
© Pearson Education, Inc., publishing as Pearson Prentice Hall. All rights reserved.
72

Name _____.   Date _____

Literary Analysis: Figurative Language

Poets often use **figures of speech**, or **figurative language**, to make their poems more musical and memorable. The chart below lists and explains three common figures of speech.

Figure of Speech	Definition	Example
simile	a comparison of two unlike things as if they are alike, using a comparing word such as *like* or *as* to state the comparison	The wind is like a cheerleader.
metaphor	a comparison of two unlike things as if they are alike, suggested by stating one thing *is* another	The wind is a cheerleader.
personification	a comparison of something nonhuman with something human, suggested by giving the nonhuman thing human characteristics	The wind sang in a loud, cheerful voice.

DIRECTIONS: *Answer these questions about the figurative language in "Ode to Enchanted Light." Include the line numbers of any examples you list.*

1. List two similes that help the reader picture the light in "Ode to Enchanted Light."
   _____

2. Which simile in the first nine lines do you think best captures the enchanted mood the poet wants to convey? Why? _____
   _____

3. Explain how the details about the cicada involve personification. _____
   _____

4. With what metaphor does "Ode to Enchanted Light" conclude? _____
   _____

5. What feelings, or mood, does the final metaphor help convey? _____
   _____

73

Name _____ Date _____

Poetry Collection: Pablo Neruda, Elizabeth Bishop, Emily Dickinson
Vocabulary Builder

Word List

uneasily	unresponsive	rut	debates

A. DIRECTIONS: *Using your knowledge of the underlined Word List words, circle* T *if the statement is true or* F *if the statement is false.*

T / F   1. A nightmare can make someone sleep <u>uneasily</u>.

T / F   2. Daydreamers are sometimes <u>unresponsive</u> when you ask them a question.

T / F   3. Every homeowner likes a big <u>rut</u> in the driveway.

T / F   4. Someone who <u>debates</u> all her decisions probably acts much too quickly.

B. DIRECTIONS: *Answer each question with a sentence that uses one of the Word List words. Use a different Word List word in each of your answers.*

1. When might a doctor conclude that someone is in a coma?

_____

_____

2. What does a person usually do when he or she has a big decision to make?

_____

_____

3. How do some people sleep when they are worried about a great danger?

_____

_____

4. What might a heavy-wheeled vehicle leave on a dirt road?

_____

_____

Name _____ Date _____

Support for Writing a Study for a Poem

Use this chart to jot down ideas about the figurative language that you hope to include in your poem about a natural setting.

Comparison to Make	Wording to Use	Type of Figurative Language

75

Poetry Collection: Pablo Neruda, Elizabeth Bishop, Emily Dickinson
Support for Extend Your Learning

Research and Technology

Use this form to record information about the poems you choose for your mini-anthology. Under "Ideas for My Introduction," jot down points to be made and details to be included.

POEM 1	
Title of Poem	Author
Subject of Poem	Source
Ideas for My Introduction	

POEM 2	
Title of Poem	Author
Subject of Poem	Source
Ideas for My Introduction	

POEM 3	
Title of Poem	Author
Subject of Poem	Source
Ideas for My Introduction	

Listening and Speaking

After choosing the poem for your poetry recitation, write it on a separate sheet of paper so you can mark how to read the poem. For example, use capital letters for any words you plan to say louder than normal and tiny letters for any words you plan to say more softly. Use a bracketed *P* where you plan to pause or *LP* for a long pause. Put other notes about tone in brackets. Here is an example of how you might map out the beginning of "Ode to Enchanted Light."

Poem: Ode to Enchanted Light
Under the trees [P] LIGHT
has dropped from the [amazed tone:] TOP of the SKY, [LP]

Name _____ Date _____

Enrichment: Wind Force

Storms can cause a great deal of destruction on small islands like the mangrove keys in "Little Exercise." Scientists use the Beaufort scale to measure the force of the winds.

Beaufort Scale of Wind Force			
Beaufort Number	**Wind Speed (mph)**	**Description**	**Effect at Sea**
0	less than 1	Calm	Sea is like a mirror.
1	1–3	Light air	Ripples look like scales without foam crests.
2	4–7	Light breeze	Small wavelets appear; crests look glassy but do not break.
3	8–12	Gentle breeze	Large wavelets appear. Crests begin to break. Foam looks glassy, perhaps with scattered whitecaps.
4	13–18	Moderate breeze	Small waves appear, becoming longer; whitecaps are fairly frequent.
5	19–24	Fresh breeze	Moderate waves arise, taking a longer form; many white caps appear (with some chance of spray).
6	25–31	Strong breeze	Large waves; whitecaps everywhere, with some spray.
7	32–38	Moderate gale (high wind)	Sea heaps up, and white foam from breaking waves begins to blow in streaks.
8	39–46	Fresh gale	Moderately high, longer waves appear; edges of crests break. Foam is blown.
9	47–54	Strong gale	High waves appear. Sea begins to roll. Spray may affect visibility.
10	55–63	Whole gale	Very high waves with long crests. Sea looks white. Rolling of the sea becomes heavy. Visibility is affected.
11	64–72	Storm	Exceptionally high waves. (Small and medium-sized ships might be lost to view behind the waves.) The sea is covered with foam and froth. Visibility is affected.
12–17	73 and above	Hurricane	The air is filled with foam and spray. Sea is completely white with a driving spray. Visibility is seriously affected.

DIRECTIONS: *On a separate sheet of paper, write your own description of a bad storm as it approaches and hits a coastal area, an island, or a ship at sea. Trace the progress from a calm day to a nasty one by using the information in the Beaufort scale. If you like, you can write your description in the form of a poem.*

Name _____ Date _____

Build Language Skills: Vocabulary

The Suffix -*ment*

The suffix -*ment* means "the act of" doing something or "the state of" being something. It is often added to verbs to turn them into nouns. For example, in the noun *restatement*, -*ment* has been added to the verb *restate*. To *restate* is to say again. The new noun, *restatement*, means "the act of saying something again" or "something in the state of being said again."

A. DIRECTIONS: *Write a sentence that uses the noun form of each verb. Form your nouns by using the suffix -ment. In number 5, make a spelling adjustment to the verb when you add -ment.*

> **Example:** (restate) His <u>restatement</u> expressed the same ideas in simpler language.

1. (require) _____

   _____

2. (involve) _____

   _____

3. (develop) _____

   _____

4. (excite) _____

   _____

5. (argue) _____

   _____

B. DIRECTIONS: *Complete each sentence using each word in the box only once.*

synonymous   restatement   context   confirm   clarify

1. The meaning of a word depends on its _____.
2. The words *poetry* and *verse* are _____.
3. Because the vocabulary in the poem is difficult, the teacher gave us a _____ in simpler language.
4. The teacher had to _____ the meaning of some of the words for us.
5. Once you have guessed the meaning of a word, you can _____ that you are correct by checking a dictionary.

Name _____ Date _____

Build Language Skills: Grammar

Direct and Indirect Objects

A **direct object** is a noun or pronoun that follows an action verb and receives the action of the verb. It answers the question *What?* or *Whom?* after the action verb. (A direct object does not appear after a linking verb.)

Sonya brewed some *tea.* [*What* did Sonya brew?]

The aroma tempted *them.* [*Whom* did the aroma tempt?]

An **indirect object** is a noun or pronoun that comes between an action verb and a direct object. It answers the question *To or for whom?* or *To or for what?* after an action verb. You cannot have an indirect object without a direct object.

Sonya brewed her *guests* some tea. [*For whom* did Sonya brew some tea?]

Sonya gave each *cup* a different flavor. [*To what* did Sonya give a different flavor?]

Pronouns used as direct or indirect objects require the object form of the pronoun.

Incorrect: We visited *Sue and he.* **Correct:** We visited *Sue and him.*

Incorrect: Sal gave *Dave and I* help. **Correct:** Sal gave *Dave and me* help.

A. PRACTICE: *Underline the direct object and circle the indirect object in each sentence that contains one or both. If the pronoun form is incorrect, cross it out and write the correct form on the line after the sentence. If there is no direct or indirect object in the sentence, write* none *on the line.*

1. Nature plays a strong role in her poetry. _____

2. The poem's speaker gives us advice about human relationships.

   _____

3. The last poem really impressed Nancy and I. _____

4. The images show readers the speaker's feelings. _____

5. The biggest fans of her poetry are Celia and Mary. _____

B. Writing Application: *Add to each subject in each item below to create a sentence that includes an action verb and a direct object. Also, include an indirect object in two of your sentences.*

1. The heavy machinery _____

2. Great poets _____

3. My thoughts _____

4. The glowing light _____

5. The islanders _____

Name _____ Date _____

Critical Reading *Identify the letter of the choice that best answers the question.*

____ 1. What kind of scene does "Ode to Enchanted Light" describe?
  A. a natural scene
  B. a city scene
  C. an underground scene
  D. an indoor scene

____ 2. What might be the light described "like a green latticework of branches" in "Ode to Enchanted Light"?
  A. moonbeams
  B. rays of sunlight
  C. rays from a searchlight
  D. none of the above

____ 3. What example of personification does "Ode to Enchanted Light" contain?
  A. It compares the light to a green latticework of branches.
  B. It compares the light to clean white sand.
  C. It describes cicadas sending their song into the air.
  D. It describes the world as a glass overflowing with water.

____ 4. How many similes do these lines from "Ode to Enchanted Light" contain?
     light
     like a green
     latticework of branches,
     shining
     on every leaf,
     drifting down like clean
     white sand.
  A. none
  B. one
  C. two
  D. three

____ 5. In "Little Exercise," what sort of scene does the speaker ask us to picture?
  A. a hot day at a crowded beach
  B. a violent storm blowing up
  C. a battle scene
  D. a magical dark night

_____ 6. What two things does this simile from "Little Exercise" compare?

> Think of a storm roaming the sky uneasily
> like a dog looking for a place to sleep in,

    A. a storm and a dog
    B. a storm and the sky
    C. the sky and a dog
    D. a dog and sleep

_____ 7. In these lines from "Little Exercise," what does the context suggest that a *heron* is?

> . . . occasionally a heron may undo his head,
> shake up his feathers, . . .

    A. an actor
    B. the speaker
    C. the poet
    D. a bird

_____ 8. What happens at the end of "Little Exercise"?
    A. Someone drowns.
    B. A bridge collapses.
    C. The storm returns.
    D. Someone sleeps through the storm.

_____ 9. What sort of day does Emily Dickinson describe in "The Sky Is Low, the Clouds Are Mean"?
    A. an unpleasantly hot summer day
    B. a cold and nasty winter day
    C. a beautiful but sad autumn day
    D. a day of fresh spring rain

_____ 10. What figure of speech does Dickinson use in this line from "The Sky Is Low, the Clouds Are Mean"?

> A narrow wind complains all day

    A. simile
    B. metaphor
    C. personification
    D. no figure

_____ 11. What does *mean* mean in the line "The sky is low, the clouds are mean"?

    A. high

    B. average

    C. cruel or nasty

    D. signify

_____ 12. Which of these words often signal a simile?

    A. *like* and *as*

    B. *so* and *and*

    C. *for* and *like*

    D. none of the above

Vocabulary and Grammar

_____ 13. In which of these places would you most likely see a *rut*?

    A. a dirt road   C. a movie theater

    B. a museum hall   D. a skyscraper

_____ 14. What is the indirect object in the following sentence?

    Celia gave me two tickets to the new play.

    A. Celia   C. tickets

    B. me   D. play

_____ 15. Which word is most nearly *opposite* in meaning to the word *unresponsive*?

    A. reacting   C. puzzled

    B. quiet   D. unanswered

Essay

16. Write a short essay in which you describe the scene in either "Ode to Enchanted Light" or "The Sky Is Low, the Clouds Are Mean." Show which details from the poem work to build the particular impression you identified.

17. Write a short composition in which you summarize the events in "Little Exercise." Trace what the speaker observes from the beginning of the poem to the end.

Name _____ Date _____

Poetry Collection: Pablo Neruda, Elizabeth Bishop, Emily Dickinson
Selection Test B

Critical Reading *Identify the letter of the choice that best completes the statement or answers the question.*

____ 1. What does the word *enchanted* suggest about the light in "Ode to Enchanted Light"?
  A. It is pleasant and mysterious.
  B. It is sad and mournful.
  C. It is unpleasant and ugly.
  D. It is the work of elves.

____ 2. Which attitude does the speaker display in "Ode to Enchanted Light"?
  A. sensitivity to the needs of others
  B. faith in human progress
  C. a deep sense of wonder
  D. a belief in scientific precision

____ 3. Which figure of speech from "Ode to Enchanted Light" is a metaphor?
  A. light / like a green / latticework of branches.
  B. drifting down like clean / white sand.
  C. A cicada sends / its sawing song / high into the empty air.
  D. The world / is a glass overflowing / with water.

____ 4. Which word in the context is a clue to the meaning of *latticework* in "Ode to Enchanted Light"?
    light
    like a green
    latticework of branches
  A. light
  B. green
  C. branches
  D. none of the above

____ 5. What impression of nature does Pablo Neruda convey in "Ode to Enchanted Light"?
  A. Nature is a source of comfort for human beings.
  B. Nature is indifferent to human suffering.
  C. Nature is not always pretty.
  D. Nature is very far removed from city life.

____ 6. In these opening lines from "Little Exercise," to what does the word *growling* refer?
    Think of the storm roaming the sky uneasily
    like a dog looking for a place to sleep in,
    listen to it growling.
  A. the storm only
  B. the dog only
  C. both the storm and the dog
  D. neither the storm nor the dog

_____ 7. Where does "Little Exercise" take place?
   A. in a tropical or semitropical coastal area
   B. on a bleak island off the coast of New England
   C. in the California desert
   D. in the Arctic

_____ 8. Which of these is an example of personification in "Little Exercise"?
   A. mangrove keys / lying out there unresponsive to the lightning
   B. a heron may undo his head, / shake up his feathers, make an uncertain comment
   C. The boulevard / and its . . . sidewalks with weeds in every crack, / are relieved to be wet,
   D. all of the above

_____ 9. In these lines from "Little Exercise," which word is a clue to the meaning of *boulevard*?
   It is raining there. The boulevard
   and its broken sidewalks with weeds in every crack,
   are relieved to be wet, the sea to be freshened.

   A. raining
   B. sidewalks
   C. weeds
   D. wet

_____ 10. In "The Sky Is Low, the Clouds Are Mean," what human behavior does the snow-flake display?
   A. It cannot make up its mind.
   B. It is mean and nasty.
   C. It is full of complaints.
   D. It has trouble getting along with others.

_____ 11. In "The Sky Is Low, the Clouds Are Mean," what human behavior does the wind display?
   A. It treats others badly.
   B. It whines about being badly treated.
   C. It keeps changing direction and is unable to make up its mind.
   D. It is narrow in outlook and insensitive to the needs of others.

_____ 12. Which of these things does Dickinson personify in her poem?
   A. the sky
   B. the sky, clouds, snowflake, and wind
   C. the barn
   D. the diadem

Vocabulary and Grammar

____ 13. Which word is an antonym of *uneasily*?
  A. restfully
  B. nervously
  C. hardly
  D. complicated

____ 14. In which sentence is *debates* used correctly?
  A. She debates the pillow as she tries to fall asleep.
  B. At the store, she debates whether or not to buy the scarf.
  C. Joe debates Jack because they agree on everything.
  D. all of the above

____ 15. Which sentence contains an indirect object?
  A. The radio warned us of the storm.
  B. The police gave everyone three hours to evacuate.
  C. Carl remained at home on the island.
  D. He escaped the storm in a boat.

____ 16. Which statement about indirect objects is accurate?
  A. An indirect object can come after an action verb or a linking verb.
  B. An indirect object is always a pronoun.
  C. An indirect object comes before a direct object.
  D. all of the above

____ 17. In which sentence is a pronoun correctly used as a direct object?
  A. The stars of the play were Pablo and me.
  B. My dad gave me his old watch.
  C. Nan invited my sister and I to her party.
  D. Ask me no more questions, please.

Essay

18. From the details in "Ode to Enchanted Light," what does Pablo Neruda seem to mean by "enchanted light"? Answer this question in a brief essay that uses details from the poem to support your explanation.

19. Explain how figurative language contributes to the theme and impact of "The Sky Is Low, the Clouds Are Mean." Be sure to provide examples of figurative language to support your ideas about the poem.

Poetry by May Swenson, Billy Collins, Dorothy Parker
Vocabulary Warm-up Word Lists

Study these words from the poetry collection. Then, complete the activities that follow.

Word List A

frosty [FRAW stee] *adj.* looking as if covered with powderlike ice
White and silver glitter made the winter dance poster look <u>frosty</u>.

glimmered [GLIM erd] *v.* shone with a bit of light
Those stars <u>glimmered</u> for years before an astronomer saw them.

inhabitants [in HAB i tuhnts] *n.* people or animals that live in a place
The <u>inhabitants</u> of the city greeted the new mayor warmly.

unlikely [un LYK lee] *adj.* not probable
Snow in July is an <u>unlikely</u> event in Rhode Island.

winding [WYND ing] *v.* twisting and turning
The road was <u>winding</u> along the curve of the shoreline for miles.

wonderment [WUN der muhnt] *n.* amazement; great surprise
I looked in <u>wonderment</u> at the new car sitting in the driveway.

Word List B

ancient [AYN shuhnt] *adj.* from times long ago
The new room of the art museum houses <u>ancient</u> Roman statues.

druid or **Druid** [DROO id] *n.* Celtic priest of long-ago Europe
The <u>Druid</u> led his followers to the forest for a religious ceremony.

flare [FLAIR] *n.* a blaze of light or flame
The <u>flare</u> suddenly shot up into the dark sky, like a firework.

illuminating [i LOO muh nayt ing] *v.* lighting up
Colorful lanterns were <u>illuminating</u> the sidewalk.

ritual [RICH oo uhl] *n.* religious or social custom
<u>Ritual</u> is part of every religion, though it differs in each one.

torchbearer [TAWRCH bair er] *n.* one who carries a burning torch
Marie was chosen to be the <u>torchbearer</u> who lit the bonfire.

Poetry by May Swenson, Billy Collins, Dorothy Parker
Vocabulary Warm-up Exercises

Exercise A *Fill in each blank in the paragraph below with an appropriate word from Word List A. Use each word only once.*

The road was [1] _____ through the dark, wintry countryside.
I had nowhere to go, so I drove slowly. I passed under a tent of trees with a
[2] _____ coating. I figured that the sun never reached this spot and
imagined that the snow might not melt until spring. Then, the car suddenly entered a
clearing. The lights of faraway houses [3] _____ faintly from a hillside.
I pictured their [4] _____ sitting down to their dinners or stretched out
on cozy recliners in front of crackling fireplaces. I wanted to knock at any door and ask
to be admitted, however [5] _____ that might be. It was probable that
anyone who even answered the door would just stare at me in [6] _____,
as if I were an alien whose spacecraft was out on the lawn.

Exercise B *Write a complete sentence to answer each question. For each answer, use a word from Word List B to replace each underlined word or phrase without changing its meaning.*

1. Do you have any interest in learning about the lives of peoples <u>from long ago</u>?
   _____

2. What could you light that would create a bright <u>flame</u>?
   _____

3. Who should be the <u>person carrying the lighted stick</u> in the nighttime parade?
   _____

4. Do Americans living in the United States have a <u>set of actions</u> that they do
   every year?
   _____

5. On the Fourth of July, were fireworks <u>lighting up</u> the sky where you live?
   _____

6. Several thousand years ago, would you have been likely to find a <u>group of priests
   who were Celts</u> living in what is now the United States?
   _____

Poetry by May Swenson, Billy Collins, Dorothy Parker
Reading Warm-up A

Read the following passage. Pay special attention to the underlined words. Then, read it again, and complete the activities. Use a separate sheet of paper for your written answers.

Anna stood in the busy square. Her eyes popped open with underline{wonderment} at the light coating of snow, the holiday decorations, and the crowds of people scurrying about. She asked herself how thousands of underline{inhabitants} managed to walk along the same streets without constantly bumping into one another.

Anna was from a small southwestern ranch where the most exciting event was a runaway calf. She had sure picked the right time of year to visit the big city.

Stepping inside the city's largest department store, Anna was no less amazed. Silver and white glitter made the columns on the main selling floor look underline{frosty}. Mirrors and lamps, wreaths and ribbons, all created a bright, festive air. Everywhere people bought things and clerks collected money. Young men and women squirted customers with perfume. Escalators carried some people up and down, out of the crowd. Then, elevator doors would open, spilling yet more people onto the floor.

Anna was underline{winding} her way through the crowded hat department when something special caught her eye. Tiny lights underline{glimmered} like stars from a dark area that was supposed to give the feeling of nighttime. For a moment, she imagined herself back home, staring up at the night sky from her favorite hilltop. Was she homesick already?

Just for fun, Anna decided to visit the toy department on the sixth floor. When she stepped off the elevator, she caught a glimpse of someone she thought she knew. An underline{unlikely} coincidence, she thought. Whom do I know here? Of course, with so many people, someone probably does look like Ray from back home!

Surprisingly, it was Ray, a shy boy whom she hardly knew from her old high school. She began to walk briskly, in order to catch up with him. She wanted to find out what he was doing here. Most of all, she wanted to hold on to him as a small piece of home, here so far from everyone she knew.

1. Circle the words that tell what caused Anna's underline{wonderment}. Rewrite the sentence using a synonym for **wonderment**.

2. Underline the synonym in the paragraph for underline{inhabitants}. Describe the **inhabitants** of your town or city.

3. Circle the words that tell what made the selling floor look underline{frosty}. Write about something you like that is **frosty**.

4. Underline the word that explains why Anna is underline{winding} her way through the hat department. Then, explain what **winding** means.

5. Circle the words that hint at the meaning of underline{glimmered}. Write about a time when something **glimmered** in your life.

6. Underline the antonym for underline{unlikely}. Describe what would be an **unlikely** event in your life.

Name _____ Date _____

Read the following passage. Pay special attention to the underlined words. Then, read it again, and complete the activities. Use a separate sheet of paper for your written answers.

The Celts were an <u>ancient</u> people who moved long ago from Central Europe into what is now France and Britain. A <u>Druid</u> was a member of the educated class of the Celts. Druids were teachers, lawmakers, and priests who spent a lot of time in oak forests. In fact, the word *druid* is Celtic for "knowing the oak tree."

The earliest information that exists about Druids comes from the third century B.C.E. Most of the information, however, comes from the Roman leader Julius Caesar, who lived some two hundred years later but came across Druids when he invaded their land.

Druids studied nature, astronomy, and the laws and poetry of their people. They based their calendar on four "fire festivals," falling around November 1, February 1, May 1, and August 1. Every year, each festival focused on a different aspect of life. In November, the Druids' <u>ritual</u> had to do with the onset of winter. In February, the focus was rebirth, the very earliest signs of spring. In May, the focus was on creativity, as nature is then in full bloom. August was the time when couples traditionally married.

Imagine a group of Druids in the clearing of an oak forest more than two thousand years ago. The chief Druid is a <u>torchbearer</u>, lighting the sticks of his companions. Now, a whole circle of flames is <u>illuminating</u> the oak grove. The <u>flare</u> of light from a shooting star goes unnoticed as they focus on the matters at hand.

Over the years, people have asked whether the Druids built Stonehenge, a huge stone circle in southwestern England. No one knows for sure. One day, however, we may know more about the Druids and their connection to Stonehenge.

1. Underline the words that are a synonym for <u>ancient</u>. Write a sentence naming some other *ancient* people.

2. Circle the phrase that tells you what a <u>Druid</u> was. Explain why these people were called by the name *druid*.

3. Underline the words in the previous sentence that help to understand what a <u>ritual</u> is. Tell about a *ritual* that has to do with a present-day holiday or celebration.

4. Circle the words telling what the <u>torchbearer</u> does. Write a sentence using the word *torchbearer*.

5. Underline what is <u>illuminating</u> the oak grove. Tell about something that is *illuminating* an area in your home.

6. Underline the example given of a <u>flare</u> of light. Then, describe a *flare* that you have seen.

Name _____ Date _____

Poetry by May Swenson, Billy Collins, Dorothy Parker
Literary Analysis: Comparing Humorous Imagery

Imagery is poetic language that uses images—words or phrases that appeal to the senses of sight, hearing, touch, taste, or smell. In addition to this sensory language, poets sometimes use the following techniques to create humorous effects with imagery:

- Pairing images that do not usually go together, such as a fish on a bicycle.
- Using imagery to describe common situations from unusual perspectives, such as showing an ant's eye view of a picnic.
- Describing a familiar situation in a humorous way, such as sitting in a traffic jam watching pedestrians moving faster than you are.

When you read a poem with humorous imagery, imagine the sights, sounds, smells, feelings, or tastes of these images.

DIRECTIONS: *In each of the three poems, find imagery that appeals to one or more of your senses. On the chart, record each word or phrase in the appropriate space. Then, answer the questions below the chart.*

Poem	Sight	Sound	Smell	Touch
"Southbound on the Freeway"				
"The Country"				
"The Choice"				

Name _____ Date _____

Poetry by May Swenson, Billy Collins, Dorothy Parker
Vocabulary Builder

Word List

billowing	smoldering	lilting	transparent	inhabitants

A. DIRECTIONS: *Write a complete sentence to answer each question. In each answer, use a vocabulary word from the box in place of underlined words with similar meanings.*

1. What is something that you have seen <u>swelling</u>, or <u>surging</u>, in the wind?

   _____

   _____

2. What is something you have in your home that is <u>clear</u>, or <u>see-through</u>?

   _____

   _____

3. Where do the <u>occupants</u>, or <u>residents</u>, of your community like to go for vacation?

   _____

   _____

4. What kind of singers do you think have <u>light</u>, <u>graceful</u> voices?

   _____

5. Where were you the last time you saw a fire <u>smoking without a flame</u>?

   _____

   _____

B. DIRECTIONS: *Each numbered item below consists of a pair of related words in CAPITAL LETTERS followed by four pairs of words. Circle the letter of the pair that best expresses a relationship similar to that expressed in the pair in capital letters.*

1. SMOLDERING : FIRE ::
   A. fizzing : soda
   B. growing : market
   C. stopping : acceleration
   D. pouring : choice

2. TRANSPARENT : HAZY ::
   A. sink : wreck
   B. live : exist
   C. single : multiple
   D. dirty : soil

3. LILTING : GRACEFUL ::
   A. caring : wicked
   B. simple : difficult
   C. near : far
   D. dangerous : hazardous

4. INHABITANT : DWELLER ::
   A. douse : dry
   B. doubt : uncertainty
   C. certain : controversial
   D. pauper : pause

Name _____ Date _____

Poetry by May Swenson, Billy Collins, Dorothy Parker
Support for Writing to Compare Humorous Imagery

Before you write your essay that compares the humorous imagery in each of these three poems, use the graphic organizer below to jot down ideas about each poem.

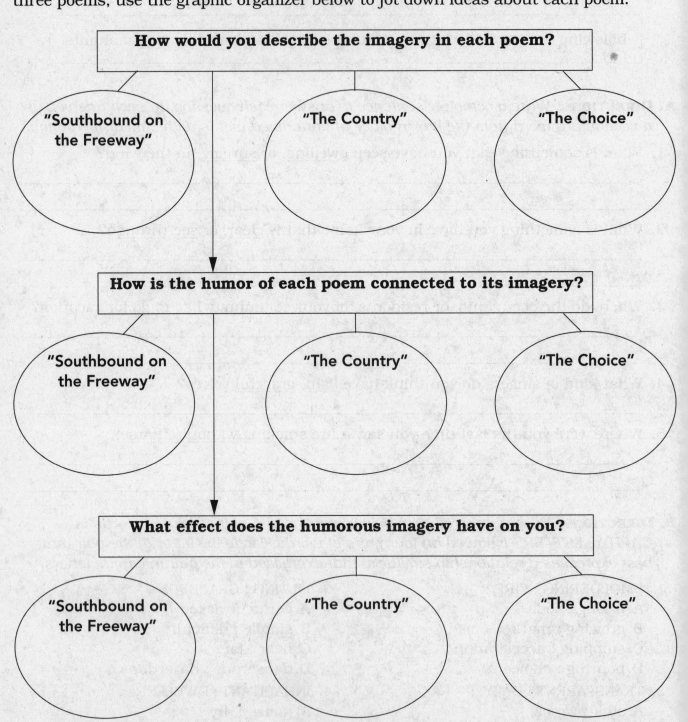

Now, use your notes to write your essay comparing the humorous imagery in the three poems.

Poetry Collection: May Swenson, Billy Collins, and Dorothy Parker
Selection Test A

Critical Reading *Identify the letter of the choice that best answers the question.*

____ 1. Which lines begin the humorous view of the freeway in "Southbound on the Freeway"?
   A. A tourist came in from Orbitville, / parked in the air . . .
   B. He must be special— / the others respect him . . .
   C. They have four eyes. / The two in the back are red.
   D. Those soft shapes, / shadowy inside / the hard bodies . . .

____ 2. What is "Southbound on the Freeway" mostly about?
   A. a midwestern tourist's view of California
   B. a long car trip across America
   C. a space alien's view of car traffic
   D. a late-night trip to the grocery store

____ 3. What is being described in these lines from "Southbound on the Freeway"?
   Their feet are round and roll
   on diagrams—or long

   measuring tapes—dark
   with white lines.

   A. cars on the road
   B. strange alien creatures
   C. a machine used in highway construction
   D. carpenters using black and white tape

____ 4. What makes the description of the freeway in "Southbound on the Freeway" humorous?
   A. The images paired together normally do not go together.
   B. The description is from the perspective of a visitor from outer space.
   C. The narrator is describing an unusual situation in a matter-of-fact way.
   D. Sights, sounds, smells, and tastes are exaggerated.

____ 5. What is the narrator warned about at the beginning of "The Country"?
   A. not to play with matches
   B. not to start a fire in the fireplace
   C. not to play around a hot stove
   D. not to leave matches lying around

____ 6. In "The Country," what does the narrator imagine a mouse doing?
   A. forgetting to put the matches away
   B. lighting a match on a wooden beam
   C. blowing out candles on a cake
   D. starting a fire in the fireplace

____ 7. What does the author imply in these lines from "The Country"?
   lit up in the blazing insulation,
   the tiny looks of wonderment on the faces
   of his fellow mice
   A. He implies that the house caught on fire because of a mouse.
   B. He implies that the mice like the warmth of the fireplace.
   C. He implies that many mice live in the walls of the house.
   D. He implies that the mice are able to communicate with one another.

____ 8. In what way is the description in "The Country" humorous?
   A. The narrator does not believe what the other person is telling him.
   B. The mice living in the walls remind readers of cartoon mice.
   C. The idea of a mouse striking a match is out of the ordinary.
   D. The description of the matches being put in a round tin is unusual.

____ 9. Who is the speaker in "The Choice"?
   A. a man who owns billowing farms
   B. someone who chooses between two men
   C. a woman who loves jewelry and horses
   D. a man with a lilting song

____ 10. Which line from "The Choice" makes the poem humorous?
   A. Only a melody, happy and high
   B. He'd have given me laces rare,
   C. Gaily I followed wherever you led.
   D. Somebody ought to examine my head!

____ 11. How are "The Choice" and "Southbound on the Freeway" similar?
   A. They both contain imagery that is suspenseful.
   B. They both describe extraordinary women.
   C. Each illustrates how love can make a person do silly things.
   D. Each ends with words that surprise readers.

Vocabulary

____ 12. Which word comes closest to the meaning of *transparent*?
   A. clear
   B. invisible
   C. cloudy
   D. shiny

____ 13. Which of these might be left *smoldering*?
   A. a bow and arrow
   B. cheerful emotions
   C. a campfire
   D. a cup of tea

____ 14. Which word is most similar in meaning to *inhabitants*?
   A. people
   B. residents
   C. animals
   D. employees

Essay

15. Write an essay comparing the humor in "Southbound on the Freeway" and "The Choice." What ordinary parts of life are described in the poems? What makes each description humorous?

16. Write an essay comparing and contrasting "Southbound on the Freeway" and "The Country." Do the poems describe normal occurrences or events that are out of the ordinary? What makes the descriptions in the poems humorous?

Poetry by May Swenson, Billy Collins, Dorothy Parker
Selection Test B

Critical Reading *Identify the letter of the choice that best completes the statement or answers the question.*

____ 1. How does the narrator in "Southbound on the Freeway" see the roads that the creatures roll on?
  A. as ribbons through the city
  B. as long measuring tapes
  C. as lighted switchboard circuits
  D. as threads of a rug

____ 2. What is described in these lines from "Southbound on the Freeway"?
  Sometimes you can see a five-eyed
  one, with a red eye turning
  on the top of his head.
  A. a police car
  B. a space alien
  C. a neon sign
  D. a costume

____ 3. What is being described in these lines from "Southbound on the Freeway"?
  . . . Those soft shapes,
  shadowy inside
  the hard bodies
  A. an X-ray of a human skull
  B. the people inside the cars
  C. the tires of a car
  D. the contents of the trunks of cars

____ 4. The poem "Southbound on the Freeway" is humorous because
  A. images that normally do not go together are paired together.
  B. it is told from the perspective of a visitor from outer space.
  C. the narrator is describing an unusual situation in a matter-of-fact way.
  D. the sights, sounds, smells, and tastes are exaggerated.

____ 5. About what is the narrator warned in "The Country"?
  A. lighting matches
  B. playing with the mice that live in the wall
  C. leaving matches lying around the house
  D. tearing up the floral wallpaper

____ 6. In "The Country," what does the narrator envision during the night?
  A. a mouse in the bed
  B. lighting a campfire
  C. insects inside the walls
  D. a mouse striking a match

___ 7. "The Country" is humorous because
   A. the description of the matches in a round tin is funny.
   B. the mice living in the walls remind readers of cartoon mice.
   C. the narrator does not believe what the other person is telling him.
   D. the idea of a mouse striking a match is out of the ordinary.

___ 8. Which sentence best describes the contrast between the two men in "The Choice"?
   A. One man is rich, and the other is joyful about life.
   B. One man is slow, and the other is swift.
   C. One man has horses, and the other has a dog.
   D. One man is a follower, and the other is a leader.

___ 9. What does the speaker of "The Choice" mean by the last line, which follows?
      Somebody ought to examine my head!

   A. She fell off the horse and hurt her head.
   B. She thinks she should see a doctor.
   C. She should have thought more about her decision.
   D. She may have been crazy to give up the rich man.

___ 10. The line from "The Choice" that makes the poem humorous is
   A. Only a melody, happy and high.
   B. He'd have given me laces rare,
   C. Gaily I followed wherever you led.
   D. Somebody ought to examine my head!

___ 11. "The Choice" and "Southbound on the Freeway" are similar because
   A. they both contain imagery that is suspenseful.
   B. they both describe visits from another planet.
   C. they both discuss how love can make a person do silly things.
   D. they both have thought-provoking last lines.

___ 12. What makes the humor in "The Country" different from the humor in "The Choice"?
   A. "The Country" describes alien creatures in the walls of a house.
   B. "The Country" describes cars in a rural area.
   C. "The Country" describes human imagination at work.
   D. "The Country" describes an alien's imagination at work.

___ 13. Which of the following images is from "Southbound on the Freeway"?
   A. They all hiss as they glide, / like inches, down the marked / tapes.
   B. You—you'd only to whistle low, / Gaily I followed wherever you led.
   C. the one unlikely mouse / padding along a cold water pipe / behind the floral
      wallpaper
   D. see him rounding a corner, / the blue tip scratching against a rough-hewn beam

Vocabulary

___ 14. *Lilting* does not refer to
A. singing.
B. sounds.
C. speaking.
D. leaning.

___ 15. In which sentence is *billowing* used correctly?
A. The train engine was billowing down the tracks with strength and power.
B. A large American flag was billowing in the wind in front of the White House.
C. When the bell rang, the students came billowing out of the crowded school.
D. Cows sometimes make billowing noises when they are startled or scared.

___ 16. Which of the following is most *opposite* to the meaning of *transparent*?
A. clear
B. invisible
C. cloudy
D. shiny

___ 17. A synonym for *inhabitants* is
A. residents.
B. people.
C. animals.
D. employees.

Essay

18. "Southbound on the Freeway" and "The Country" contain unusual perspectives that make everyday people, places, or things seem extraordinary. Write a brief essay identifying those perspectives.

19. In an essay, compare and contrast the speakers in "The Choice" and "Southbound on the Freeway." Use the following questions to help you describe the speakers: What does each speaker see when looking at his or her subject? How does each speaker feel about his or her subject? What does each speaker learn from his or her subject? Be sure to include examples from the poems to support your answers.

Name _____ Date _____

Prewriting: Choosing Your Topic

Use the chart below to determine which writing prompt you know the most about.

Answer the following questions about each topic.	An important historical event in the past twenty years	Two people in literature or life who acted heroically
How long do you think it will take you to develop a response?		
Which topic do you know best or which have you reviewed or studied?		
List three facts, arguments, or other details you know about each topic.		

Drafting: Planning an Organization

To present your ideas clearly, use the graphic organizer below to list your key points in order of importance above the line or chronological order below the line.

Order of Importance (Least Important ⟶ Most Important)

Chronological Order (First ⟶ Last)

Writing Workshop—Unit 4, Part 1
Writing for Assessment: Integrating Grammar Skills

Revising Active and Passive Voice

A verb is in the **active voice** when the subject performs the action. A verb is in the **passive voice** when its subject does not perform the action. Writing is stronger when most sentences use the active voice, but the passive voice may be used to stress the action or when the performer of the action is unknown.

Active Voice	Passive Voice
Lightning **struck** the barn. My family **is painting** the house.	The barn **was struck** by lightning. The house **is being painted** by my family. **Perfromer Unknown:** The office was closed. **To stress action:** The goal was exceeded.

Identifying Active and Passive Voice

A. DIRECTIONS: *On the line before each sentence, write* active *or* passive *to identify the voice.*

_____ 1. Fire broke out in the dry preserve area.

_____ 2. Sparks were carried by the wind.

_____ 3. A passing motorist called 9-1-1 from her car phone.

_____ 4. Before the fire engines arrived, nearby houses were threatened.

Revising Active and Passive Voice

B. DIRECTIONS: *On the lines provided, rewrite these sentences to make them active voice.*

1. Energy is released by a flash of lightning.

_____

2. Thunder is produced by rapid heating of the air.

_____

3. Lightning rods are used by owners of buildings.

_____

4. Lightning is attracted by the metal in an umbrella.

_____

Unit 4: Poetry
Part 1 Benchmark Test 7

MULTIPLE CHOICE

Reading Skill: Context *Read the selection, and answer the questions that follow.*

Be still, sad heart! and cease repining;
Behind the clouds is the sun still shining;
Thy fate is the common fate of all,
Into each life some rain must fall,
Some days must be dark and dreary.

—from "The Rainy Day" by Henry Wadsworth Longfellow

1. Which of these is a possible meaning for the word *repining* in the poem?
   A. expressing uncertainty
   B. expressing determination
   C. expressing happiness
   D. expressing discontent

2. In the poem, what type of context clue for *repining* is the word *shining*?
   A. explanation
   B. definition
   C. synonym
   D. antonym

3. What is the probable meaning of *dreary* in the poem?
   A. gloomy
   B. cheerful
   C. dry
   D. windy

4. Which words most clearly help you determine the meaning of *dreary*?
   A. *sad, rain* and *dark*
   B. *clouds, sun*, and *fate*
   C. *fate, life*, and *rain*
   D. *still, sad*, and *shining*

Read the selection from the poem "Boat Song." Then, answer the questions.

THE RIVER calmly flows,
Through shining banks, through lonely glen,
Where the owl shrieks, though ne'er the cheer of men
Has stirred its mute repose,
Still if you should walk there, you would go there again.

—from "Boat Song" by Ralph Waldo Emerson

5. What is the probable meaning of *glen* in the poem?
   A. a type of tree
   B. a small stream
   C. a narrow valley
   D. a farmer's house

6. Which phrase most clearly helps determine the meaning of *glen*?
   A. The river calmly flows . . . through
   B. Through shining banks
   C. Where the owl shrieks
   D. stirred its mute repose

7. Which of these is the best definition of *repose* in Emerson's poem?
   A. silence
   B. depth
   C. rest
   D. liveliness

8. Which word in the first stanza of Emerson's poem is a clue to the meaning of *repose*?
   A. calmly
   B. mute
   C. shining
   D. lonely

Read the selection from a recipe. Then, answer the questions that follow.

Whisk together the flour and eggs until they are thoroughly mixed. Gradually add the milk and water, stirring to combine. Add the salt and butter, and beat until smooth. Then heat a lightly oiled frying pan over medium high heat. Pour the batter into the pan. Cook the crepe for about 2 minutes. Then loosen the crepe with a spatula, turn, and cook the other side.

9. What context clue best helps you figure out the meaning of *whisk* in the selection?
   A. gradually
   B. mixed
   C. add
   D. heat

10. Based on the context in which it is used, what is the most likely meaning of *spatula*?
    A. a tool for heating food
    B. a tool for frying food
    C. a tool for mixing food
    D. a tool for lifting food

Literary Analysis: Sound Devices

11. What type of sound device is used in the following lines of poetry?

    A tapering turret overtops the work,

    A. alliteration
    B. onomatopoeia
    C. rhyme
    D. rhythm

12. Which sound device uses words to imitate sounds?
    A. rhythm
    B. onomatopoeia
    C. alliteration
    D. rhyme

13. Which of these is the best example of the use of rhythm as a sound device?
    A. A snail trail streamed across the summer porch.
    B. The water in the hot pan hissed and sputtered.
    C. When I wished upon a star, the star winked back at me.
    D. Four farmers toiled tirelessly in their fields.

Literary Analysis: Figurative Language

14. Which of these is an example of the use of figurative language?
    A. The breeze rustled the leaves of the tall elms.
    B. The grain stalks bowed to one another in the breeze.
    C. A sudden breeze cooled our hot faces as we worked.
    D. The wind chimes dinged and clanged in the breeze.

15. Which choice contains a simile?
    A. The sheriff was a hearty, loud-talking fellow.
    B. Her curiosity led her to learn a great deal.
    C. The stream gurgled its way over the rocks.
    D. Pynchon's Pond was as smooth as glass.

16. Which of the following is an example of personification?
    A. A rusted stove crouched in the corner.
    B. In the race, Evan ran like a gazelle.
    C. The trail bent left, toward the creek.
    D. She sat sleepily, nodding her head.

17. Which of these best defines the use of personification in making comparisons?
    A. Two unlike things are compared using *like* or *as.*
    B. Two unlike things are compared by saying that one is the other.
    C. A nonhuman subject is given human characteristics.
    D. Human behavior is described in terms of animal behavior.

Literary Analysis: Humor *Read the selection, and answer the questions that follow.*

> The sneer is gone from Casey's lip, his teeth are clenched in hate;
> He pounds with cruel violence his bat upon the plate;
> And now the pitcher holds the ball, and now he lets it go,
> And now the air is shattered by the force of Casey's blow.
>
> Oh, somewhere in this favored land the sun is shining bright,
> The band is playing somewhere, and somewhere hearts are light:
> And somewhere men are laughing, and somewhere children shout,
> But there is no joy in Mudville—mighty Casey has struck out.
>
> —from "Casey at the Bat" by Ernest L. Thayer

18. Which of these best describes the use of humor in the excerpt from "Casey at the Bat"?
    A. pairing images that do not usually go together
    B. using personification and metaphor for effect
    C. describing a situation from an unusual perspective
    D. using words that appeal to the senses of sight and sound

19. Which technique best contributes to the poem's humorous effect?
    A. using irony so that readers are surprised to learn what happens at the end
    B. combining two points of view in an unusual way
    C. using images that appeal to the senses of touch and taste
    D. describing a common situation from an unusual perspective

Vocabulary: Suffixes

20. What is the meaning of *virtuous* in the following sentence?

    The poem is about a virtuous man who is tricked into committing a crime.

    A. one who suffers bad luck
    B. the process of doing good
    C. relating to hard work
    D. full of good qualities

21. What is the best definition of *development* in the following sentence?

    Development of a good poem can take months or even years.

    A. having many parts
    B. relating to the act of writing
    C. concerned with outcome
    D. the act of putting together

22. Which definition best fits the word *nervous* in the following sentence?

Paulie felt nervous as he mounted the stage to recite his poem.

   A. having the quality of uneasiness
   B. relating to being proud
   C. one who has courage
   D. a state of readiness

23. Which of these best defines *amusement* in the following sentence?

For amusement, Oscar read aloud a humorous poem by Ogden Nash.

   A. the state of being entertained
   B. in order to pass the time
   C. one who enjoys poetry
   D. relating to recreation

24. Which definition best fits the word *wondrous* in the following sentence?

The poet Mary Oliver can make ordinary things seem wondrous.

   A. in an amazing manner
   B. one who inspires wonder
   C. having an extraordinary quality
   D. the act of marveling

25. What is the meaning of *contentment* in the following sentence?

True contentment is writing a poem that says exactly what you feel.

   A. a process that brings happiness
   B. full of pleasant feelings
   C. one who is feeling happy
   D. the state of being satisfied

Grammar

26. Which sentence contains a predicate adjective as a subject complement?
   A. Maggie is walking with her dog.
   B. The small farm on the hill was tidy.
   C. Jay and Art are both photographers.
   D. The salesperson who called was he.

27. Which sentence contains a predicate pronoun as a subject complement?
   A. We wondered what happened to him.
   B. The best person for the job is she.
   C. Are they coming to our play?
   D. He was the Poet Laureate in 2001.

28. Which sentence contains a predicate noun used as a subject complement?
    A. The walk through the tunnel was eerie.
    B. What nationality are you?
    C. My dog is master of the household.
    D. The ground is sloping and uneven.

29. What is the direct object in the following sentence?

    Olivia fed a cracker to the gray mule in the pen.

    A. Olivia
    B. cracker
    C. mule
    D. pen

30. Which sentence contains an indirect object?
    A. Elyssa handed her dad the purple iris.
    B. Jack hung the lantern on the nail.
    C. Dad gave the horse's reins to me.
    D. That coat is too large for Marco.

31. Which sentence shows a verb in the active voice?
    A. A loud screech was heard in the tree.
    B. Are the streets really paved in gold?
    C. The baby is sleeping soundly.
    D. The new park was finished at last.

ESSAY

Writing

32. Imagine that you have been asked to write an introduction for a favorite recorded song that you will play for other students. You want to draw students' attention especially to the words of the song and their effect on you. Jot down two or three ideas about how you will explain why the words of this song are important to you. Mention any use of sound devices such as alliteration, onomatopoeia, rhyme, or rhythm in the song.

33. Jot down notes for a study for a poem about a walk in the woods. Begin by listing some things you might see, hear, smell, touch, and taste in the woods. Then choose three things on your list and write phrases that make comparisons using one example each of a simile, a metaphor, and personification, such as *The tall pines looked like sharpened pencils.*

34. Imagine that you are writing for assessment and have expressed the following main idea in response to a writing prompt. List at least three details that you might use to support this main idea: Poetry often reassures us that someone else shares our thoughts and feelings.

Name _____

Unit 4: Poetry
Part 2 Concept Map

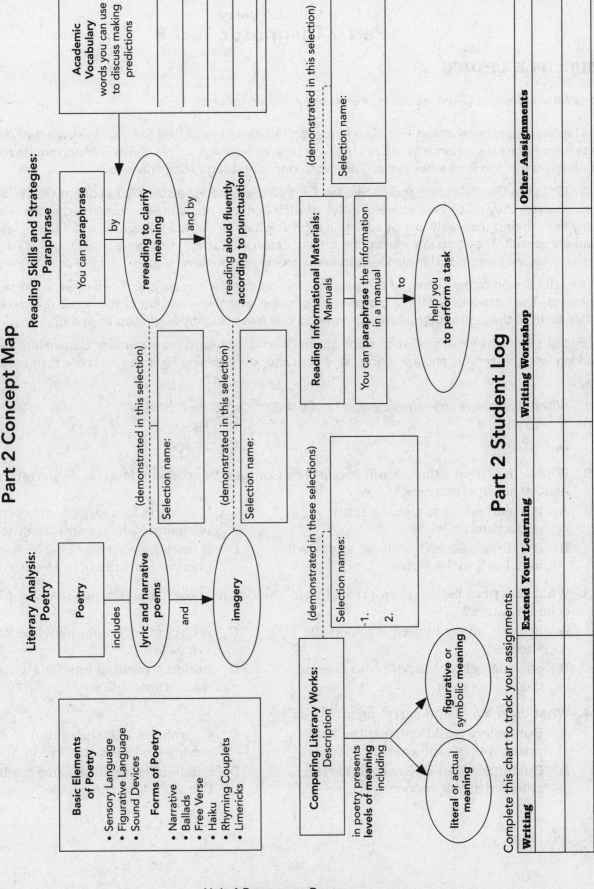

Reading Skills and Strategies:
Paraphrase

You can paraphrase

by

rereading to clarify meaning

and by

reading aloud fluently according to punctuation

(demonstrated in this selection)

Selection name: _____

(demonstrated in this selection)

Selection name: _____

Academic Vocabulary
words you can use to discuss making predictions

_____
_____
_____
_____

Reading Informational Materials:
Manuals

You can paraphrase the information in a manual

to

help you **to perform a task**

(demonstrated in this selection)

Selection name: _____

Literary Analysis:
Poetry

Poetry

includes

lyric and narrative poems

and

imagery

Basic Elements of Poetry

• Sensory Language
• Figurative Language
• Sound Devices

Forms of Poetry

• Narrative
• Ballads
• Free Verse
• Haiku
• Rhyming Couplets
• Limericks

Comparing Literary Works:
Description

in poetry presents **levels of meaning** including

figurative or symbolic meaning

literal or actual meaning

(demonstrated in these selections)

Selection names:
1. _____
2. _____

Part 2 Student Log

Complete this chart to track your assignments.

Writing	Extend Your Learning	Writing Workshop	Other Assignments

Unit 4: Poetry
Part 2 Diagnostic Test 8

MULTIPLE CHOICE

Read the selection. Then, answer the questions that follow.

The word *supermarket* was first used in the late 1920s in the United States. However, early supermarkets were not nearly as large as today's high-volume, self-service stores. Several important developments mark this transition from small general stores to one-stop mega-supermarkets.

In 1910, the Great Atlantic and Pacific Tea Company opened the so-called economy store format. On their shelves, they placed attractive displays of such items as tea, coffee, and canned foods. This company kept their prices fairly low by selling in high volume. This practice became a feature of later supermarkets as well. They also introduced the idea of "cash and carry." Customers had to pay cash, and delivery was not offered. This also helped keep grocery prices low.

Any discussion of the history of the supermarket must include mention of two more important developments. The introduction of the motor vehicle is one, and the invention of the home refrigerator is the other. Both of these products allowed people to buy large quantities of food at one time.

By the 1930s, the supermarket concept was becoming more and more popular. Convenient locations, parking lots, self-service, and low prices have kept shoppers flowing to stores for more than seventy years.

1. When was the word *supermarket* first used in the United States?
   A. 1910
   B. 1920s
   C. 1930s
   D. 1940s

2. Why is the Great Atlantic and Pacific Tea Company's economy store so important in the history of supermarkets?
   A. It was the first to use the term *supermarket.*
   B. It did not succeed, so it set supermarkets back many years.
   C. It was the first supermarket to offer refrigerated foods and parking lots.
   D. It introduced many new ideas that became features of later supermarkets.

3. What practices helped keep prices low in the Great Atlantic and Pacific Tea Company's economy store?
   A. keeping a very limited stock on the shelves
   B. offering delivery service and lines of credit
   C. selling in high volume while keeping prices low
   D. building parking lots for customers with automobiles

4. What does "cash and carry" mean?
   A. Customers could only get the low prices if they paid cash.
   B. Customers had to pay cash for the store's delivery service.
   C. Customers had the option of either paying cash or using credit.
   D. Customers could not use credit, and the store was self-service.

5. Based on the information in the selection, what can you assume about how people shopped before supermarkets were introduced?

   A. They bought large amounts of food at one time so they would not have to shop as often.

   B. They had to go to many small stores to buy all the goods they needed.

   C. They had to park their cars far away since the stores did not have parking lots.

   D. They paid cash and carried their groceries home themselves.

6. Why was the invention of motor vehicles important to the development of supermarkets?

   A. Shoppers would not go to stores without parking lots.

   B. People could carry more food home much more easily.

   C. Store owners had to charge more to pay for their vehicles.

   D. People needed all their products in one place to save gasoline.

7. The selection states that shoppers were able to buy much more food at one time after the invention of refrigerators. What does this imply about how people shopped before the invention of refrigerators?

   A. They had to pay far more for perishable foods but did not have to worry about spoilage.

   B. They were able to buy great quantities of perishable foods.

   C. They had to buy perishable foods in smaller amounts and much more frequently.

   D. They were unable to buy or eat any perishable foods.

8. What is the main idea of this selection?

   A. Supermarkets keep their prices low and sell in volume.

   B. Many factors influenced the development of supermarkets.

   C. The invention of home refrigerators helped supermarkets grow.

   D. The concept of a supermarket was introduced in the early 1900s.

Read the selection. Then, answer the questions.

Born in 1847, Alexander Graham Bell was a distinguished scientist and educator who is best known today for inventing the telephone.

With the help of his partner, Thomas Watson, Bell began to work on an electrical device that would transmit sound over telegraph wires. The two men struggled vainly for years in their efforts to get the device to work. Then, one day in 1876, Bell and Watson were working on their invention in separate rooms. Bell spilled some acid on himself. Agitated by the accident, he said, "Mr. Watson, come here. I want you!" To the astonishment of both men, Watson heard Bell's voice through the device on his workbench. Bell's telephone had become a reality!

Bell and Watson were soon giving demonstrations of the amazing new invention. It was not long before the first telephone company was established. Bell and his new wife then set sail for England to introduce the telephone to the people of Europe. When the French government awarded him a prize for his important work, Bell used the money to set up a laboratory devoted to helping the deaf. Bell continued to make many important contributions to science throughout his life. Forty-five years after inventing the telephone, Alexander Graham Bell died.

9. Which of the following is a direct result of the invention of the telephone?
   - A. It took years for Bell and Watson to succeed.
   - B. Bell wanted to work with the deaf.
   - C. The first telephone company was established.
   - D. Bell spilled acid on himself.

10. How did Bell and Watson discover that their invention worked?
   - A. Bell called out for Watson, who heard Bell's voice through the device.
   - B. Bell spilled acid on the device, and Watson saw that it started working.
   - C. They took it to Europe to show to other scientists, who told them that it worked.
   - D. They were able to call someone in the French government.

11. How did Bell use his award money from the French government?
   - A. He retired and never invented anything again.
   - B. He used it to invent the first working telephone.
   - C. He opened the first telephone service company.
   - D. He set up a laboratory devoted to helping the deaf.

12. Which of the following details from the selection helps explain why Bell and Watson were completely surprised when their invention worked?
   - A. Watson was Bell's partner for many years.
   - B. Bell was a distinguished scientist and educator.
   - C. Bell and his wife took the telephone to Europe.
   - D. They had been trying for years without success.

13. What is the main idea of this selection?
   - A. The invention of the telephone changed the course of history.
   - B. Thomas Watson rarely gets credit for inventing the telephone.
   - C. Bell and Watson were surprised when their invention worked.
   - D. Alexander Graham Bell is best known for inventing the telephone.

14. What is the main purpose of this selection?
   - A. to persuade readers to use telephones more often
   - B. to inform readers about Bell's invention of the telephone
   - C. to give Thomas Watson credit for inventing the telephone
   - D. to entertain readers with amusing stories about Bell and Watson

15. About how old was Bell when he died?
   - A. 45 years old
   - B. 29 years old
   - C. 74 years old
   - D. 50 years old

Vocabulary Warm-up Word Lists

Study these words from the poetry of Robert Hayden, William Shakespeare, and Ricardo Sánchez. Then, complete the activities that follow.

Word List A

aromas [uh ROH muhz] *n.* strong, pleasant smells
   The <u>aromas</u> of cooking, made my mouth water.

benefits [BEN uh fits] *n.* advantages or help that you get from something
   The <u>benefits</u> of Grandma's visit were three great meals every day.

brethren [BRETH ruhn] *n.* brothers; comrades or fellows
   Native Americans treated the early white settlers like <u>brethren</u>, as if they were family.

familial [fuh MIL yuhl] *adj.* having to do with a family
   Jenna's <u>familial</u> duties included watching her little brother.

resolution [rez uh LOO shuhn] *n.* the quality of having strong beliefs and the desire to do something
   Though painting the house was not easy work, he completed the task with <u>resolution</u>.

thicketed [THIK it ed] *adj.* covered with a thick growth of shrubs or small trees
   The island was <u>thicketed</u> with berry-producing shrubs.

Word List B

bonanza [buh NAN zuh] *adj.* having to do with a sudden gain of money or good luck (usually used as a noun)
   Lydia's long-lost, wealthy uncle left her a <u>bonanza</u> inheritance in his will.

dart [DAHRT] *v.* to move suddenly and quickly in a direction
   When prairie dogs sense danger, they <u>dart</u> underground.

folly [FAHL ee] *n.* foolishness; a silly thing
   When the first steamboat appeared, some people thought it was a <u>folly</u>.

shackles [SHAK uhlz] *n.* metal rings joined by chains put around the wrists or ankles to prevent escape
   The prisoner arrived in court in <u>shackles</u>, along with two guards.

summoning [SUH muhn ing] *n.* a calling of people together
   When a meal on the ranch was ready, there came a <u>summoning</u> from the "dinner bell."

yonder [YAHN duhr] *adj.* being at a certain distance, usually within view
   "Run to <u>yonder</u> shed and get the shears for me," said Pa.

Poetry Collection: Robert Hayden, William Shakespeare, Ricardo Sánchez
Vocabulary Warm-up Exercises

Exercise A *Fill in each blank in the paragraph below with an appropriate word from Word List A. Use each word only once.*

Claire was firm in her [1] _____ to become a great chef, so she went to

cooking school for a summer. The school was deep in the country. It had a comfortable,

[2] _____ feel, and Claire felt at home right away. One of the

[3] _____ of being in the country was that there was plenty of room

to grow fresh vegetables to use in recipes. The tomato and bean plants grew so well

that they [4] _____ part of the garden. During the day, the young

chefs worked in the big kitchens. Mouth-watering [5] _____ filled the air.

Each evening, they all enjoyed a fine meal and the company of their cooking

[6] _____.

Exercise B *Revise each sentence so that the underlined vocabulary word is used in a logical way. Be sure to keep the vocabulary word in your revision.*

1. The bonanza find did not produce any gold.

   _____

2. If it begins to rain at the party, you can dart out from under the canopy.

   _____

3. In modern times, believing that the earth is round is sheer folly.

   _____

4. Wearing shackles, the animals ran gracefully through the meadow.

   _____

5. The awards assembly began hours before the summoning of all winners to
   the stage.

   _____

6. Pick peaches from yonder tree, the one on the other side of the hill.

   _____

Poetry Collection: Robert Hayden, William Shakespeare, Ricardo Sánchez

Reading Warm-up A

Read the following passage. Pay special attention to the underlined words. Then, read it again, and complete the activities. Use a separate sheet of paper for your written answers.

I was so excited when my parents told me that we were going to a family reunion! I had never been to one before. All I knew was that there would be more than 300 Santoros in one place at one time, and that all of us were related, all of us were <u>brethren</u>. I realized that I had more cousins than I had ever dreamed of.

We got on the road early on the morning of the reunion, and started on our way. The family had rented an entire campground by the seashore for the event. We drove on and on, past the city, past small towns, and then through an area that was <u>thicketed</u> with low shrubs and berry bushes. The air smelled salty. We were almost there.

Soon I saw lines of cars parked by the sand, all with signs that said, "Santoro Family Reunion." Even the vehicles seemed to have a <u>familial</u> likeness—there were several that looked the same as ours, as if they were relatives. We parked and jumped out of the car to join in the party. <u>Aromas</u> of grilling meats and vegetables filled my nose, and those delicious smells made me hungry right away. I was given a T-shirt with the family name on it, and before I knew it, I was in the middle of a game of beach volleyball.

One of the <u>benefits</u> of having a big group is the advantage of having plenty of helping hands. As if by magic, big tables were set up, and heaping platters of food were appearing on them. As I ate, laughed, and chatted with Santoros of every shape and size, I realized what a great thing a big family is. I decided then and there, with complete determination and <u>resolution</u>, that I would stay in touch with everyone and that I would organize another family reunion when I was older.

1. Circle the words that explain the meaning of <u>brethren</u>. Then, give a synonym for *brethren*.

2. Underline the words that tell what made the area <u>thicketed</u>. Describe a *thicketed* area that you know about.

3. Circle the words that give a clue about the meaning of <u>familial</u>. Are there *familial* resemblances in your family?

4. Underline the words that tell what is making the <u>aromas</u>. Name some of your favorite *aromas*.

5. Underline the word that is similar to <u>benefits</u>. Tell about some *benefits* you have by being a member of a family, a club, or a team.

6. Circle the word that helps you understand the meaning of <u>resolution</u>. Tell about something you have done with *resolution*.

Poetry Collection: Robert Hayden, William Shakespeare, Ricardo Sánchez
Reading Warm-up B

Read the following passage. Pay special attention to the underlined words. Then, read it again, and complete the activities. Use a separate sheet of paper for your written answers.

Stories of the Old West rarely include African Americans. Freed from the <u>shackles</u> of slavery, many blacks did make their way to the frontier in search of better lives. Even before the Civil War, black miners turned up to hunt for gold in California. <u>Bonanza</u> gold made some rich; others opened businesses and started newspapers or schools.

After the Civil War, many former slaves became homesteaders, buying land from the government for next to nothing. Life was hard out on the plains. The land was tough to plow, and the weather was often unkind.

Supplies were hard to come by, too. Parents couldn't say to their kids, "Go over to <u>yonder</u> store and buy some rope" for the nearest store might be hundreds of miles away.

Some freed slaves heeded the army's <u>summoning</u> of soldiers to fight Indians on the Great Plains. The Indians nicknamed them "buffalo soldiers." This name was given out of respect; the Native Americans held the buffalo in high regard since it fed, clothed, and sheltered them.

About one of four cowboys in the Old West was black, and Nat Love was one of the most famous. He rode well and shot well. When a bull would <u>dart</u> this way and that, trying to avoid being caught, Nat was ready to bring it down with his rope.

Mary Fields, a freed slave, was rough and tough, too. Making her way to Montana, she hauled supplies and did other "heavy" work. She was always ready with her fists to convince people who thought it was <u>folly</u> for her to do such work. Later in life, she mellowed and began delivering mail. She became known as Stagecoach Mary for her ability to ride her stagecoach through any kind of weather and still show up on time.

Nat and Mary are just two of the "characters" that were part of the westward movement of African Americans. Many more stories remain to be told.

1. Underline the words that help you figure out the meaning of <u>shackles</u>. Define two meanings of **shackles** as it is used in this passage.

2. Circle the two words that give a clue to the meaning of <u>bonanza</u>. Explain what **bonanza** means.

3. Circle the phrase in the next sentence that contrasts strongly with <u>yonder</u>. Write a sentence with **yonder**, using real locations in your life.

4. Rewrite the sentence that includes <u>summoning</u>, replacing it with a synonym. Tell about an experience in which you did or did not respond to a **summoning**.

5. Underline the words that give a picture of what it means to <u>dart</u>. Describe something you know that can **dart**.

6. Underline what Mary Fields did to convince people who thought her work was <u>folly</u>. Tell about something that you think is **folly**.

Name _____ Date _____

Reading: Reread to Paraphrase

To make their poems more powerful and memorable, poets often use language that is rarely used in everyday speech. To understand a poem, it may therefore be helpful to paraphrase it in simple, everyday language. When you **paraphrase,** you restate text in your own words. First, **reread the poem to clarify** the writer's meaning. Identify the most basic information in each sentence or phrase—what is being done and who or what is doing it. Use a dictionary or text aids like footnotes, if provided, to help you with unfamiliar terms. Once you understand the poet's meaning, restate the sentences in everyday English. Eliminate repetition, use simpler synonyms, and put unusual sentence structures into a word order that is easier to understand.

DIRECTIONS: *Use this chart to paraphrase the poems by Shakespeare and Sánchez in this collection. One example has been done for you.*

Poem	Original Lines	Paraphrased Lines
"Blow, Blow, Thou Winter Wind"	Line 1: "Blow . . . wind."	Winter wind, go ahead and blow.
	Lines 2–3: "Thou . . . ingratitude."	
	Lines 4–6: "Thy . . . rude."	
	Line 7: "Heigh-ho! . . . holly."	
	Line 8: "Most . . . folly."	
	Lines 9–10: "Then . . . jolly."	
	Lines 11–13: "Freeze . . . forgot."	
	Lines 14–16: "Though . . . not."	
"Old Man"	Lines 1–6: "old . . . freely;"	
	Lines 7–14: "old . . . life . . ."	
	Lines 15–21: "you . . . albuquerque . . ."	
	Lines 22–28: "old . . . there:"	
	Lines 29–36: "some . . . painful . . ."	
	Lines 37–47: "old . . . you . . ."	

Name _____ Date _____

Poetry Collection: Robert Hayden, William Shakespeare, Ricardo Sánchez
Literary Analysis: Lyric and Narrative Poetry

A **lyric poem** expresses the thoughts and feelings of a single speaker and uses images and other details to create a single, unified impression. A **narrative poem** tells a story in verse and has all the elements of a short story, including plot, conflict, setting, characters, and theme.

DIRECTIONS: *Choose one lyric poem and one narrative poem in this collection. Write the title of each poem on the line provided, and then answer the questions about it.*

A. Lyric Poem Title:_____

1. Why is this poem a lyric poem? _____
   _____

2. What are two feelings or emotions that the speaker expresses? _____
   _____

3. List two images that the speaker uses and the ideas they convey. _____
   _____
   _____

4. What main impression would you say the poem conveys? _____
   _____

B. Narrative Poem Title: _____

1. Why is this poem a narrative poem? _____
   _____

2. Summarize the plot in one or two sentences. _____
   _____
   _____

3. What is the main conflict or struggle, and how is it resolved in the end?
   _____
   _____

4. As specifically as possible, identify the poem's main setting.
   _____
   _____

5. Who is the main character? What minor characters does the poem feature?
   _____
   _____

Name _____ Date _____

Poetry Collection: Robert Hayden, William Shakespeare, Ricardo Sánchez
Vocabulary Builder

Word List

ingratitude legacy beckoning anguish

A. DIRECTIONS: *Answer each question with a sentence that uses one of the Word List words. Use a different Word List word in each of your answers.*

1. What might someone get from a rich relative when that relative dies?

   _____

   _____

2. How would you describe a person who fails to give thanks to those who help him or her?

   _____

   _____

3. What do some students feel on the night before a big test?

   _____

   _____

4. How would you describe the smells that tempt you to visit someone's kitchen?

   _____

   _____

B. DIRECTIONS: *For each pair of related words in CAPITAL LETTERS, circle the letter of the pair that best expresses a similar relationship.*

1. THANKS : INGRATITUDE : :
   A. cold : iciness
   B. welcome : unfriendliness
   C. scream : fear
   D. hello : greeting
2. LEGACY : INHERITANCE : :
   A. contract : signature
   B. marriage : wedding
   C. birth : death
   D. news : newspaper
3. BECKONING : DISMISSING : :
   A. calling : yelling
   B. blending : merging
   C. reading : writing
   D. coming : going
4. SUFFER : ANGUISH : :
   A. confuse : puzzlement
   B. whisper : shy
   C. anger : apologetic
   D. boredom : yawn

Unit 4 Resources: Poetry
117

Name _____ Date _____

Poetry Collection: Robert Hayden, William Shakespeare, Ricardo Sánchez
Support for Writing a Lyric or Narrative Poem

Use this sheet to jot down your notes for your lyric or narrative poem. If you plan to write a lyric poem, fill in the information called for on the first chart. If you plan to write a narrative poem, fill in the information called for on the second chart.

Lyric Poem
Person:
Qualities:
Achievements:

Narrative Poem
Events:
Characters:
Details of Setting:

Name _____ Date _____

Support for Extend Your Learning

Research and Technology

On the chart below, fill in the information for your list of sources about fugitive slaves and the abolitionist movement. Under Information About Source, list all the information needed to find each source. For example, if your source is a document that appears in a printed book, list the title, editor, publisher, publication date, and pages of the book. If your source is on the Internet, list the title and URL (address) of the Web site.

	Title of Document	Date Written or Published	Information About Source
Primary Source 1			
Primary Source 2			
Secondary Source 1			
Secondary Source 2			
Secondary Source 3			

Listening and Speaking

Create your evaluation form using the chart below. Add at least two more qualities to the first column. Decide on a scale for scoring—for example, a four-point scale with *1* being "poor" and *4* being "outstanding." Then, photocopy the form, or copy it by hand, and use it to evaluate each person's reading of a poem in the collection.

Title:		
Qualities	**Score**	**Comments**
Varied Tone		
Proper Pauses		
Clear Reading		

Name _____ Date _____

Enrichment: Old Age and Harriet Tubman

In the past hundred years, advances in medicine and social policy have helped increase the number of Americans who are 65 years old or more. Social attitudes toward old age have also changed. Today, under federal law, workers in most jobs can no longer be forced to retire when they reach 65. Senior citizens remain more physically active than they did fifty years ago, and many enjoy good health well into their seventies and eighties.

A. DIRECTIONS: *Society's attitudes toward the elderly are reflected in books and magazines, on television, and in other media. Using magazines in the library or available to you at home, explore how old age is represented in magazine advertisements. Make copies of at least three ads that feature elderly people. Then, answer these questions.*

Ad #1: What product or service is being sold? _____

What are the elderly people doing? _____

Ad #2: What product or service is being sold?_____

What are the elderly people doing?_____

Ad #3: What product or service is being sold?_____

What are the elderly people doing?_____

From these ads, what do you conclude about our society's attitude toward old age?

_____

_____

_____

_____

B. DIRECTIONS: *Harriet Tubman, the heroine mentioned in "Runagate Runagate," was born into slavery about 1820 and lived to be about 93 years old. Do research online or in a printed reference source to find out some of Tubman's achievements in the later part of her life. List at least three on the lines below.*

_____

_____

_____

_____

_____

Name _____ Date _____

Poetry Collection: Robert Hayden, William Shakespeare, Ricardo Sánchez
Selection Test A

Critical Reading *Identify the letter of the choice that best answers the question.*

_____ 1. In "Blow, Blow, Thou Winter Wind," what does the speaker say is worse than the winter wind?
A. the summer rain
B. the freezing cold
C. human beings who behave unkindly
D. life without friends or family

_____ 2. Which is the best paraphrase of this line from "Blow, Blow, Thou Winter Wind"?
Most friendship is feigning,
A. Most people only pretend to be a friend.
B. Most friends are true.
C. Most friends fawn over you.
D. Friendship is demanding and tiring.

_____ 3. What main feeling does the lyric poem "Blow, Blow, Thou Winter Wind" express?
A. friendship
B. admiration
C. annoyance
D. disappointment

_____ 4. Which word best describes the mood of these lines from "Blow, Blow, Thou Winter Wind"?
Then, heigh-ho, the holly!
This life is most jolly.
A. embarrassed
B. disappointed
C. bitter
D. cheerful

_____ 5. In "Old Man," what is the cultural heritage of the speaker and his grandfather?
A. Indian (or Native American) only
B. Indian (or Native American) and Spanish
C. Spanish only
D. Spanish and Portuguese

____ 6. What main feeling does the speaker in "Old Man" express for his grandfather?

    A. sorrow

    B. contempt

    C. admiration

    D. envy

____ 7. What was the most significant thing the speaker in "Old Man" learned from his grandfather at family gatherings?

    A. pride in his heritage

    B. patience

    C. recipes for cooking with green chiles

    D. distrust for modern ways

____ 8. What is the best paraphrase for these lines from "Old Man"?

    some of our blood was here, . . .

    before the coming of coronado

    A. Some of us bled in the fight with Coronado.

    B. Some of our ancestors were here before the Spaniard named Coronado came.

    C. Some of us lost blood in battles fought long before Coronado came.

    D. Some of our ancestors lost blood in the Coronado River.

____ 9. In the narrative poem "Runagate Runagate," what is the story mainly about?

    A. farm life in the South during the 1800s

    B. the Civil War

    C. escaping from slavery

    D. the civil rights movement of the 1950s

____ 10. What do these lines show about the people running in "Runagate Runagate"?

    Runs falls rises stumbles on from darkness into darkness

    and the darkness thicketed with shapes of terror

    and the hunters pursuing and the hounds pursuing

    A. They have reason to feel frightened.

    B. They are cowardly.

    C. They are fine athletes.

    D. They are running in circles.

____ 11. In "Runagate Runagate," how do the wanted posters describe Harriet Tubman?

    A. as a coward

    B. as a foolish, misguided person

    C. as a great heroine of her people

    D. as an armed, dangerous criminal

_____ **12.** If you were paraphrasing the following line from "Runagate Runagate," what word or phrase would be best to use in place of *dart*?

They'll dart underground when you try to catch them

A. dig

B. dash

C. dare

D. pointy object

Vocabulary and Grammar

_____ **13.** Which word means the same as *legacy*?

A. contract   C. stocking

B. lawyer   D. inheritance

_____ **14.** Which word means the opposite of *beckoning*?

A. calling   C. drying

B. commanding   D. dismissing

_____ **15.** How many prepositional phrases does the following line contain?

No more auction block for me

A. none   C. two

B. one   D. three

Essay

16. Write a paraphrase of a part you remember from "Blow, Blow, Thou Winter Wind" or "Runagate Runagate." Your paraphrase should be in paragraph form.

17. Write an essay about the grandfather in "Old Man." Explain what he is like, what he has done for the speaker, and how the speaker feels about him.

Name _____ Date _____

Poetry Collection: Robert Hayden, William Shakespeare, Ricardo Sánchez
Selection Test B

Critical Reading *Identify the letter of the choice that best completes the statement or answers the question.*

____ 1. In "Blow, Blow, Thou Winter Wind," what can you infer about the speaker?
   A. He behaves cruelly to others.
   B. He has been treated unkindly by others.
   C. He loves warm weather.
   D. He loves cold weather.

____ 2. What main point does "Blow, Blow, Thou Winter Wind" make about the harshness of nature?
   A. It is not as bad as the harshness of humans toward one another.
   B. It is worse than the harshness of humans toward one another.
   C. It reflects the harshness of human relationships.
   D. It is caused by forces human beings cannot understand.

____ 3. Which is the best paraphrase of this line from "Blow, Blow, Thou Winter Wind"?
   Thy tooth is not so keen,

   A. Your bite is not so sharp.
   B. Your appetite is not so hungry.
   C. Your attitude is not so enthusiastic.
   D. My imagination is not so vivid.

____ 4. What main emotion does the lyric poem "Blow, Blow, Thou Winter Wind" express?
   A. love for friends and family
   B. admiration for nature
   C. irritation with bad weather
   D. disappointment with human behavior

____ 5. In the lyric poem "Old Man," what main emotions does the speaker express for his grandfather?
   A. love but disappointment
   B. contempt and biting humor
   C. admiration and respect
   D. puzzlement and indifference

____ 6. What does the speaker in "Old Man" think about the past times of which his grandfather speaks?
   A. Those times are out of date and best forgotten.
   B. Life in those times was in some ways freer.
   C. Life in those times was full of pain and misery.
   D. No one today can understand or appreciate those times.

___ 7. What is the main thing that the grandfather in "Old Man" teaches the speaker to value?
   A. his cultural heritage
   B. the family business in Albuquerque
   C. nature
   D. friendship

___ 8. Which is the best paraphrase for the term *pueblos* in "Old Man"?
   A. small stones
   B. large farms
   C. Indian (Native American) communities
   D. annual family gatherings in the Southwest

___ 9. What is the setting of the narrative poem "Runagate Runagate"?
   A. a June evening just after World War I
   B. a late afternoon in biblical times
   C. a dark night before the Civil War
   D. the morning of July 4, 1776

___ 10. What is the main conflict in the narrative poem "Runagate Runagate"?
   A. the battle between North and South in the Civil War
   B. the attempt by American slaves to escape using the Underground Railroad
   C. Susyanna's struggle not to show her emotions
   D. the struggle of the slaves to remain quiet as they escape to freedom

___ 11. What does the North Star represent in "Runagate Runagate"?
   A. faith
   B. freedom
   C. brotherly love
   D. old mysteries

___ 12. What are these lines from "Runagate Runagate"?
   If you see my Pompey, 30 yrs of age,
   new breeches, plain stockings, negro shoes;
   if you see my Anna, likely young mulatto
   branded E on the right cheek, R on the left

   A. lyrics to old Negro spirituals that contain coded messages about slavery
   B. letters from slaves hoping to learn the whereabouts of runaway slaves in their families
   C. ads or posters from slave owners seeking the capture and return of runaway slaves
   D. dialogue spoken by Harriet Tubman and other "conductors" on the Underground Railroad

_____ 13. Which is the best paraphrase of these lines from "Runagate Runagate"?
    and she's turned upon us, leveled pistol
    glinting the moonlight
    A. And she turned around, offering us her pistol, which sparkled in the moonlight.
    B. And she turned toward us and raised her pistol, which shone in the moonlight.
    C. And she rotated her pistol, trying to make it level with the shining moonlight.
    D. And she pointed her pistol upward, trying to shoot the glowing rays of moonlight.

Vocabulary and Grammar

_____ 14. Which of the following choices is a *legacy*?
    A. a contract signed by two partners
    B. a good grade in school
    C. the origin of a word
    D. a wedding ring passed down in a family

_____ 15. Which sentence uses both underlined vocabulary words correctly?
    A. She thanked us with <u>ingratitude</u> for offering help in a time of <u>anguish</u>.
    B. She thanked us with <u>anguish</u> for offering help in a time of <u>ingratitude</u>.
    C. Their <u>ingratitude</u> caused joy and <u>anguish</u>.
    D. Their cruelty and <u>ingratitude</u> caused pain and <u>anguish</u>.

_____ 16. How many prepositional phrases does this line contain?
    They'll dart underground when you try to catch them

    A. none   C. two
    B. one   D. three

_____ 17. In these lines from "Old Man," what sort of prepositional phrase is "of our blood"?
    some of our blood was here,
    he would say,
    A. an adjective modifying the noun *blood*
    B. an adjective modifying the pronoun *some*
    C. an adverb modifying the verb *would say*
    D. an adverb modifying the adverb *here*

Essay

18. Write a brief essay in which you explain what a lyric poem is and why "Blow, Blow, Thou Winter Wind" or "Old Man" qualifies as a lyric poem.

19. Like all good stories, good narrative poems often contain suspense—the feeling of tension or excitement that makes readers keep reading to learn what happens next and what happens in the end. In an essay, discuss the details that build suspense in the narrative poem "Runagate Runagate."

Vocabulary Warm-up Word Lists

Study these words from the poetry of Emma Lazarus, Henry Wadsworth Longfellow, and Paul Laurence Dunbar. Then, complete the activities that follow.

Word List A

cruelties [KROO uhl teez] *n.* actions that cause pain or suffering
 The prisoners of war suffered many <u>cruelties</u> in prison.

defiance [di FY uhns] *n.* disobedience; standing up against
 In <u>defiance</u> of the law, many northerners aided runaway slaves.

hovel [HUHV uhl] *n.* a small, dirty hut
 The lovely cottage promised in the advertisement was really a <u>hovel</u>.

huddled [HUHD ld] *adj.* crowded or gathered together
 The <u>huddled</u> crowd stood under the canopy until the rain stopped.

peril [PER uhl] *n.* great danger
 In times of <u>peril</u>, the bell rang out a warning to the townsfolk.

refuse [REF yoos] *n.* the leftover part of something
 Who could toss a fine painting in the garbage as if it were <u>refuse</u>?

Word List B

consciences [KAHN shuhns ez] *n.* the feelings that tell you whether what you are doing is right or wrong
 The team members' <u>consciences</u> bothered them after they let their manager take the blame for their bad playing.

dread [DRED] *n.* great fear of something that may happen
 Harold experienced a sense of <u>dread</u> before every math test.

masses [MAS ez] *n.* all the ordinary people
 To be sure of victory, the candidates spent time meeting the <u>masses</u>.

steed [STEED] *n.* a horse, especially one with spirit used in war
 The black <u>steed</u> had a will of its own but it was brave.

teeming [TEEM ing] *adj.* being full of people
 On December 26, the mall was <u>teeming</u> with shoppers looking for sales.

transfigured [trans FIG yuhrd] *adj.* changed for the better, usually in ways that can be seen
 The sculptor <u>transfigured</u> a pile of junk into an amazing work of art.

Name _____ Date _____

Poetry Collection: Emma Lazarus, Henry Wadsworth Longfellow, Paul Laurence Dunbar
Vocabulary Warm-up Exercises

Exercise A *Fill in each blank in the paragraph below with an appropriate word from Word List A. Use each word only once.*

Yesterday, in the city, I saw the [1] _____ of protesters. They marched together in the cold, outside of a [2] _____ where some homeless people [3] _____ for warmth. As people passed, the protesters spoke out about the [4] _____ of allowing people to live like [5] _____ on the streets. The protesters were in [6] _____ of being arrested, but their efforts paid off when a Red Cross van pulled up and took the homeless people to a shelter for food, clothing, and a warm place to sleep.

Exercise B *Write a complete sentence to answer each question. For each answer, use a word from Word List B to replace each underlined word or words without changing its meaning.*

1. Does going to the dentist fill you with <u>fear</u>?

   _____

2. Would you buy a <u>horse with lots of spirit</u> for a young child learning to ride?

   _____

3. After a long vacation, why do some people look <u>greatly changed</u>?

   _____

4. What times of day would you want to avoid <u>crowded</u> highways?

   _____

5. Why is it important for the <u>ordinary people</u> to vote in elections?

   _____

6. What happens when people do not listen to their <u>senses of right and wrong</u>?

   _____

Poetry Collection: Emma Lazarus, Henry Wadsworth Longfellow, Paul Laurence Dunbar
Reading Warm-up A

Read the following passage. Pay special attention to the underlined words. Then, read it again, and complete the activities. Use a separate sheet of paper for your written answers.

If I asked you to define the word *liberty*, you might say it means "freedom." Then, I might ask, "Freedom from what?" or "Freedom to do what?" You would probably have to stop and think before answering those questions.

Over the years, to different groups of people, *liberty* has meant different things. In early American colonial times, it meant freedom to practice one's own religion. Later, it came also to mean <u>defiance</u> of the taxes and other controls that the British put upon the colonists. Americans were not going to stand for any laws being forced on them!

When war broke out with the British, *liberty* mostly meant independence from Britain. After the American victory, it came to mean "citizenship for certain white males and a handful of free men of color."

Slaves brought over from Africa had no liberty. They arrived in this country <u>huddled</u> and chained together in the worst conditions one can imagine. Many of them died at sea. Those who survived often had to endure the <u>cruelties</u> of their masters. How could a slave owner enjoy his own "liberty" when there was none for the people he beat or sold? How could he enjoy living in a fine home while his slaves lived in a <u>hovel</u>? As you know, slavery ended in 1865. The freeing of slaves gave a new definition to *liberty*.

With the great number of immigrants entering the United States in the 1840s, *liberty* began to mean other things as well. It stood for freedom from <u>peril</u> at the hands of a cruel ruler's soldiers who knocked down your door and attacked you. It meant freedom from hunger. It meant freedom to earn a living at a job of one's choosing. It stood for *not* being treated like <u>refuse</u> by a government that regarded your beliefs as worthless garbage.

One might say that the meaning of *liberty* continues to change even today. Do you agree?

1. Underline a sentence that helps you understand <u>defiance</u>. Explain a time you have been in *defiance* of something you felt was unjust.

2. Circle the word that hints at the meaning of <u>huddled</u>. Describe a time you had to remain *huddled* for some reason.

3. Circle two <u>cruelties</u> mentioned. Describe *cruelties* that people do today.

4. Underline what the author contrasts with a <u>hovel</u>. Describe what a *hovel* might look like.

5. Underline the <u>peril</u> from which some immigrants were fleeing. Describe a time when someone you know or read about was in *peril*.

6. Circle a synonym for <u>refuse</u>. Write a sentence that tells people what to do with their *refuse*.

Name _____ Date _____

Poetry Collection: Emma Lazarus, Henry Wadsworth Longfellow, Paul Laurence Dunbar
Reading Warm-up B

Read the following passage. Pay special attention to the underlined words. Then, read it again, and complete the activities. Use a separate sheet of paper for your written answers.

Sitting atop his strong <u>steed</u>, Paul Revere looked across the Charles River on the night of his famous ride. He saw two lanterns hanging high up in the Old North Church. They were his signal to warn the people that the British were coming by sea, but they were also lights of freedom.

By 1775, Boston had already been a center for freedom for more than a hundred years. Puritans had settled in nearby Plymouth in 1620 for religious freedom. Ten years later, a number of them followed a preacher, William Blackstone, to an area now known as Boston.

Before long, this new colony became a booming community. In 1680, the British took control of the growing colony. In the 1760s, they began to tax Bostonians heavily without allowing them a voice in the British government. The people resented it. Not only the town's leaders, but also its <u>masses</u>, felt a growing desire to rise up against the British. In 1775, despite the <u>dread</u> of war against the much stronger British army, the colonists fired "the shot heard round the world." The American Revolution had begun.

After years of fighting, Americans won their freedom from the British. Boston was at peace. New buildings began rising up everywhere. Docks for ships stretched out into the sea. Slowly, Boston was being <u>transfigured</u> into a real city. Boston was a busy place, <u>teeming</u> with people and industry.

In the 1830s, Boston again became a light for freedom. Horace Mann, a former lawyer and strong supporter of education, helped to shape the public school system of Massachusetts. More people now could learn to read and write. Publisher William Lloyd Garrison and writer Harriet Beecher Stowe stirred the people's <u>consciences</u> by attacking slavery in the United States. A growing number of people began to believe that freedom should extend to all, and eventually, it did.

1. Underline the words that help you figure out what a <u>steed</u> is. Describe what Revere's **steed** might be like.

2. Circle the people whom the author contrasts with the <u>masses</u>. Give an example from history of rulers being cruel to the **masses**.

3. Circle the words that tell you why the colonists had a <u>dread</u> of war. Describe a time when you had a **dread** of something.

4. Underline two sentences that describe a <u>transfigured</u> Boston. Describe a person or place you know that has been **transfigured**.

5. Circle the two things with which Boston was <u>teeming</u>. Describe a **teeming** city.

6. Underline what people's <u>consciences</u> led them to believe. Describe a time you and friends followed your **consciences**.

Unit 4 Resources: Poetry
© Pearson Education, Inc., publishing as Pearson Prentice Hall. All rights reserved.
130

Name _____ Date _____

Reading: Reread to Paraphrase

To understand a poem, it often helps to paraphrase it in simple, everyday language. When you **paraphrase,** you restate text in your own words. First, **reread the poem to clarify** the writer's meaning. Identify the most basic information in each sentence or phrase—what is being done and who or what is doing it. Use a dictionary or text aids like footnotes, if provided, to help you with unfamiliar terms. Once you understand the poet's meaning, restate the sentences in everyday English. Eliminate repetition, use simpler synonyms, and put unusual sentence structures into a word order that is easier to understand.

DIRECTIONS: *Use this chart to paraphrase the two shorter poems in this collection. An example has been done for you.*

Poem	Original Lines	Paraphrased Lines
"The New Colossus"	Lines 1–2: "Not . . . land;"	Not like the giant bronze statue on the Greek island of Rhodes
	Lines 3–6: "Here . . . Exiles."	
	Lines 6–8: "From . . . frame."	
	Lines 9–10: "Keep . . . lips."	
	Lines 10–11: "Give . . . free,"	
	Lines 13–14: "Send . . . door!"	
"Harriet Beecher Stowe"	Lines 1–3: "She . . . alone."	
	Line 4: "She . . . slept:"	
	Lines 5–6: "Her message . . . throne."	
	Lines 7–8: "Command . . . leapt."	
	Lines 9–10: "Around . . . flame"	
	Lines 11–13: "Blest . . . priestess!"	
	Lines 13–14: "At . . . fame."	

Name _____ Date _____

Poetry Collection: Emma Lazarus, Henry Wadsworth Longfellow, Paul Laurence Dunbar
Literary Analysis: Lyric and Narrative Poetry

A **lyric poem** expresses the thoughts and feelings of a single speaker and uses images and other details to create a single, unified impression. A **narrative poem** tells a story in verse and has all the elements of a short story, including plot, conflict, setting, characters, and theme.

DIRECTIONS: *Choose one lyric poem and one narrative poem in this collection. Write the title of each poem on the line provided, and then answer the questions about it.*

A. Lyric Poem Title: _____

1. Why is this poem a lyric poem? _____
_____

2. What are two feelings or emotions that the speaker expresses? _____
_____

3. List two images that the speaker uses and the ideas they convey. _____
_____
_____

4. What main impression would you say the poem conveys? _____
_____

B. Narrative Poem Title: _____

1. Why is this poem a narrative poem? _____
_____

2. Summarize the plot in one or two sentences. _____
_____
_____

3. What is the main conflict or struggle, and how is it resolved in the end?
_____
_____

4. As specifically as possible, identify the poem's main setting.
_____
_____

5. Who is the main character? What minor characters does the poem feature?
_____
_____

Name _____ Date _____

Poetry Collection: Emma Lazarus, Henry Wadsworth Longfellow, Paul Laurence Dunbar

Vocabulary Builder

Word List

yearning	complacent	somber	aghast

A. DIRECTIONS: *Answer each question with a sentence that uses one of the Word List words. Use a different Word List word in each of your answers.*

1. What is the mood at a funeral usually like?

_____

_____

2. How might a powerful person feel about his or her future?

_____

_____

3. How might a shocking accident affect someone?

_____

_____

4. What adjective describes a person who craves a piece of candy?

_____

_____

B. DIRECTIONS: *For each pair of related words in CAPITAL LETTERS, circle the letter of the pair that best expresses a similar relationship.*

1. WANTING : YEARNING : :
   A. smiling : grinning
   B. smiling : frowning
   C. laughing : crying
   D. sitting : standing

2. PLEASED : COMPLACENT : :
   A. joyous : unhappy
   B. safe : harmful
   C. annoyed : irritated
   D. donated : stingy

3. SOMBER : SUNNY : :
   A. jolly : bright
   B. hectic : crowded
   C. young : foolish
   D. plain : colorful

4. AGHAST : GASP : :
   A. shock : puzzle
   B. laugh : giggle
   C. timid : yell
   D. sleepy : yawn

Poetry Collection: Emma Lazarus, Henry Wadsworth Longfellow, Paul Laurence Dunbar
Support for Writing a Lyric or Narrative Poem

Use this sheet to jot down your notes for your lyric or narrative poem. If you plan to write a lyric poem, fill in the information called for on the first chart. If you plan to write a narrative poem, fill in the information called for on the second chart.

Lyric Poem
Person:
Qualities:
Achievements:

Narrative Poem
Events:
Characters:
Details of Setting:

Poetry Collection: Emma Lazarus, Henry Wadsworth Longfellow, Paul Laurence Dunbar
Support for Extend Your Learning

Research and Technology

On the chart below, fill in the information for your list of sources about Paul Revere and his ride. Under Information About Source, list all the information needed to find each source. For example, if your source is a document that appears in a printed book, list the title, editor, publisher, publication date, and pages of the book. If your source is on the Internet, list the title and URL (address) of the Web site.

	Title of Document	Date Written or Published	Information About Source
Primary Source 1			
Primary Source 2			
Secondary Source 1			
Secondary Source 2			
Secondary Source 3			

Listening and Speaking

Create your evaluation form using the chart below. Add at least two more qualities to the first column. Decide on a scale for scoring—for example, a four-point scale with *1* being "poor" and *4* being "outstanding." Then, photocopy the form, or copy it by hand, and use it to evaluate each person's reading of a poem in the collection.

Title:		
Qualities	**Score**	**Comments**
Varied Tone		
Proper Pauses		
Clear Reading		

Poetry Collection: Emma Lazarus, Henry Wadsworth Longfellow, Paul Laurence Dunbar
Enrichment: American Heroes

Paul Revere is just one of a long list of American heroes. Heroes possess qualities that we admire. They are people whose actions inspire and help others. Our stories, poems, and films are filled with the deeds of heroes. They provide examples of noble behavior and lessons in how to overcome difficulties and rise to challenges. We also see heroes in our daily lives—the firefighter who risks his or her life to rescue someone from a burning building, the driver who stops to help people injured in a car accident, the surgeon who donates his skills to help cure a child in need. A closer look at our society's heroes reveals a lot about ourselves—about what we value, and why.

A. DIRECTIONS: *Use your own knowledge and experience to answer these questions.*

1. What are some character traits common to American heroes?

   _____

   _____

2. Why do you think there are more male than female heroes depicted in American history?

   _____

   _____

3. Do we have heroes who are artists, scholars, physicians, or scientists? Explain.

   _____

   _____

4. Do you think it is important for a society to have heroes? Why?

   _____

   _____

5. Do you think our idea of heroism will change in the next hundred years? Explain.

   _____

   _____

B. DIRECTIONS: *Think of someone you consider a hero. Your hero might be someone famous or a lesser-known person from your everyday life. Describe this person's heroic qualities.*

   _____

   _____

   _____

   _____

   _____

Poetry Collections: Robert Hayden, William Shakespeare, Ricardo Sánchez; Emma Lazarus, Henry Wadsworth Longfellow, Paul Laurence Dunbar

Build Language Skills: Vocabulary

Word Origins

Most dictionaries provide information on the origins of words as well as their meanings. For example, if you look up the word *reflect* in a dictionary, the origin will indicate that the word began in Latin as *reflectere,* meaning "to bend" or "to throw back." Knowing the origin of a word can sometimes help you understand its meaning. For instance, knowing that *reflect* is from the Latin for "to throw back" helps you understand that when a mirror *reflects* your image, it throws back your image so that you can see it.

A. DIRECTIONS: *Answer these questions on the lines provided.*

1. *Corral,* an English word for the enclosed outdoor area on a ranch where horses and other animals are penned in, comes from the Spanish word for "circle" or "ring." How does knowing the origin help you understand what a corral looks like?

   _____

   _____

2. The English word *lyric* is from *lyra,* the name of a stringed musical instrument in ancient Greece. What does this origin suggest is an important quality of lyric poetry?

   _____

   _____

3. *Pundit,* our term for someone who appears on a television news show to discuss a particular issue, comes from Sanskrit, the language of ancient India. A Sanskrit word similar to *pundit* meant "a learned person." What does this origin suggest about the qualities a television pundit should display?

   _____

   _____

4. The English word *fascinate* comes from the Latin word for "a magic charm." How does this information help you understand what something does when it fascinates you?

   _____

   _____

B. DIRECTIONS: *Circle* T *if the statement is probably true or* F *if the statement is probably false.*

T / F 1. To paraphrase is to *restate* text in your own words.

T / F 2. Someone who likes to *reflect* on his or her decisions often acts without thinking.

T / F 3. A symbol can sometimes *convey* different meanings to different people.

T / F 4. Someone who finds it easy to *adapt* to new situations is very stubborn and rigid.

T / F 5. When you *emphasize* an idea, you try to ignore it.

Poetry Collections: Robert Hayden, William Shakespeare, Ricardo Sánchez;
Emma Lazarus, Henry Wadsworth Longfellow, Paul Laurence Dunbar

Build Language Skills: Grammar

Prepositions and Prepositional Phrases

A **preposition** is a word that relates a noun or pronoun to another word in the sentence. The noun or pronoun is called the **object of the preposition**. A **prepositional phrase** consists of a preposition, its object, and any words that modify the object. The entire phrase serves as an adjective or an adverb. Study this example:

> The boy *with Mary* danced *around the empty room.*

The first preposition, *with,* relates its object, the noun *Mary,* to another word in the sentence, *boy.* The preposition and its object form the prepositional phrase *with Mary.* The phrase serves as an adjective, describing the noun *boy*—it tells you *which* boy. The second preposition, *around,* relates its object, the noun *room,* to another word in the sentence, *danced.* The preposition, its object, and the words *the* and *empty,* which modify the object, form the prepositional phrase *around the empty room.* The phrase serves as an adverb, describing the verb *danced*—it tells you *where* the boy danced.

The chart shows some words that are often used as prepositions.

Sequence	Location	Direction	Other Relationships
after	above	around	about
before	in	down	at
during	near	from	for
until	under	up	of

A. PRACTICE: *Circle the prepositional phrase in each sentence, labeling the preposition P and its object OP. Draw an arrow to the word that the phrase modifies. On the line before the sentence, indicate whether the phrase serves as an* adjective *or an* adverb.

_____ 1. The study of poetry is not always easy.

_____ 2. To understand a poem, you often read between the lines.

_____ 3. I enjoyed that poem by an African American poet.

_____ 4. He wrote poetry after the Civil War.

_____ 5. Read it with me as I recite it aloud.

B. Writing Application: *Expand each sentence by adding a prepositional phrase to describe the underlined word. Write the new sentence on the line.*

1. The <u>dog</u> barked all night. _____

2. The moonlight <u>streamed</u>. _____

3. We <u>sat</u> together. _____

Name _____ Date _____

Selection Test A

Critical Reading *Identify the letter of the choice that best answers the question.*

_____ 1. In "The New Colossus," what or who is "the brazen giant of Greek fame"?
  A. the Statue of Liberty
  B. an ancient Greek statue, to which the Statue of Liberty is compared
  C. the United States of America
  D. Emma Lazarus, who wrote the poem, which is very popular in Greece

_____ 2. Which is the best paraphrase of this line from "The New Colossus"?
  "Keep, ancient lands, your storied pomp!" cries she
  A. "Old nations, keep your stuffy elegance that we read about in stories," she cries.
  B. "Old Europeans, stay where you live, and do not come here," she cries.
  C. "Old countries, build your tall castles with their many floors," she cries.
  D. "Own up to the truth, old countries, instead of telling tales," she cries.

_____ 3. What is the main message of the words that the Statue of Liberty speaks in "The New Colossus"?
  A. I am a tired, old woman, but I am still strong.
  B. Welcome to needy immigrants in search of a new home.
  C. America is a beacon of knowledge and education.
  D. It is better to light one candle than curse the darkness.

_____ 4. What makes "The New Colossus" a lyric poem?
  A. It has fourteen lines.
  B. It has a complex rhyme scheme.
  C. It refers to ancient Greece.
  D. It gives a speaker's thoughts and feelings.

_____ 5. In "Harriet Beecher Stowe," what does the speaker most admire about Stowe?
  A. her kindness
  B. her fame
  C. her help in the struggle for freedom
  D. her style of writing

_____ 6. Which is the best paraphrase of this line from "Harriet Beecher Stowe"?
And from its sheath the sword of justice leapt.

A. And from its pages the pen of justice jumped to the public's attention.

B. And from its case the sword of justice jumped.

C. Justice burst out of a tight dress and became a deadly weapon.

D. Stowe's book proves that the pen is mightier than the sword.

_____ 7. What do the details in "Harriet Beecher Stowe" suggest about the influence of Stowe's novel, *Uncle Tom's Cabin*?

A. It had little impact on America.

B. It had a strong impact on America.

C. It had a strong impact on white Americans, but no impact on African Americans.

D. It had a strong impact on black Americans, but no impact on white Americans.

_____ 8. Why is "Harriet Beecher Stowe" *not* a narrative poem?

A. It does not focus on telling a story.

B. It does not contain dialogue.

C. It has no theme.

D. Stowe was a real person.

_____ 9. When does the narrative poem "Paul Revere's Ride" take place?

A. on the night of April 18, 1775

B. on the evening of July 4, 1776

C. on a night in the middle of winter

D. on the morning of December 7, 1941

_____ 10. What is Paul Revere's mission in "Paul Revere's Ride"?

A. to fight the British troops until reinforcements arrive

B. to carry a secret message to the British troops

C. to carry a secret message from the British troops

D. to warn the other colonists of the movements of the British troops

_____ 11. What main qualities does Paul Revere display in "Paul Revere's Ride"?

A. recklessness and foolishness

B. daring and patriotism

C. anger and jealousy

D. patriotism and ambition

___ **12.** Which is the best paraphrase of this line from "Paul Revere's Ride"?

Hang a lantern aloft in the belfry arch

A. Put a light in the hayloft, which is shaped like an arch in a church.

B. Send an arc of light out of the small lamp located on the church's roof.

C. Put a small glass lamp high in the church tower.

D. Ring the bells in the church tower as loudly as you can.

Vocabulary and Grammar

___ **13.** Which word is most nearly *opposite* in meaning to the word *aghast*?

A. calm   C. amazed

B. surprised   D. breathless

___ **14.** To which of the following would you apply the adjective *complacent*?

A. to someone who never worries and is always satisfied

B. to someone who always worries and is never satisfied

C. to someone who never yells and is always shy

D. to someone who always yells and is never shy

___ **15.** How many prepositional phrases do these lines contain?

It was one by the village clock,
When he galloped into Lexington.

A. one   C. three

B. two   D. none

Essay

16. Write a brief essay in which you show that "Paul Revere's Ride" is a narrative poem. Sum up the events, tell where they take place, and tell who the characters are.

17. Paul Revere and Harriet Beecher Stowe both made a mark on American history. Choose one of them, and write a short essay explaining why he or she is considered an American hero. Use details from the poem by Longfellow or the poem by Dunbar to support your ideas.

Name _____ Date _____

Poetry Collection: Emma Lazarus, Henry Wadsworth Longfellow, Paul Laurence Dunbar
Selection Test B

Critical Reading *Identify the letter of the choice that best completes the statement or answers the question.*

____ 1. At the end of "The New Colossus," the statue says, "I lift my lamp beside the golden door!" What is "the golden door"?
   A. a door that lets tourists climb to the top of the Statue of Liberty
   B. the gate of heaven, to which the statue's raised arm points
   C. the gangplank of the ship bringing immigrants to America
   D. New York harbor, doorway to America

____ 2. In "The New Colossus," what does the speaker point out about the old Colossus of Rhodes?
   A. The Colossus of Rhodes was small.
   B. The Colossus of Rhodes was the model for the Statue of Liberty.
   C. The Colossus of Rhodes represented power and conquest.
   D. The Colossus of Rhodes cast bolts of lightning at ships that passed by.

____ 3. Which is the best paraphrase of this line from "The New Colossus"?
   The wretched refuse of your teeming shore.

   A. the miserable outcasts of a crowded continent
   B. the awful litter on crowded beaches
   C. the miserable people who insist on leaving a crowded land
   D. the selfish people who spurn people from slums

____ 4. What main emotion does the speaker in "The New Colossus" express?
   A. the speaker's feelings about the Statue of Liberty and immigration to America
   B. the speaker's feelings about the Colossus of Rhodes and ancient Greece
   C. the Statue of Liberty's joy about holding lightning in her torch
   D. the Statue of Liberty's angry feelings toward her children

____ 5. Which is the best paraphrase of these lines from "Harriet Beecher Stowe"?
   Her message, Freedom's clear reveille, swept
   From heedless hovel to complacent throne.

   A. Stowe's message of freedom was ignored in both rich and poor households.
   B. Stowe's message awoke rich and poor alike to the cause of freedom.
   C. Stowe's message about freedom turned poor hovels into glorious mansions.
   D. Reveille inspired Stowe to write her sweeping message, which affects us all.

____ 6. In "Harriet Beecher Stowe," who are the "two peoples" that the speaker says were transfigured?
   A. African Americans and white Americans
   B. slaves and their descendants
   C. Americans and Europeans
   D. Northerners and Southerners

_____ 7. In "Harriet Beecher Stowe," what is it the speaker assumes you know about the subject of the poem?
A. that Stowe fought in the Civil War
B. that Stowe was related to Dunbar
C. that Stowe exposed the horrors of slavery
D. that Stowe was a descendant of slaves

_____ 8. What main emotion does the speaker in "Harriet Beecher Stowe" express toward the subject?
A. admiration
B. anger
C. amazement
D. sorrow

_____ 9. What is the main conflict in the poem "Paul Revere's Ride"?
A. Paul Revere's struggle to stay on his horse
B. the British troops' struggle to arrest Paul Revere and put him on trial for treason
C. Paul Revere's internal struggle about whether or not to betray Britain
D. Paul Revere's struggle to warn the colonists of the advancing British troops

_____ 10. What is the setting of the poem "Paul Revere's Ride"?
A. the start of the American Revolution
B. the War of 1812
C. the first Thanksgiving
D. the Civil War

_____ 11. What is the meaning of "One, if by land, and two, if by sea" in "Paul Revere's Ride"?
A. One man will signal if the troops come by land, and two will signal if they come by sea.
B. There will be one hour's notice if the troops come by land and two if they come by sea.
C. One spy will hide among the British troops on land and two on a ship off the coast.
D. If the British come by land, one lantern will glow; if they come by sea, two will glow.

_____ 12. Which is the best paraphrase of these lines from "Paul Revere's Ride"?
And the spark struck out by that steed in his flight,
Kindled the land into flame with its heat.

A. Sparks from Paul Revere's horse started a brush fire.
B. Paul Revere's horse sparked fear in everyone who saw it riding across the land.
C. Paul Revere wiped out the spark of victory in the British troops.
D. Paul Revere's ride helped ignite a rebellion across the colonies.

_____ 13. *Lyric* describes which of the poems in this collection?
A. "The New Colossus" only
B. "Harriet Beecher Stowe" only
C. "The New Colossus" and "Harriet Beecher Stowe"
D. "Paul Revere's Ride" and "Harriet Beecher Stowe"

Vocabulary and Grammar

___ 14. Which sentence uses its underlined vocabulary word correctly?
   A. Their laughter was loud and <u>somber</u>.
   B. The car <u>aghast</u> smelled peculiar.
   C. The children, <u>yearning</u> to run around, felt cooped up in the classroom.
   D. She is a <u>complacent</u> customer, always demanding top service or a refund.

___ 15. How many prepositional phrases do these lines contain?
   > Creeping along from tent to tent,
   >
   > And seeming to whisper, "All is well!"

   A. one in the first line; one in the second
   B. two in the first line; none in the second
   C. two in the first line; one in the second
   D. two in the first line; two in the second

___ 16. What does *complacent* mean in the following sentence?
   > Before reading *Uncle Tom's Cabin*, many people felt *complacent* regarding slavery.

   A. satisfied   C. gloomy
   B. resentful   D. horrified

___ 17. In these lines, what sort of prepositional phrase is "at our sea-washed, sunset gates"?
   > Here at our sea-washed, sunset gates shall stand
   >
   > A mighty woman with a torch. . . .

   A. an adjective that modifies *gates*   C. an adverb that modifies *mighty*
   B. an adjective that modifies *woman*   D. an adverb that modifies *Here*

Essay

18. Write a brief essay in which you identify a work that is a lyric poem and explain why it qualifies as one. Select from "The New Colossus," "Harriet Beecher Stowe," and "Paul Revere's Ride."

19. Paul Revere, Harriet Beecher Stowe, and the Statue of Liberty are all figures or symbols important to America's heritage. Choose two, and explain their significance in a brief essay. Use details from the poems to illustrate your points.

Vocabulary Warm-up Word Lists

Study these words from the poetry of John Updike, N. Scott Momaday, and Alice Walker. Then, complete the activities that follow.

Word List A

continent [KAHN tuh nuhnt] *n.* one of the large land masses on Earth
   My aunt has visited every <u>continent</u> except Antarctica.

dusk [DUSK] *n.* the time before it gets dark, just after sunset
   Mom says that she has trouble seeing when she drives at <u>dusk</u>.

planes [PLAYNZ] *n.* flat surfaces
   A simple box has six different <u>planes</u>.

shimmer [SHIM er] *v.* to shine with a soft light that seems to shake a bit
   When the moon is full, I see its reflection <u>shimmer</u> on the lake.

swarm [SWAWRM] *n.* a large group of insects that move together
   They say that a <u>swarm</u> of killer bees can take down a large animal.

withdraw [with DRAW] *v.* to go away or leave
   Since the room was full of noisy five-year-olds, I decided to <u>withdraw</u> from it.

Word List B

accents [AK sents] *n.* the different ways people pronounce words because of where they were born or live
   Traveling through the South, I heard about a dozen different <u>accents</u>.

behold [bi HOHLD] *v.* to look at or to see something
   Fans, <u>behold</u> how incredible his guitar-picking skills are!

cedars [SEE derz] *n.* evergreen trees with red, sweet-smelling wood
   As we walked through the forest of tall <u>cedars</u>, I felt very small.

parkas [PAR kuhz] *n.* thick, warm coats with hoods
   The warmest <u>parkas</u> are filled with soft feathers, called down.

radiator [RAY dee ay tuhr] *n.* a heating unit in a room
   I loved the hissing sound the old <u>radiator</u> made as it heated the cold room.

stiffen [STI fuhn] *v.* to become difficult to move
   Grandpa's knee would <u>stiffen</u> at the first sign of any bad weather.

Poetry Collection: John Updike, N. Scott Momaday, Alice Walker
Vocabulary Warm-up Exercises

Exercise A *Fill in each blank in the paragraph below with an appropriate word from Word List A. Use each word only once.*

On the huge [1] _____ of North America, there is a great variety of weather. For example, May can be hot in some places and cool in others. People in the Central American countries may stay indoors in May, to avoid fighting off a [2] _____ of annoying insects in the heat. At the same time, people around the Great Lakes are enjoying the outdoors. They might sit peacefully in the afternoon, watching the sun [3] _____ on the water. In the western part of North America, beautiful sunsets bring the calm of [4] _____, a time just to sit quietly. In the far northeast, chilly weather makes people [5] _____ from the night air. All over North America, clear days of May make the [6] _____ of objects seem to stand out more sharply.

Exercise B *Answer the questions with complete explanations.*

1. Would you use a <u>radiator</u> in a place where the temperature averages ninety degrees all year?
   _____

2. What emotion might cause a person to <u>stiffen</u> his or her whole body?
   _____

3. During which sports might athletes wear <u>parkas</u>?
   _____

4. When might you tell someone to <u>behold</u> something?
   _____

5. Which <u>accents</u> can you recognize as being from a particular place?
   _____

6. Why is the wood from <u>cedars</u> often used to build chests in which clothes are stored?
   _____

Name _____ Date _____

Poetry Collection: John Updike, N. Scott Momaday, Alice Walker
Reading Warm-up A

Read the following passage. Pay special attention to the underlined words. Then, read it again, and complete the activities. Use a separate sheet of paper for your written answers.

People around the world listen to rock music today. Yet, this popular form of music had its beginnings right here on our own <u>continent</u>. It began in the 1950s. At this time, three unique American musical styles came together. These were pop, rhythm and blues, and country and western.

Elvis Presley was the first huge star to put it all together. His rock-and-roll music was incredibly popular among American teenagers. His voice was great. The beat of his music was strong, fast, and exciting.

Presley also put on quite a show. He was famous for his way of dancing and for wearing fancy clothes and flashy jewelry that would <u>shimmer</u> under the spotlights. Presley was also very good-looking. He had dazzling eyes and cheekbones that looked like chiseled <u>planes</u>. Girls swooned over Presley and followed him everywhere like a <u>swarm</u> of bees.

Because rock and roll really appealed to the young, many stars would <u>withdraw</u> from the main stage as they aged. Plenty of young musicians were always waiting in the wings to take their place. Today, however, some successful, older rock stars perform to audience of all ages.

Perhaps the biggest force for change in the American rock-and-roll generation came from England. A group of four young British lads named the Beatles stormed the United States. In 1964, people went wild when they heard the Beatles' music for the first time.

New influences have always kept rock music fresh and surprising. Folk, soul, disco, heavy metal, punk, hip hop, rap . . . you can hear bits of all of it in rock music. Chances are, if you walk down the street on any summer day at <u>dusk</u>, you will hear rock-and-roll music coming from someone's open window. Its energy, messages for young and old alike, and inclusion of different styles will always keep it popular.

1. Underline the word in the paragraph that gives a clue about which *continent* is "our own." Then, list the name of each *continent*.

2. Circle the words describing what would <u>shimmer</u> under the lights. Then, explain what *shimmer* means.

3. Underline the word in the previous sentence that tells what dazzling eyes and cheekbones like chiseled <u>planes</u> add up to. Then, explain why cheekbones might look like *planes*.

4. Circle the word defining the type of <u>swarm</u> the girls resembled. Then, describe a time when you have seen a *swarm* of people.

5. Underline the words telling when rock stars would <u>withdraw</u> from the action. Then, tell about a time when you had to *withdraw* from somewhere.

6. Circle the words telling when you might hear rock music at <u>dusk</u>. Explain why people would be home listening to music at *dusk*.

Poetry Collection: John Updike, N. Scott Momaday, Alice Walker
Reading Warm-up B

Read the following passage. Pay special attention to the underlined words. Then, read it again, and complete the activities. Use a separate sheet of paper for your written answers.

I had always wanted to visit Boston. In my mind, I pictured myself walking through Boston Common, going to a Red Sox game, and feeling excited to <u>behold</u> the historical places along the Freedom Trail. I knew I would <u>stiffen</u> as I saw the spot where the Boston Massacre occurred, frozen in awe to see such an important part of our country's fight for freedom.

I always imagined these events happening during the summer months. Yet, my first visit to Boston occurred in the dead of winter, in January. It was a time when I did not like to leave the quiet, snow-covered <u>cedars</u> in the woods behind our house. My friends and I loved to don <u>parkas</u> and walk on snowshoes through the forest. With our ice skates slung over our shoulders, we would reach our own frozen pond and play hockey for hours. These were great days for me, and I hated to miss them. Nevertheless, I could not turn down an opportunity to see Boston.

My father, who had to go there on business, took me with him for a long weekend. We stayed in a famous old hotel right downtown. An old-fashioned hissing <u>radiator</u> heated the room, and the furniture, I think, dated back to the time of Paul Revere's ride.

The weather was bitter cold, so Dad and I stuck to indoor activities. We rode an elevator to the top of the tallest building to see the splendid city spread out before us. We went to the brightly lit shops and restaurants of historic Faneuil Hall. There, I enjoyed listening to the <u>accents</u> of the Bostonians who were chatting with shopkeepers and friends. We also visited the Museum of Fine Arts and Harvard University in Cambridge.

The highlight of the trip for me, however, was not the history or the culture. It was sports! We got tickets to a Celtics basketball game. Now, what could be more exciting than that?

1. Underline the words naming what the writer would <u>behold</u> along Freedom Trail. Then, explain what *behold* means.

2. Circle a word in the sentence that gives a clue about the meaning of <u>stiffen</u>. Then, explain how someone looks who would *stiffen*.

3. Underline the words telling where the <u>cedars</u> are located. Then, describe what *cedars* look like.

4. Circle the word naming something else besides <u>parkas</u> that the narrator and his or her friends would wear. Then, explain why they would wear *parkas*.

5. Underline the words that tell what a <u>radiator</u> does. Then, write a sentence using *radiator*.

6. Circle the word naming whose <u>accents</u> the writer heard. Then, list three types of *accents* that you have heard.

Name _____ Date _____

Poetry Collection: John Updike, N. Scott Momaday, Alice Walker
Reading: Read According to Punctuation to Paraphrase

When you **paraphrase** a poem, you restate it in your own words. First, read the poem through carefully and try to determine the complete thoughts it contains. **Use the punctuation** on the page—as well as the words themselves—to help you identify complete thoughts. Next, restate the meaning of each complete thought in your own words. Eliminate unneeded repetition. Mentally fill in any missing words to complete thoughts that are not fully stated. If the vocabulary is difficult, use simpler synonyms. Put unusual sentence structures into a word order that is easier to understand.

DIRECTIONS: *Use this chart to paraphrase the first two parts of "New World" by N. Scott Momaday. An example has been done for you.*

Complete Thoughts	Paraphrased Lines
Lines 1–2: "First Man, behold:"	Look, First Man
Lines 3–5: "the earth . . . leaves;"	
Lines 6–8: "the sky . . . rain."	
Lines 9–15: "Pollen . . . mountains."	
Lines 16–19: "Cedars . . . pines."	
Lines 20–28: "At . . . pools."	
Lines 29–31: "Grasses . . . shine."	
Lines 32–36: "Shadows . . . smoke."	

Name _____ Date _____

Literary Analysis: Imagery

Poetry often makes use of **imagery,** language that appeals to one or more of the five senses. Each instance of imagery is called an **image**. If you take note of the images as you read a poem, you will often understand it better. As you read, imagine that you are actually seeing, smelling, hearing, tasting, or touching the things described by the poet. Put yourself at the scene mentally, and experience the images.

DIRECTIONS: *Use this chart to help you focus on the imagery in the three poems in this collection. From each poem, list words or phrases that appeal to the senses in the corresponding boxes. Remember that many images appeal to more than one sense.*

	Sight	Sound	Touch	Smell	Taste
"January"					
"New World"					
"For My Sister Molly . . ."					

Name _____ Date _____

Poetry Collection: John Updike, N. Scott Momaday, Alice Walker
Vocabulary Builder

Word List

| borne | glistens | recede |

A. DIRECTIONS: *Using your knowledge of the underlined Word List words, circle T if the statement is true or F if the statement is false.*

T / F 1. Many a star <u>glistens</u> in the clear nighttime sky.

T / F 2. Elephants are often <u>borne</u> on the wind.

T / F 3. After a wave comes up on the shore, it begins to <u>recede</u>.

B. DIRECTIONS: *For each pair of sentences, circle the letter of the sentence in which the underlined Word List word is used correctly.*

1. A. A diamond <u>glistens</u> on her finger.

   B. A dark object <u>glistens</u> in a dark room.

2. A. The bottle was <u>borne</u> on the waves.

   B. Johnny was <u>borne</u> on April 4, 1988.

3. A. She was very ambitious and tried hard to <u>recede</u>.

   B. He is not bald, but his hairline has begun to <u>recede</u>.

C. DIRECTIONS: *Circle the letter of the word that is closest in meaning to the Word List word in CAPITAL LETTERS.*

1. GLISTENS
   A. dims   B. shines   C. hears   D. moistens
2. BORNE
   A. carried   B. involved   C. existed   D. supreme
3. RECEDE
   A. triumph   B. grow   C. retreat   D. increase

Name _____ Date _____

Poetry Collection: John Updike, N. Scott Momaday, Alice Walker

Support for Writing a Review of Poetry

Use this chart to help you evaluate the poems in this collection. To rate each element, use *A+, A, A–, B+, B*, and so on. Consider *C* a passing grade and *F* failure. In the third column, include examples as well as your general comments. Then, use the information on the chart to help you write your review.

"January"		
Element	**Rating**	**Details**
sound		
word choice		
imagery		

"New World"		
Element	**Rating**	**Details**
sound		
word choice		
imagery		

"For My Sister Molly . . ."		
Element	**Rating**	**Details**
sound		
word choice		
imagery		

Unit 4 Resources: Poetry

Poetry Collection: John Updike, N. Scott Momaday, Alice Walker
Support for Extend Your Learning

Research and Technology

Use this modified timeline to record important events in the life of the poet you investigate. Include information on the author's birth date, education, employment, changes of residence, publications, awards, and death date, if relevant.

Poet: _____

Year	Important Event	Source of Information

Listening and Speaking

Complete this chart with information about the piece of music that you choose as background music for your dramatic reading.

Poem: _____

Title of Music	
Composer of Music	
Description of Music	
Portion of Music To Be Used	
Reason(s) the Music Suits the Poem	
CD or Audiocassette Source Information	

Poetry Collection: John Updike, N. Scott Momaday, Alice Walker

Enrichment: The Pulitzer Prize

All three writers in this collection are past winners of the Pulitzer Prize. Pulitzers have been given since 1917 for achievements in American journalism, letters, drama, and music. *Letters* means fiction, history, poetry, biography or autobiography, and general nonfiction. N. Scott Momaday and Alice Walker won their prizes for poetry; John Updike won his for fiction. Although these awards have little financial value in themselves, it is a great honor to receive them.

The Pulitzer Prizes were the idea of Joseph Pulitzer, an American newspaper publisher. Pulitzer was born in Hungary and immigrated to the United States in 1847. In 1878, he became the owner and publisher of the *St. Louis Post-Dispatch*, a newspaper that, under his guidance, became a success. In 1883, he bought the *New York World* and made that a success too. People liked his use of cartoons and other illustrations, bold news coverage and news stunts, and crusades against corruption.

In 1890, Pulitzer suffered partial blindness, but he continued to direct his newspapers. He gave money to establish the Pulitzer Prizes and what is now the Columbia School of Journalism, which administers the Pulitzer Prizes.

DIRECTIONS: *Refer to the information in the passage above to answer these questions.*

1. How do you think Joseph Pulitzer felt about his adoptive country? Why do you think so?

   _____

   _____

2. Why do you think Pulitzer established what is now the Columbia School of Journalism?

   _____

   _____

3. How might winning a Pulitzer Prize help a writer's career?

   _____

   _____

4. Can a writer for a British newspaper win a Pulitzer Prize? Why?

   _____

   _____

Name _____ Date _____

Selection Test A

Critical Reading *Identify the letter of the choice that best answers the question.*

____ 1. What does the speaker describe in "January"?
   A. a cold time of year
   B. a typical school day
   C. a winter holiday
   D. a summer day in South America

____ 2. To what senses does this image from "January" appeal most?
   The radiator
      Purrs all day.
   A. sight, sound, touch
   B. sight, taste, smell
   C. touch and taste
   D. sight and smell

____ 3. Which is the best paraphrase of these lines from "January"?
   And parkas pile up
      Near the door.
   A. And cars crash near the front door.
   B. And we get lots of visitors parking near the door.
   C. And warm jackets form a heap near the door.
   D. And animals form a pile trying to get in the door.

____ 4. In "New World," what seems to be the speaker's relationship with the world of nature?
   A. He dislikes it and prefers city life.
   B. He likes it but knows very little about it.
   C. He admires it and observes it carefully.
   D. He considers it harsh and cruel to most living things.

____ 5. What three specific times does "New World" describe?
   A. yesterday, today, and tomorrow
   B. dawn, noon, and dusk
   C. spring, summer, and fall
   D. the past, the present, and the future

____ 6. Which is the best paraphrase of these lines from "New World"?

eagles / hie and / hover / above / the plain

A. Eagles hurry and hang above the flatland.

B. Eagles hang in midair and wave their wings.

C. Eagles race and rush in an ugly way.

D. Eagles soar and swoop in a simple, everyday way.

____ 7. To which senses do these lines from "New World" appeal most strongly?

At noon / turtles / enter / slowly / into / the warm / dark loam.

A. sight and sound

B. sight and touch

C. touch and taste

D. sound and smell

____ 8. Which is the best paraphrase of these lines from "For My Sister Molly Who . . ."?

For my sister Molly who in the fifties
Knew Hamlet well . . .

A. for my sister Molly who, by the time she was fifty, knew Shakespeare's play *Hamlet* well

B. for my sister Molly who met a man named Hamlet when they were both in their fifties

C. for my sister whom Molly knew in the 1950s in a small village

D. for my sister Molly who in the 1950s understood Hamlet, a character in Shakespeare

____ 9. In "For My Sister Molly Who . . . ," how does the speaker feel about her sister?

A. She is jealous of her sister.

B. She barely knows her sister.

C. She admires her sister.

D. She thinks her sister is very foolish.

____ 10. In "For My Sister Molly Who . . . ," to which senses do these lines appeal most?

Who walked among the flowers
And brought them inside the house
And smelled as good as they
And looked as bright.

A. smell and sight

B. smell and sound

C. taste and smell

D. sight and sound

Vocabulary and Grammar

____ 11. Which word is most nearly *opposite* in meaning to the word *borne* in the sentence "Pollen is borne on winds"?

A. died

B. carried

C. froze

D. identified

____ 12. What does *glistens* mean in these lines?

the sky

glistens

with rain.

A. thickens

B. moistens

C. hears

D. shines

____ 13. What is the infinitive phrase in the following sentence?

To read poetry aloud is something new to me.

A. to read

B. to read poetry aloud

C. to read poetry aloud is something new

D. to me

Essay

14. Write a composition in which you paraphrase "New World" or "For My Sister Molly Who in the Fifties." Your paraphrase should be in paragraph form, not line for line.

15. Do you think John Updike got his description of January right? In a short essay, explain what January is like for you, and compare and contrast it with Updike's description in the poem.

Name _____ Date _____

Poetry Collection: John Updike, N. Scott Momaday, Robert Hayden
Selection Test B

Critical Reading *Identify the letter of the choice that best answers the question.*

____ 1. What is the landscape that the speaker describes in "January"?
  A. a snowy place
  B. a tropical climate
  C. Antarctica
  D. Montana

____ 2. Which word or phrase best describes how the speaker feels in "January"?
  A. frightened
  B. sad to be home
  C. exhausted
  D. glad to be home

____ 3. In the following stanza of "January," what does the image "trees' black lace" capture?
  The river is
    A frozen place
  Held still beneath
    The trees' black lace.
  A. on the tree branches, the tiny leafless twigs that form a dark lace pattern
  B. on the trees, the green leaves that form a leaf pattern often seen on lace
  C. on the trees, the dark thin branches that wave in the wind like black shoelaces
  D. the shadow of the trees interlaced with the dark frozen river

____ 4. In "January," what does the speaker mean by the image in the following lines?
  The sun a spark
  Hung thin between
  The dark and dark.
  A. The sun barely shows behind the dark clouds.
  B. The sun sends off thin sparks in the night.
  C. The sun appears for only a short time between the long winter nights.
  D. The sun is unable to relieve the depression of winter.

____ 5. Which is the best paraphrase of these lines from "January"?
  Fat snowy footsteps
    Track the floor,
  A. Thick snowy footprints show where animals walked.
  B. Thick snowy outlines of feet mark the floor.
  C. Large snow boots lie on the floor of the house.
  D. A fat snowy creature followed us into the house.

____ 6. Which word best describes the speaker's feeling about the scene in "New World"?
  A. fear
  B. wonder
  C. pride
  D. sorrow

_____ 7. What do these lines from "New World" describe?

> Shadows / withdraw / and lie / away / like smoke.

    A. a forest fire
    B. a magic trick
    C. the end of the speaker's depression
    D. the sun lighting up the morn

_____ 8. Which of these images from "New World" most strongly appeals to the sense of touch?
    A. the earth glittering with leaves
    B. light gathering in pools
    C. gray foxes stiffening in the cold
    D. rivers following the moon

_____ 9. Which is the best paraphrase of these lines from "New World"?

> Pollen / is borne / on winds / that low / and lean / upon / mountains.

    A. The Roman god of plants is swept up on winds blowing between the mountains.
    B. Small flower cells carried by low-blowing winds help make the mountains fertile.
    C. The wind gives birth to dustlike flower grains that drop onto the mountains.
    D. Flower powder is carried on winds that moan and press on the mountains.

_____ 10. In "For My Sister Molly Who . . . ," how did Molly treat the speaker in the fifties?
    A. She treated her as a complete equal.
    B. She was a devoted older sister, entertaining and teaching the speaker.
    C. She was a spoiled girl who usually ignored the speaker but was sometimes kind.
    D. She was an opinionated older sister who bossed around the speaker.

_____ 11. Which is the best paraphrase of these lines from "For My Sister Molly . . ."?

> Waking up the story buds
> Like fruit.

    A. whetting our appetite for stories
    B. picking stories out of the air like buds and fruit off trees
    C. telling stories about morning in a garden
    D. making stories more flowery and appealing by adding details

_____ 12. From the details in "For My Sister Molly . . . ," what did Molly teach the speaker?
    A. literature
    B. creativity
    C. their heritage
    D. all the above

_____ 13. How do the quotation marks in these lines from "For My Sister Molly . . . " help you understand and paraphrase the lines?

> And taught me not to say us for we
> No matter what "Sonny said." . . .

    A. They indicate that the speaker is not sure Sonny said *us.*
    B. The indicate that "Sonny said" is a lie.
    C. The indicate that a reader should say the two words slowly.
    D. They indicate that the speaker had claimed that Sonny spoke well.

Vocabulary and Grammar

____ **14.** Which word is most nearly *opposite* in meaning to the word *recede*?
   A. enter
   B. lead
   C. win
   D. fail

____ **15.** Which of these things usually *glistens*?
   A. a headache
   B. a song
   C. a new dime
   D. an old hat

____ **16.** How many infinitive phrases do these lines contain?
   Who had been to school
   And knew (and told us too) that certain
   Words were no longer good
   And taught me not to say us for we
   A. none
   B. one
   C. two
   D. three

____ **17.** Identify the infinitive phrase and in its function in the following line.
   And loved to read "Sam McGee from Tennessee"
   A. *To read* is an adjective modifying "Sam McGee from Tennessee."
   B. *To read* is a noun, the direct object of the verb *loved*.
   C. *To read "Sam McGee from Tennessee"* is an adverb modifying *loved*.
   D. *To read "Sam McGee from Tennessee"* is the direct object of the verb *loved*.

Essay

18. Based on the poem "For My Sister Molly Who in the Fifties," write a short essay in which you identify the conclusions you draw about Molly's personality, background, attitudes, and talents.

19. Write a brief essay discussing the use of imagery in one of the poems—"January," "New World," or "For My Sister Molly Who in the Fifties." Examine the ways in which the poem uses images to convey the emotions or thoughts of its speaker.

Vocabulary Warm-up Word Lists

Study these words from the poetry of Amy Ling, Wendy Rose, and E. E. Cummings. Then, complete the activities that follow.

Word List A

century [SEN chuh ree] *n.* a period of one hundred years
  A <u>century</u> ago, there was no television or Internet.

delicious [di LISH uhs] *adj.* delightful
  My grandfather described ballet as a <u>delicious</u> treat for his eyes.

eldest [EL dist] *adj.* oldest
  My <u>eldest</u> brother is four years older than me and two years older than my other brother.

image [IM ij] *n.* a representation; a likeness
  People in our family often say that I am the perfect <u>image</u> of my Aunt Caroline.

perch [PERCH] *v.* to sit or stand on the top or edge of something
  I wish my cat would not <u>perch</u> on the upstairs windowsills when the windows are open.

twinkling [TWING kling] *v.* sparkling; shining with quick flashes
  In the country, the stars were <u>twinkling</u> brightly.

Word List B

aqua [AH kwuh] *adj.* bluish-green in color
  The cool, <u>aqua</u> water of the pool looked so inviting!

exquisite [EK skwiz it] *adj.* beautiful
  For fancy occasions, my mother wears an <u>exquisite</u> ruby necklace.

humorous [HYOO mer uhs] *adj.* funny and enjoyable
  We went to a <u>humorous</u> play put on by the local junior college.

jostling [JAHS ling] *n.* the act of pushing or bumping into others
  I often feel upset by the <u>jostling</u> that I experience when riding the subway.

slippered [SLIP uhrd] *adj.* wearing soft, light shoes
  My little sister's <u>slippered</u> feet made her walk as quiet as a mouse.

woodpecker [WOOD pek er] *n.* a tree-climbing bird that pecks holes in trees to get insects
  I like watching the red head of that <u>woodpecker</u>, but I don't like listening to its racket.

Poetry Collection: Amy Ling, Wendy Rose, E. E. Cummings
Vocabulary Warm-up Exercises

Exercise A *Fill in each blank in the paragraph below with an appropriate word from Word List A. Use each word only once.*

In our small town, we have had a Fourth of July parade every year for more than a

[1] _____. The [2] _____ person in town always leads

off the parade, seated in a fancy car. We eat [3] _____ hot dogs while

watching parade participants like the marching band, fancy floats, dancers and

jugglers, and funny clowns. Bringing up the rear is someone dressed to be the exact

[4] _____ of Uncle Sam. It's amazing what a likeness to the cartoons this

costume has. Usually, the whole town turns out for the parade. Chairs line the streets,

and some people [5] _____ high up on rooftops so as to get a bird's-eye

view. The town's good feelings last until the evening's fireworks outshine the stars that

are [6] _____ in the sky.

Exercise B *Decide whether each statement below is true or false. Circle* T *or* F. *Then, explain your answer.*

1. You are likely to see a <u>woodpecker</u> in the treeless areas of the Great Plains.
   T / F _____

2. Shopping during quiet weekday mornings can help you avoid the crowds and
   their <u>jostling</u>.
   T / F _____

3. You can expect to see many <u>slippered</u> feet on a hike.
   T / F _____

4. Mother Nature gives us <u>exquisite</u> gifts such as earthquakes.
   T / F _____

5. The sky, the ocean, and some people's eyes all can be described as <u>aqua</u>.
   T / F _____

6. A <u>humorous</u> line that you read in a book can cause you to laugh aloud.
   T / F _____

Unit 4 Resources: Poetry
162

Poetry Collection: Amy Ling, Wendy Rose, E. E. Cummings
Reading Warm-up A

Read the following passage. Pay special attention to the underlined words. Then, read it again, and complete the activities. Use a separate sheet of paper for your written answers.

My name is Amazing. At least, that is what people always say when they see me: "He is 'Amazing!'" They yell these words from the decks of small boats and big ships, as they watch me swimming in the ocean. Some of them pay money just to go out to sea, hoping for a glimpse of me.

It is a <u>delicious</u> feeling for me, to be so admired just for doing what a giant sea turtle does best. I try to think about why my <u>image</u> is so impressive.

I suppose it is my size, but what these people should find really incredible is my age. I know that seeing a three-hundred-pound turtle might be shocking, but these people should imagine how it feels to be swimming around at my age. I wish I could stop and rest some-times. Think about the birds, for example. They get to quit flying and <u>perch</u> on something for a nice long nap whenever they feel like it.

I believe that I am the <u>eldest</u> sea turtle in the world. I have lived more than eighty years, outliving three of my own children. Each year, I have seen the fireworks that are <u>twinkling</u> in the sky as people around the world wel-come a new year. I even saw the world usher in a new <u>century</u>.

During my years on Earth, I have watched the ocean waters grow more and more polluted. I have seen people pull more and more of my food out of the seas. As I near the end of my life, I hope that people who see me, who call me "Amazing," will make some changes so that giant sea turtles will thrive in this world. I hope humans know that what they really should call us is "Endangered."

1. Underline the words describing what the turtle finds <u>delicious</u>. Then, tell about something other than a food or drink that is *delicious* to you.

2. Circle a word in the next sen-tence that names what the turtle believes is impressive about its <u>image</u>. Then, explain what *image* means.

3. Underline the word telling what birds are doing before they <u>perch</u> on something. Then, describe a good place for a bird to *perch*.

4. Circle the words in the para-graph naming how long the <u>eldest</u> turtle has lived. Then, tell about the *eldest* member of your family.

5. Underline the word naming what was <u>twinkling</u> in the sky. Then, tell about something else you have seen that was *twinkling* in the sky.

6. Circle the word in the previ-ous sentences that hints at the meaning of <u>century</u>. If the turtle is speaking today, what new *century* did it see the world celebrate?

Name _____ Date _____

Read the following passage. Pay special attention to the underlined words. Then, read it again, and complete the activities. Use a separate sheet of paper for your written answers.

Nonverbal communication is vital to expressing people's true thoughts and feelings. We watch how others move and stand when they speak. We hear the tone of their voice and notice their facial expressions and body language. All of this information is extremely important. Just think about it—has a person's <u>exquisite</u> smile ever meant more to you than a hundred words that this individual might have spoken?

Signing is another critical form of communication. For those who can neither hear nor communicate verbally, signing is a powerful tool for listening and speaking. Many parents today are teaching their very young children to sign so that they can communicate before they are able to talk.

Going beyond these forms of daily nonverbal communication are art forms created to speak to us without words. For example, the ancient art of drumming is considered a universal form of communication. As you listen to people playing in a drum circle, for example, you can feel their emotions. A drumbeat can sound serious or <u>humorous</u>, powerful or lighthearted. Drummers can tell entire stories. A drumbeat can take you to the top of a mountain or to the depths of the brilliant <u>aqua</u> ocean.

Other art forms work wordlessly, too. Rather than hearing a message, you see it. For example, a mime is a person who acts out complete scenes without speaking a word. Often appearing in <u>slippered</u> feet, mimes try to avoid creating any sounds. Even when a scene calls for <u>jostling</u> or other usually noisy encounters, a mime succeeds in showing the action quietly. Watching a mime perform is like seeing a <u>woodpecker</u> at work through a soundproof window. You can hear what is happening but only in your mind. Through the silence, you can think more deeply about the action you see.

1. Underline the word naming something <u>exquisite</u>. Then, describe an *exquisite* nonverbal communication you have seen.

2. Circle the word that means the opposite of <u>humorous</u>. Then, describe something *humorous* you have heard lately.

3. Underline the word naming something <u>aqua</u>. Then, explain what *aqua* means.

4. Circle the words explaining why mimes often have <u>slippered</u> feet. Then, describe how your feet look when they are *slippered*.

5. Circle the word that tells what calls for <u>jostling</u>. Explain why *jostling* might be described as a noisy action.

6. Underline what the writer compares to watching a <u>woodpecker</u> through a soundproof window. Then, explain the work of a *woodpecker*.

Reading: Read According to Punctuation to Paraphrase

When you **paraphrase** a poem, you restate it in your own words. First, read the poem through carefully and try to determine the complete thoughts it contains. **Use the punctuation** on the page—as well as the words themselves—to help you identify complete thoughts. Next, restate the meaning of each complete thought in your own words. Eliminate unneeded repetition. Mentally fill in any missing words to complete thoughts that are not fully stated. If the vocabulary is difficult, use simpler synonyms. Put unusual sentence structures into a word order that is easier to understand.

DIRECTIONS: *Because the poem "Your Little Voice" does not use standard punctuation or capitalization to make complete thoughts clear, try to figure them out from the poem's words and the spacing of the words on the page. On the chart below, list your paraphrase on the right. An example has been done for you.*

Complete Thoughts	Paraphrased Lines
Lines 1–2: "your . . . leaping"	I heard your little voice over the telephone.
Lines 3–4: "and . . . dizzy"	
Lines 5–10: "With . . . faces"	
Line 11: "floating . . . me"	
Lines 12–17: "I . . . moon"	
Lines 18–19: "dear . . . crazy"	
Lines 19–24: "how . . . voice"	

Poetry Collection: Amy Ling, Wendy Rose, E. E. Cummings
Literary Analysis: Imagery

Poetry often makes use of **imagery,** language that appeals to one or more of the five senses. Each instance of imagery is called an **image.** If you take note of the images as you read a poem, you will often understand it better. As you read, imagine that you are actually seeing, smelling, hearing, tasting, or touching the things described by the poet. Put yourself at the scene mentally, and experience the images.

DIRECTIONS: *Use this chart to help you focus on the imagery in the three poems in this collection. From each poem, list words or phrases that appeal to the senses in the corresponding boxes. Remember that many images appeal to more than one sense.*

	Sight	Sound	Touch	Smell	Taste
"Grandma Ling"					
"Drum Song"					
"Your Little Voice"					

Name _____ Date _____

Vocabulary Builder

Word List

burrow	impertinently	vertical

A. DIRECTIONS: *Using your knowledge of the underlined Word List words, circle* T *if the statement is true or* F *if the statement is false.*

T / F **1.** A skyscraper is a tall <u>vertical</u> structure.

T / F **2.** An animal that makes its home in a passage underground lives in a <u>burrow</u>.

T / F **3.** Most teachers like students who speak <u>impertinently</u>.

B. DIRECTIONS: *For each pair of sentences, circle the letter of the sentence in which the underlined Word List word is used correctly.*

1. **A.** The <u>vertical</u> line was parallel to the ground.

   B. A telephone pole is a large <u>vertical</u> length of wood posted in the ground.

2. **A.** The chipmunk lived in a <u>burrow</u> underground.

   B. The bird made its nest in a tall <u>burrow</u> in the tree.

3. **A.** Polite children often speak <u>impertinently</u>.

   B. Mr. Dana punished his son for speaking <u>impertinently</u>.

C. DIRECTIONS: *Circle the letter of the word that is closest in meaning to the Word List word in capital letters.*

1. VERTICAL
   A. normal   B. upright   C. green   D. horizontal
2. BURROW
   A. hole   B. whole   C. lend   D. donkey
3. IMPERTINENTLY
   A. relevantly   B. intelligently C. rudely   D. eagerly

Name _____ Date _____

Poetry Collection: Amy Ling, Wendy Rose, E. E. Cummings
Support for Writing a Review of Poetry

Use this chart to help you evaluate the poems in this collection. To rate each element, use *A+, A, A-, B+, B,* and so on. Consider *C* a passing grade and *F* failure. In the third column, include examples as well as your general comments. Then, use the information on the chart to help you write your review.

"Grandma Ling"		
Element	**Rating**	**Details**
sound		
word choice		
imagery		

"Drum Song"		
Element	**Rating**	**Details**
sound		
word choice		
imagery		

"Your Little Voice"		
Element	**Rating**	**Details**
sound		
word choice		
imagery		

Name _____ Date _____

Research and Technology

Use this modified timeline to record important events in the life of the poet you investigate. Include information on the author's birth date, education, employment, changes of residence, publications, awards, and death date, if relevant.

Poet: _____

Year	Important Event	Source of Information

Listening and Speaking

Complete this chart with information about the piece of music that you choose as background music for your dramatic reading.

Poem: _____

Title of Music	
Composer of Music	
Description of Music	
Portion of Music To Be Used	
Reason(s) the Music Suits the Poem	
CD or Audiocassette Source Information	

Name _____ Date _____

Enrichment: The Telegraph and the Telephone

Before the 1840s, messages had to be physically transported from one place to another. The invention of the telegraph changed all that. By using electrical wires, the telegraph enabled people to send messages over great distances in a short time. However, these messages were sent one letter of the alphabet at a time in a code made up of long and short sounds. The sender at point A would give a message to a telegraph operator, who would put the message into code and send it over the wires to another telegraph operator at point B. The second operator would translate the coded message back into letters of the alphabet and get it to the person the sender wanted to reach near point B.

By the 1870s, two American inventors working to improve the telegraph separately came up with a way of using electrical wires to transmit actual human voices. Their names were Alexander Graham Bell and Elisha Gray. Because Bell reached the patent office a few hours ahead of Elisha Gray, he got the credit for the invention of the telephone. It took decades, however, before telephones became everyday objects in American homes. The poem "Your Little Voice" was first published in 1923, when having a telephone was still a fairly new experience for many Americans.

A. DIRECTIONS: *Answer these questions based on the information in the passage above and your own knowledge, including your understanding of the poem "Your Little Voice."*

1. How did the telegraph improve communications?

   _____

   _____

2. How is the telephone an improvement over the telegraph?

   _____

   _____

3. How do you think people reacted to telephones when the first ones began to appear?

   _____

   _____

4. What details in "Your Little Voice" suggest that the telephone was still fairly new?

   _____

   _____

B. DIRECTIONS: *On the lines below, or on a separate sheet of paper, describe the effects of the cell phone or another recent invention. Your description may be in the form of a poem.*

_____

_____

_____

Poetry Collections: John Updike, N. Scott Momaday, Alice Walker;
Amy Ling, Wendy Rose, E. E. Cummings

Build Language Skills: Vocabulary

Word Origins and Related Words

The word *adapt* comes from the Latin word *adaptare*, which means "to fit to." When you adapt, you fit yourself to new circumstances. When you adapt something else, you change it to fit a particular need. Related words include *adapter*, *adaptable*, *adaptability*, and *adaptation*.

A. DIRECTIONS: *On the lines provided, answer these questions about words related to* adapt.

1. Why do you need to be *adaptable* when times change?

   _____

   _____

2. What changes might be made in a musical *adaptation* of a play that originally had no music?

   _____

   _____

3. Why do you think you need an *adapter* when you want to put a plug with three prongs into a wall socket with only two holes?

   _____

   _____

4. Why is *adaptability* a useful personality trait for someone who travels a lot?

   _____

   _____

B. DIRECTIONS: *Complete each sentence with the vocabulary word that makes the most sense in the sentence. Use each word in the box only once.*

reflect	convey	emphasize	restate	adapt

1. If your explanation is not clear, _____ it in simpler language.
2. Sometimes a symbol can _____ different meanings to different people.
3. A shiny surface will often _____ an image almost as clearly as a mirror.
4. When he printed up the instructions, he used italic print to _____ key ideas.
5. It is important to be able to _____ to a new situation.

Poetry Collections: John Updike, N. Scott Momaday, Alice Walker;
Amy Ling, Wendy Rose, E. E. Cummings

Build Language Skills: Grammar

Infinitives and Infinitive Phrases

An **infinitive** is the form of a verb that includes the word *to* and acts as a noun, an adjective, or an adverb. Each of these sentences contains the infinitive *to dance.*

Noun:	*To dance* is difficult for some people. [serves as the subject of the sentence]
Noun:	Many people love *to dance.* [serves as the direct object of the verb *love*]
Adjective:	That catchy music is an invitation *to dance.* [modifies the noun *invitation*]
Adverb:	It is easy *to dance* to that music. [modifies the adjective *easy*]

An **infinitive phrase** is an infinitive with modifiers or a complement. The entire phrase acts as a single part of speech. The following sentences show some ways in which infinitives are expanded into infinitive phrases. In each sentence, the infinitive phrase is in italics.

With Adverb:	I would love *to dance well.* [phrase serves as noun (direct object)]
With Direct Object:	He gave me an invitation *to dance a mambo.* [phrase serves as adjective (modifies *invitation*)]
With Prepositional Phrase:	I find it easy *to dance to that music.* [phrase serves as adverb (modifies *easy*)]

A. PRACTICE: *Circle the infinitive phrase in each sentence. On the line after the sentence, indicate whether the phrase serves as a* noun, *an* adjective, *or an* adverb. *If it serves as a noun, tell whether it is a subject, a direct object, or another part of the sentence. If it serves as an adjective or an adverb, tell what it modifies.*

1. I like to read poetry aloud._____

2. It is easiest to recite poetry with a strong rhythm._____

3. We had an assignment to do a poetry reading._____

4. To set the poem to music was difficult._____

5. We were able to rehearse twice._____

B. Writing Application: *Complete each sentence by adding an infinitive phrase on the line.*

1. I really want _____

2. It is fun _____

3. My cousin gave me tips _____

Name _____ Date _____

Poetry Collection: Amy Ling, Wendy Rose, E. E. Cummings
Selection Test A

Critical Reading *Identify the letter of the choice that best answers the question.*

_____ 1. According to "Grandma Ling," where does the speaker first meet Grandma Ling?
A. Pennsylvania
B. Taiwan
C. in her backyard
D. in a mirror

_____ 2. Which word best describes the speaker's feelings toward Grandma Ling when they met?
A. frightened
B. shy
C. warm
D. bored

_____ 3. To what senses does this image from "Grandma Ling" appeal most strongly?
Before she came to view, I heard
her slippered feet softly measure
the tatami floor with even step;
A. sound and touch
B. sight and touch
C. touch and taste
D. sight and smell

_____ 4. Which is the best paraphrase of these lines from "Grandma Ling"?
and there I faced
my five foot height, sturdy legs and feet,
A. And there I saw someone the same height as me, with strong legs and feet.
B. And there I stood as tall as I could on strong legs and feet to face someone much shorter.
C. And there I accepted that I was five feet tall, with thick legs and feet.
D. And there I observed someone else who was five feet tall, with slim legs and feet.

_____ 5. In "Drum Song," what or whom does the speaker describe?
A. animals and children
B. animals, men, women, and children
C. children only
D. animals and women

Unit 4 Resources: Poetry
© Pearson Education, Inc., publishing as Pearson Prentice Hall. All rights reserved.
173

____ 6. In "Drum Song," to what sense does the first line of each stanza appeal?

    A. With the command "Speak," it appeals to the sense of sound.

    B. With the command "Watch," it appeals to the sense of sight.

    C. With the command "Look," it appeals to the sense of sight.

    D. With the command "Listen," it appeals to the sense of sound.

____ 7. Which is the best paraphrase of these lines in "Drum Song"?

    . . . Snowhare . . .

    your whiskers dance

    bush to burrow

    A. Your whiskers move as you dig under a bush.

    B. Your whiskers shake as you move from a bush to your hole.

    C. Your dance whisks you from a bush to a hole in the ground.

    D. You tell lies as you look for a bush to dig up.

____ 8. Which of these attitudes does "Drum Song" express?

    A. a positive attitude toward nature

    B. a negative attitude toward nature

    C. a positive attitude toward science

    D. a negative attitude toward people

____ 9. In "Your Little Voice," where does the speaker hear the voice?

    A. in a garden

    B. at a dance

    C. on an airplane

    D. on the phone

____ 10. In "Your Little Voice," how does the speaker feel about the person whose voice he hears?

    A. angry

    B. loving

    C. confused

    D. jealous

____ 11. Which is the best paraphrase of this line from "Your Little Voice"?

    With the jostling and shouting of merry flowers . . .

    A. with the pushing and shouting of happy flowers

    B. with the shoving and shouting of angry flowers

    C. with the pushing and shouting, I was reminded of jolly flowers

    D. with the joking and cheering of happy flowers

____ 12. To which sense does this image from "Your Little Voice" appeal most strongly?

I was whirled and tossed into delicious dancing

A. smell

B. touch

C. taste

D. sound

Vocabulary and Grammar

____ 13. Which word is most nearly *opposite* in meaning to the word *impertinently*?

A. politely

B. unnecessarily

C. thoughtlessly

D. strongly

____ 14. What does *burrow* mean in this sentence?

The woodchuck went into its burrow.

A. fur

B. period of sleep in winter

C. hole providing shelter

D. to dig in the ground

____ 15. Identify the infinitive phrase in the following sentence.

I went to the stadium because I like to watch baseball games.

A. to the stadium

B. because I like

C. to watch

D. to watch baseball games

Essay

16. Write a composition in which you paraphrase the four stanzas of the poem "Drum Song" by Wendy Rose. Present your paraphrase in paragraph form, not as a poem.

17. Write a brief essay about the speaker's situation in either "Grandma Ling" or "Your Little Voice." If you write about "Grandma Ling," be sure to explain how the speaker feels about her grandmother. If you write about "Your Little Voice," be sure to explain how the speaker feels about the person who has the little voice.

Poetry Collection: Amy Ling, Wendy Rose, E. E. Cummings
Selection Test B

Critical Reading *Identify the letter of the choice that best completes the statement or answers the question.*

____ 1. In "Grandma Ling," how does the speaker meet her grandmother?
   A. She leaves China and joins her grandmother in Pennsylvania.
   B. She travels to Taiwan and meets her grandmother there.
   C. She meets her every time she looks in a mirror, since the resemblance is so strong.
   D. She "digs a hole to China" and meets her grandmother in the world of imagination.

____ 2. Which is the best paraphrase of these lines from "Grandma Ling"?
   my image stood before me,
   acted on by fifty years.

   A. A photograph of me had faded over time.
   B. Something in a fifty-year-old mirror stood before me.
   C. I saw someone who looked like me but fifty years older.
   D. I saw something I had not seen in fifty years.

____ 3. In "Grandma Ling," how do the speaker and her grandmother communicate?
   A. in English
   B. in Chinese
   C. through an interpreter
   D. with smiles and hugs

____ 4. Which of these images from "Grandma Ling" most strongly appeals to the senses of sight, sound, and touch?
   A. the hole dug deep enough to reach China
   B. the slippered feet softly measuring the tatami floor
   C. the aqua paper-covered door sliding open
   D. the grandmother's square forehead, high cheeks, and wide-set eyes

____ 5. Each stanza in "Drum Song" begins "Listen," and then presents an image—of a turtle, woodpecker, snowhare, and women. Together, what do these images imply?
   A. Human beings are part of nature.
   B. Human beings have conquered nature.
   C. Modern life is no longer close to nature.
   D. Nature is cruel to animals and humans.

____ 6. From the details in "Drum Song," what can you conclude about the speaker?
   A. The speaker has observed animals in the wild.
   B. The speaker has a lot of pets.
   C. The speaker would like to have a turtle as a pet.
   D. all of the above

Name _____ Date _____

___ 7. Which is the best paraphrase of these lines from "Drum Song"?
    . . . perch
    on vertical earth
    of tree bark and
    branch.
    A. sit on a fallen log
    B. squat down on bark-covered ground
    C. sit in or on a living tree
    D. dive between the trees

___ 8. In "Drum Song," what might the image "your tongues melt" mean?
    A. The women are working in desert heat.
    B. The snow on the mountains melts.
    C. The drum speaks.
    D. Women unfreeze their tongues and talk.

___ 9. How does the speaker in "Your Little Voice" feel about hearing the voice?
    A. delighted
    B. puzzled
    C. angry
    D. gloomy

___ 10. What seems to be the relationship between the speaker in "Your Little Voice" and the person with the "little voice"?
    A. co-workers
    B. couple in love
    C. parent-child
    D. teacher-pupil

___ 11. In "Your Little Voice," what is the purpose of the image of the merry flowers skipping?
    A. to show that the people in the poem are part of nature
    B. to help us picture the garden where the poem takes place
    C. to capture the sound and rhythm of the little voice
    D. to convey the speaker's happiness on hearing the little voice

___ 12. Which of these images from "Your Little Voice" most strongly appeals to the sense of touch?
    A. pale important stars
    B. i felt suddenly dizzy
    C. skipping high-heeled flames
    D. floating hands were laid upon me

____ **13.** Which is the best paraphrase of these lines from "Your Little Voice"?

    Looked up

    with impertinently exquisite faces

    A. admired the beautiful though irrelevant appearance

    B. looked up with boldly beautiful faces

    C. looked up at the bold, beautiful sky

    D. admired the rude beauty that could not be met

Vocabulary and Grammar

____ **14.** Which of the following people is behaving *impertinently*?

    A. a doctor saving lives

    B. a student answering a teacher rudely

    C. an actress whose hair is blown by wind

    D. a farmer carefully planting a crop of corn

____ **15.** Which sentence uses the underlined vocabulary word correctly?

    A. Draw a straight line from left to right; then draw a <u>vertical</u> line that crosses it.

    B. A car should not cross double <u>vertical</u> lines painted down the center of the highway.

    C. A person needs to be completely <u>vertical</u> when he or she sleeps.

    D. Climbing the tall mountain gave me <u>vertical</u>.

____ **16.** How many infinitive phrases do these lines contain?

    go slow, go steady,

    from rock to water

    to land to rock to

    water.

    A. none   **B.** one   **C.** two   **D.** five

____ **17.** Identify the infinitive phrase and in its function in these lines.

    She smiled, stretched her arms

    to take to heart the eldest daughter

    A. The infinitive phrase *to take* serves as an adjective modifying *heart*.

    B. The infinitive phrase *to take to heart* serves as an adjective modifying *daughter*.

    C. The infinitive phrase *to take to heart* is a noun, the object of the verb *stretched*.

    D. The infinitive phrase *to take to heart* is an adverb modifying *stretched*.

Essay

18. Write a brief essay about the view of nature presented in "Drum Song." Cite details from the poem to support your general comments about its theme.

19. Write a brief essay discussing the use of imagery in both "Grandma Ling" and "Your Little Voice." Examine the ways in which each poem uses images to convey the emotions or attitudes of its speaker.

Vocabulary Warm-up Word Lists

Study these words from the poetry of Robert Frost and Walt Whitman. Then, complete the activities that follow.

Word List A

fearful [FEER fuhl] *adj.* terrible; bad
  The <u>fearful</u> mudslides luckily did not reach our house.

flung [FLUHNG] *v.* thrown suddenly with force
  When our team won, many hats were <u>flung</u> happily into the air.

grim [GRIM] *adj.* gloomy and depressing
  The house, closed up for years, had a <u>grim</u>, unloved appearance.

swaying [SWAY ing] *adj.* moving slowly from side to side
  The <u>swaying</u> crowd chanted loudly in support of the home team.

trodden [TRAHD n] *v.* walked or stepped on
  The hunters have <u>trodden</u> a path into the deep woods.

victor [VIK tuhr] *adj.* being the winner in a struggle or battle (old-fashioned form of *victorious*)
  The <u>victor</u> team celebrated by going out to dinner.

Word List B

bouquets [boo KAYZ] *n.* bunches of flowers
  We arranged six <u>bouquets</u> of fresh flowers to place on the tables.

claim [KLAYM] *n.* a right to have or do something
  The farmer said he had a <u>claim</u> on all the land up to the fence.

hence [HENS] *adv.* from this time on; from this point on
  From that happy day <u>hence</u>, they never had to work again.

mournful [MAWRN fuhl] *adj.* very sad; full of sorrow
  Her beautiful but <u>mournful</u> voice brought us all to tears.

trills [TRILZ] *v.* makes a sound in music by quickly repeating two notes that are similar
  The flute player <u>trills</u> the same two notes throughout the first four measures of the song.

undergrowth [UN der grohth] *n.* bushes and small trees that grow around and beneath larger trees
  The rabbit hopped across the lawn and disappeared in the <u>undergrowth</u>.

Name _____ Date _____

Poetry by Robert Frost and Walt Whitman
Vocabulary Warm-up Exercises

Exercise A *Fill in each blank in the paragraph below with an appropriate word from Word List A. Use each word only once.*

Our backpacks are [1] _____ over our shoulders and tightened. James

has a [2] _____ expression on his face. "Come on. Cheer up," I tell him.

"It's not a real survival test, only a game." Still, James, feeling scared, eyes the thick,

dark, [3] _____ woods as if his life depends on getting through them

safely. We start out along a path through the trees where leaves lie just as they fell. No

one has [4] _____ there recently. High, thin, [5] _____

branches shift with the breeze, but the thicker, lower ones don't move a hair. The only

sounds are our footsteps and our breathing. James cares a lot more about being the

[6] _____ than I do. I'm just happy to be outdoors, using my compass

and my wits to get through the woods.

Exercise B *Decide whether each statement below is true or false. Circle T or F. Then, explain your answer.*

1. On Valentine's Day, people sometimes send <u>bouquets</u> to their loved ones.
   T / F _____

2. You might be annoyed if a bird <u>trills</u> outside your window at 5:00 A.M.
   T / F _____

3. You will find a lot of <u>undergrowth</u> in a desert.
   T / F _____

4. When you are feeling sad, you can be cheered up by <u>mournful</u> music.
   T / F _____

5. Starting today you have an eleven o'clock curfew, and <u>hence</u>, you should be home
   before that hour.
   T / F _____

6. If you are babysitting two children, only one has a <u>claim</u> on your attention.
   T / F _____

Unit 4 Resources: Poetry

Name _____ Date _____

Read the following passage. Pay special attention to the underlined words. Then, read it again, and complete the activities. Use a separate sheet of paper for your written answers.

The weather looked grim. The snow had been coming down for hours, and now the winds had reached blizzard speed. The best thing to do in such harsh, gloomy conditions was to stay indoors, warm and safe.

Doreen knew, however, that her mother was out there somewhere. In such weather, even a strong, capable woman driving a reliable van could get into trouble. Risking her own safety, Maureen bundled up, grabbed a shovel, and headed out into the fearful storm.

Doreen wrapped her scarf—which she usually flung over her shoulder—tightly around her face. Only her eyes peeked out.

For some reason, the phrase "the road not taken" suddenly popped into her mind. Why was she thinking of the title of a poem at a time like this? She considered it a moment. Then, she realized that she was indeed taking an unusual road by going to look for her mother.

Doreen walked along the shoulder of the road through snow that no one else had trodden. She stopped every few seconds to scan the distance for her mother, but she couldn't see far. Bare, swaying trees caught in the wind and occasional headlights were her only company.

There was a side road just about where Doreen was now standing—or there would have been, had it not been covered in one continuous snow bank. "The road not taken" crept into her mind again. She knew it meant something different this time, something literal. She quickly turned onto the side road.

For a second, Doreen imagined herself part of a victor team, having saved the most travelers stranded in the blizzard. However, there was just one traveler she wanted to save now. Suddenly, she could hear a motor grinding and wheels rocking on the slick snow. She sighed as she recognized her mother's van.

1. Circle the two words in the paragraph that define grim. Write about something you have seen or read that was *grim*.

2. Underline the sentence in the first paragraph that tells what made the storm fearful. Tell about a *fearful* storm you've been in or heard about.

3. Circle the word that tells that Doreen's scarf was not flung over her shoulder. Tell what would happen to a glass bowl that was *flung*.

4. Circle a word that is close in meaning to trodden. Rewrite the sentence with *trodden*, replacing the word with a synonym.

5. Circle what causes swaying trees. Describe another *swaying* object.

6. Underline the part of the sentence that explains what a victor team would have done. Write about a time that you were a *victor*.

Poetry by Robert Frost and Walt Whitman
Reading Warm-up B

Read the following passage. Pay special attention to the underlined words. Then, read it again, and complete the activities. Use a separate sheet of paper for your written answers.

April 1865 was a fateful month for Abraham Lincoln. The Confederate government abandoned its capital of Richmond, Virginia. On the fourth, President Lincoln walked through its streets. On the ninth, General Lee surrendered to General Grant, and the Civil War was over. On the fourteenth, however, while Lincoln was watching a play at Washington, D.C.'s Ford Theater, John Wilkes Booth shot and killed him.

Although the country needed Lincoln to help heal its wounds, death had the stronger <u>claim</u>. A week later, Mr. Lincoln's funeral train left Washington. It traced most of the route he had taken to greet the people after his election, before he took office. Its destination was Springfield, Illinois, which Lincoln thought of as his hometown.

The train steamed slowly toward Philadelphia and on to New York. <u>Mournful</u> crowds stood by the tracks wherever the train passed. In rural areas, people stood in the <u>undergrowth</u> beneath towering trees. When the train stopped in major cities, hundreds of thousands of people waited in lines for hours to view President Lincoln's body. Some brought <u>bouquets</u> of spring flowers and other tokens of their love for the fallen leader.

At Albany, the train turned west and traveled across New York State. It went through Ohio and Indiana. It entered Chicago, where it stopped, and then it steamed on to Springfield.

When an important leader dies these days, many a bugle <u>trills</u> with the sad notes of "Taps," a tune that always sends sorrow through the crowd. Perhaps the most touching aspect of Lincoln's arrival in Springfield, however, was the attendance of his horse, Old Bob, and his dog, Fido. They were silently led in to see their master one last time.

The nation had lost its leader. Now, it was more important than ever for people to put aside differences and help the country heal. However, it would be a long time <u>hence</u> before that healing would begin.

1. Circle the two things that had a <u>claim</u> on President Lincoln. Write about two things that both have a *claim* on you now.

2. Underline two words in the previous paragraph that give clues to what <u>mournful</u> means. Write about an event in which crowds would be the opposite of *mournful*.

3. Circle the phrase that gives a clue to the meaning of <u>undergrowth</u>. Describe what you might find in *undergrowth*.

4. Underline the words that help you figure out the meaning of <u>bouquets</u>. Describe another event when people might bring *bouquets*.

5. Circle the words that tell you that <u>trills</u> has something to do with music. Write about a creature that *trills*.

6. Circle the word that hints at the meaning of <u>hence</u>. Rewrite the sentence with *hence*, replacing the word with a phrase that has the same meaning.

Name _____ Date _____

Literary Analysis: Comparing Types of Description

Descriptive writing paints word pictures for readers. A variety of descriptions can be used in poetry to present **levels of meaning.**

- **Literal meaning** is the actual, everyday meaning of words.
- **Figurative meaning** relies on figures of speech and the symbolic nature of language.

An **analogy** is a figurative description that compares two or more things that are similar in some ways, but otherwise unalike. For example, a poem that literally describes the ocean also can be read as an analogy: it may compare the ocean to life because both are vast, deep, and ever-changing. The poem, therefore, has two levels of meaning—one literal and one figurative.

DIRECTIONS: *On the following chart, for each quotation from a poem, note words and images that give you clues about its figurative meaning. The first one is done for you.*

Passages from "The Road Not Taken"	Which words and images give you clues about the figurative meaning of the passage?
1. "Two roads diverged in a yellow wood,"	Two roads = choices; yellow wood = life
2. "Then took the other, as just as fair, / And having perhaps the better claim, / Because it was grassy and wanted wear;"	

Passages from "O Captain! My Captain"	Which words and images give you clues about the figurative meaning of the passage?
3. "O Captain! my Captain! our fearful trip is done, / The ship has weather'd every rack, the prize we sought is won,"	
4. "My Captain does not answer, his lips are pale and still, / My father does not feel my arm, he has no pulse nor will."	

Name _____ Date _____

Poetry by Robert Frost and Walt Whitman
Vocabulary Builder

Word List

diverged   exulting

A. DIRECTIONS: *Complete the following word map by filling in the appropriate information.*

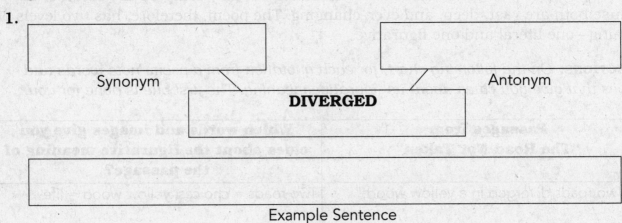

1.

Synonym _____   Antonym _____

DIVERGED

Example Sentence

2.

Synonym _____   Antonym _____

EXULTING

Example Sentence

B. DIRECTIONS: *Circle the letter of the pair that best expresses a relationship similar to that expressed in the pair in CAPITAL LETTERS.*

1. DIVERGED : SEPARATED ::
   A. converged : split
   B. removed : extracted
   C. weighed : calculated
   D. dressed : appeared

2. EXULTING : LAMENTING ::
   A. talk : converse
   B. barrel : basket
   C. seldom : often
   D. dwindle : decrease

Unit 4 Resources: Poetry

Poetry by Robert Frost and Walt Whitman
Support for Writing to Compare Description in Literary Works

Before you write your essay, use the graphic organizer below to list ideas about each poem.

"The Road Not Taken"

How common are the experiences the poets describe?	How universal are the emotions that prompt the descriptions?	Which poet better expresses his emotions through the descriptions? Why?	Which message is easier for you to interpret? Why?

"O Captain! My Captain"

Now, use your notes to write your essay comparing the descriptions in the "The Road Not Taken" and "O Captain! My Captain!"

Name _____ Date _____

Poetry by Robert Frost and Walt Whitman
Selection Test A

Critical Reading *Identify the letter of the choice that best answers the question.*

____ 1. At the beginning of "The Road Not Taken," what decision does the speaker face?
   A. which road to take
   B. where to eat lunch
   C. whether to go forward or go back
   D. whether to keep walking or stop and rest

____ 2. What do the following lines from "The Road Not Taken" mean?
   And sorry I could not travel both
   And be one traveler,
   A. He thinks both paths are equally good.
   B. He is only one man and cannot go down two roads at the same time.
   C. He wishes that he were traveling with someone, so they could each explore a path.
   D. He regrets not taking the other road as he looks back.

____ 3. What is the difference between the two roads in "The Road Not Taken"?
   A. one road is wider
   B. one road has a better view
   C. one road is less traveled
   D. one road is rockier

____ 4. What does the speaker mean in these lines from "The Road Not Taken"?
   Oh, I kept the first for another day!
   Yet knowing how way leads on to way,
   I doubted if I should ever come back.
   A. After walking the first road, he will come back and go down the road he did not take.
   B. He does not like to travel in the same part of the woods over and over again.
   C. He likes to walk in the woods by himself and knows the way very well.
   D. He wants to take the other path later, but realizes he will probably never have that chance.

____ 5. Whom does the speaker in "The Road Not Taken" stand for?
   A. someone lost in the woods
   B. a person who made a decision
   C. a person now standing at a fork
   D. a person who likes a well-beaten path

6. What do the "two roads" represent in "The Road Not Taken"?
   A. significant people who impact our lives
   B. paths that fate leads us to
   C. the beginnings of new phases in life
   D. important decisions made in life

7. On the surface, "The Road Not Taken" is about a walk in the woods. What is the meaning of the poem on a deeper level?
   A. It is about traveling through life with others to help you make decisions.
   B. It is about loving and protecting nature by not disturbing natural habitats.
   C. It is about what to do when faced with life's important decisions.
   D. It is about the importance of exercise and enjoying the outdoors.

8. Who is the Captain in "O Captain! My Captain!"?
   A. Walt Whitman
   B. General McClellan
   C. a ship's captain
   D. President Lincoln

9. In "O Captain! My Captain!" which historical event is the poet mourning?
   A. the defeat of the Confederacy
   B. the victory of the Union
   C. the assassination of President Lincoln
   D. the death of Walt Whitman's father

10. In the following lines from "O Captain! My Captain!" what does the *ship* represent?
    The ship has weather'd every rack,
    the prize we sought is won.

    A. the United States
    B. the North
    C. the South
    D. the presidency

11. Why does the speaker of "O Captain! My Captain!" say the following lines?
    It is some dream that on the deck,
       You've fallen cold and dead.

    A. He dreamt the President had died.
    B. He wishes the President were not dead.
    C. He dreamt while sleeping on the deck.
    D. He is afraid of dying on a ship.

____ 12. What do the following lines from "O Captain! My Captain!" mean?

> My Captain does not answer, his lips are pale
> and still,

    A. The Captain is dead.

    B. The Captain is too cold to talk.

    C. The Captain is mad.

    D. The Captain is sleeping.

____ 13. In "O Captain! My Captain!" what does "fearful trip" refer to when the speaker says, "From fearful trip the victor ship comes in"?

    A. the Civil War

    B. a fierce storm at sea

    C. the presidency

    D. Lincoln's life

Vocabulary and Grammar

____ 14. Which would be an appropriate word to replace *diverged*?

    A. divided

    B. presented

    C. conformed

    D. unequaled

____ 15. In which of the following instances would you most likely find someone *exulting*?

    A. at a funeral

    B. during a test

    C. after a dental appointment

    D. after winning a championship game

Essay

16. The poems "The Road Not Taken" and "O Captain! My Captain!" present images with a literal meaning. In an essay, compare the literal meaning of the images in each poem. What is a "literal meaning"? What is the literal meaning of the images in "The Road Not Taken"? How would you summarize what happens on the surface of the poem? What is the literal meaning of the images in "O Captain! My Captain!"? How would you summarize what happens on the surface of the poem?

17. The images in "The Road Not Taken" and "O Captain! My Captain!" have figurative meanings. Write an essay comparing the figurative descriptions in the two poems. What is a "figurative meaning"? What is the figurative meaning of "The Road Not Taken"? What is the figurative meaning of "O Captain! My Captain!"?

Poetry by Robert Frost and Walt Whitman
Selection Test B

Critical Reading *Identify the letter of the choice that best completes the statement or answers the question.*

____ 1. The speaker in "The Road Not Taken" is a person who
    A. is lost in the woods.
    B. remembers making a decision.
    C. is currently standing at a fork in the road.
    D. likes to walk on a well-beaten path.

____ 2. In "The Road Not Taken," the description of the wood as yellow
    A. tells us the wood is very young, not yet full grown.
    B. makes the setting seem churchlike.
    C. tells us the scene is taking place at noon.
    D. helps us see the scene as autumnal.

____ 3. Which is the best restatement of these lines from "The Road Not Taken"?
    And sorry I could not travel both
    And be one traveler, . . .
    A. I regret I couldn't take both roads.
    B. I regret I am only one person.
    C. I regret that I am traveling alone.
    D. I am sorry to be far from home.

____ 4. In "The Road Not Taken," when Frost says two roads ". . . that morning equally lay / In leaves no step had trodden black," he means that
    A. both roads were covered in yellow leaves.
    B. both roads were wet with dew.
    C. neither road led to a place the speaker wanted to go.
    D. neither road had been walked on yet that morning.

____ 5. Which line or lines from "The Road Not Taken" describe the setting?
    I. I shall be telling this with a sigh / Somewhere ages and ages hence:
    II. Yet knowing how way leads on to way, / I doubted if I should ever come back.
    III. Though as for that, the passing there / Had worn them really about the same.
    A. I
    B. II
    C. III
    D. I, II, and III

____ 6. What is "The Road Not Taken" about below its surface meaning?
    A. It closely observes the impact of humans on the woods.
    B. It urges readers to take chances.
    C. It raises questions of choice and decision making.
    D. It urges readers to exercise and enjoy the outdoors.

_____ 7. In "O Captain! My Captain!" the poet is mourning
    A. the defeat of the Confederacy.
    B. the victory of the Union.
    C. the assassination of President Lincoln.
    D. the endlessness of war.

_____ 8. The Captain in "O Captain! My Captain"
    A. represents Walt Whitman.
    B. is buried at sea.
    C. is a ship's captain.
    D. represents President Lincoln.

_____ 9. In the first line from "O Captain! My Captain!" what does "our fearful trip" refer to?
    A. the Civil War
    B. the battle at Antietam Creek
    C. the presidency
    D. Lincoln's life

_____ 10. Which statement best expresses the underlying meaning of this line from "O Captain! My Captain!"?

    The ship has weather'd every rack, the prize we

    sought is won.

    A. Despite its hardships, the North will now be richer than the South.
    B. The Union has survived great difficulties and won the war.
    C. The Union has been greatly weakened by the war.
    D. The ship has withstood every peril and returns home safely.

_____ 11. In "O Captain! My Captain!" what is the underlying meaning of this line?

    The port is near, the bells I hear, the people all

    exulting.

    A. Many Americans will greet the ship and pay their respects to President Lincoln.
    B. The goal of keeping America one country is within reach, and people are joyous.
    C. I am glad to be approaching victory and returning to my church and my people.
    D. We're are not quite home yet. We still have to quell riots.

_____ 12. Why are the people acting as they are in the following lines of "O Captain! My Captain!"?

    For you bouquets and ribbon'd wreaths—for you

    the shores a-crowding,

    For you they call, the swaying mass, their eager

    faces turning:

    A. They are paying tribute to Lincoln because he has died.
    B. They are welcoming the general who won many battles, but died in the last one.
    C. They are celebrating Lincoln's election to a second term.
    D. They are paying tribute to a great sailor who is bringing them wealth.

____ 13. What does the *ship* represent in this line from "O Captain! My Captain!"?
The ship is anchor'd safe and sound, its voyage
closed and done,
A. the North
B. the South
C. the United States
D. the war

Vocabulary

____ 14. In which sentence is *diverged* used correctly?
A. Where the two roads *diverged* into one road, the traffic became backed up.
B. The river flowed south and then *diverged* to the southeast and the southwest.
C. The crowd was happy to be *diverged* into the waterpark.
D. When it started to rain, we *diverged* and canceled the picnic.

____ 15. Which word is most *opposite* in meaning to *diverged*?
A. divided
B. presented
C. conformed
D. unequaled

____ 16. In which sentence is *exulting* used correctly?
A. We enjoyed the wedding, *exulting* in the love of the happy couple.
B. The tribal people, *exulting* the hunter with fire power, thought he was a god.
C. The *exulting* rain was pleasant to walk in, even if it made us wet.
D. When the guest of honor arrived late, the *exulting* group got up and left.

Essay

17. Both "The Road Not Taken" and "O Captain! My Captain!" address personal feelings. In an essay, compare and contrast the speakers in the two poems. What does each speaker say about his subject? How does each speaker feel about his subject?

18. Both "The Road Not Taken" and "O Captain! My Captain!" are analogies. Write an essay comparing the authors' use of analogy. What is analogy? How does Frost use analogy in his poem? How does Whitman use analogy in his poem? Why has each of these analogy poems become so famous?

Writing Workshop—Unit 4, Part 2
Comparison-and-Contrast Essay

Prewriting: Gathering Details

Use the Venn diagram below to list ideas and details about your two subjects. Use the center section to record similarities and the outer sections of each circle to record differences.

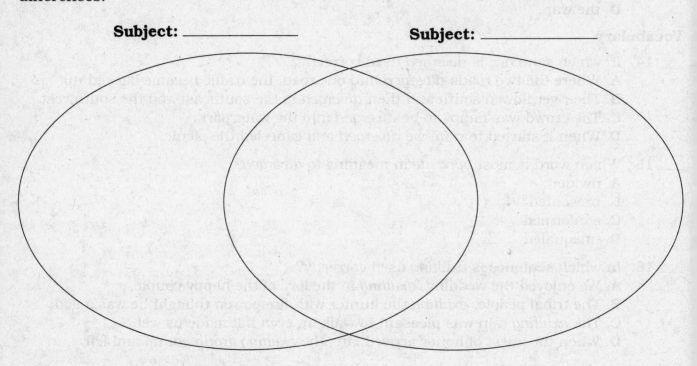

Subject: _____   Subject: _____

Drafting: Providing Elaboration

Use the chart below to develop the main point of each supporting paragraph in your essay.

Paragraphs	First Paragraph	Second Paragraph
State the topic of each paragraph.		
Extend the idea by restating it in a new way, applying it to a particular case, or contrasting it with another point.		
Elaborate with specific examples, facts, statistics, explanations, or quotations.		

Writing Workshop—Unit 4, Part 2
Comparison-and-Contrast Essay: Integrating Grammar Skills

Revising to Vary Sentence Beginnings

To keep your writing lively, avoid starting each sentence the same way. You can start sentences with different parts of speech or with prepositional phrases.

Start with a noun:	The <u>diner</u>, tapping impatiently, called for the check.
Start with an adjective:	<u>Surprised</u>, the waiter rushed over.
Start with a prepositional phrase:	<u>After a brief discussion</u>, the waiter delivered the bill.

Common Prepositions			
Sequence	**Location**	**Direction**	**(Other)**
after	in	around	about
before	near	down	for

Identifying a Variety of Sentence Beginnings

A. DIRECTIONS: *Circle the word that describes the sentence beginning.*

1. In ancient Egypt, pharaohs built pyramids. *(noun, prepositional phrase)*

2. The pyramids, enormous and grand, held treasures. *(noun, adjective)*

3. During an expedition, archaeologists found a sealed door. *(prepositional phrase, noun)*

4. Excited, they entered a room filled with objects. *(prepositional phrase, adjective)*

Fixing Repetitive Sentence Beginnings

B. DIRECTIONS: *On the lines provided, rewrite these sentences so that they begin with either an* adjective *or a* prepositional phrase.

1. The mummy of King Tutankhamen was in the tomb.

   _____

2. The body was preserved by Egypt's dry climate and was in excellent condition.

   _____

3. King Tut was wearing a mask of solid gold, and he looked magnificent!

   _____

4. Archaeologists found objects to study in King Tut's tomb.

   _____

Name _____ Date _____

Words With Prefixes and Suffixes

Prefixes are affixes added to beginnings of base words. **Suffixes** are affixes added to ends of words. When using the prefix *in-*, choose the correct form (*il-*, *im-*, or *ir-*) to match the base word. Memorize the spellings of words with *-ance* and *-ence*, and *-able* and *-ible*, as there are no sound clues to help you.

Word List

cooperate	existence	irresponsible	questionable
correspondence	impatient	performance	reversible

A. DIRECTIONS: *Write the word in parentheses that is correctly spelled.*

1. (correspondance, correspondence) between the brothers _____
2. a very (iresponsible, irresponsible) attitude _____
3. got (impatient, inpatient) with the delay _____
4. received (questionable, questionible) advice _____
5. gave a great (preformance, performance) _____
6. refused to (coperate, cooperate) _____
7. a pretty boring (existance, existence) _____
8. a new (reversible, reversable) jacket _____

B. DIRECTIONS: *Write two or three sentences using each group of words below.*

1. *irresponsible, inheritance,* and *existence*

_____

_____

_____

2. *impatient, cooperate, questionable,* and *reversible*

_____

_____

_____

3. *correspondence, persihable,* and *performance*

_____

_____

_____

Name _____ Date _____

Evaluating Media Messages

After choosing your commercial, fill out the following chart to evaluate the content and techniques of what you see.

Title of commercial: _____

What are some of the images presented in the commercial?

What is the message behind them?

What mood is created by key words, music, or sound effects?

What media techniques are used to persuade you to agree with this meassage?

How would you rate the credibility of this message?

For Further Reading—Unit 4

DIRECTIONS: *Think about the books you have read. Then, on a separate sheet of paper, answer the discussion questions and take notes for your Literature Circle.*

Trouble the Water: 250 Years of African American Poetry edited by Jerry W. Ward, Jr.

Discussion Identify two poems that express insights about strong African American women. Cite a detail from each poem that supports this theme.

Connections—Literature Circle Summarize what these poems, taken together, reveal about the importance of poetry in the African American experience.

Johnny Tremain by Esther Forbes

Discussion After Johnny injures his hand, he becomes friends with Rab Silsbee. What qualities does Rab have that makes him a role model for Johnny?

Connections—Literature Circle When the novel begins, Johnny is a fourteen-year-old boy. When the story ends, he is a sixteen-year-old man. What causes this change in Johnny? How are his experiences in the novel a journey into adulthood for him?

Reflections on a Gift of Watermelon Pickle: and Other Modern Verse compiled by Stephen Dunning, Edward Lueders, and Hugh Smith

Discussion In "The Builders" by Sara Henderson Hay, who is the speaker in this poem? What story is he telling? How does this version of the old story differ from the original?

Connections—Literature Circle In "The Forecast" by Dan Jaffe, what kind of forecast is the speaker describing? What has it replaced in our lives? Is he at all optimistic about the people who have snapped their locks and pulled down their shades? Explain.

Poems by Robert Frost: A Boy's Will and North of Boston: Prentice Hall Anthology

Discussion Which seasons do the poems in Part I of *A Boy's Will* evoke? Give examples of lines that refer to a specific time of year.

Connections—Literature Circle Compare and contrast the two attitudes toward walls expressed in "Mending Wall." Identify which view you agree with and explain why you agree.

Unit 4: Poetry
Part 2 Benchmark Test 8

MULTIPLE CHOICE

Reading Skill *Read the selection, and answer the questions that follow.*

> 1 Announced by all the trumpets of the sky,
> 2 Arrives the snow, and, driving o'er the fields,
> 3 Seems nowhere to alight: the whited air
> 4 Hides hill and woods, the river, and the heaven,
> 5 And veils the farmhouse at the garden's end.
>
> —from "The Snowstorm" by Ralph Waldo Emerson

1. What is the best paraphrase of lines 1 through 3, up to the colon?
   A. The sky is full of wonder, and trumpets blow everywhere.
   B. While we were driving over the fields, the snow started.
   C. The snow comes, blown about with great force by the wind.
   D. The wind is blowing hard and sounds like trumpets.

2. Which best restates the clause in lines 3 through 5 beginning "the whited air"?
   A. The snow falls softly on the land.
   B. The snow blots out everything.
   C. Snow falls but does not stick.
   D. The weather is cold and gloomy.

Read the selection from a poem by John Masefield. Then, answer the questions that follow.

> 1 I must go down to the seas again, for the call of the running tide
> 2 Is a wild call and a clear call that may not be denied;
> 3 And all I ask is a windy day with the white clouds flying,
> 4 And the flung spray and the blown spume, and the sea-gulls crying.
>
> 5 I must go down to the seas again, to the vagrant gypsy life,
> 6 To the gull's way and the whale's way where the wind's like a whetted knife;
> 7 And all I ask is a merry yarn from a laughing fellow-rover,
> 8 And quiet sleep and a sweet dream when the long trick's over.
>
> —from "Sea Fever" by John Masefield

3. Reading Masefield's verse according to punctuation, where would you come to a complete stop?
   A. after lines 4 and 8
   B. after lines 2 and 6
   C. after lines 3, 6, and 7
   D. at the end of every line

4. Which of these should the reader do in line 5?
   A. Pause only after the end comma.
   B. Pause only after the first comma.
   C. Come to a stop after the end comma.
   D. Pause briefly after each comma.

5. Which is the best paraphrase of the excerpt from Masefield's poem?
   A. I love the wind and the salt spray when I am near the sea.
   B. I cannot resist the call of the wild, free life on the seas.
   C. I love to sail the sea on a clear, windy day.
   D. I envy the wild, free life of seagulls and whales.

Read the selection from a computer manual. Then answer the questions that follow.

Try these steps if your computer display goes blank or if your system freezes:

1. Unplug all external devices that are connected to your computer except the power adapter.
2. Simultaneously depress the Command and Control keys, as well as the Power button, to reactivate the system.
3. Allow the battery to charge at least ten percent before plugging in an external devices.

6. Which sentence is the best paraphrase of step 2?
   A. Press the Command key, followed by the Control key.
   B. Press the Command key, and then press the Control and Power buttons.
   C. Press the Command, Control, and Power buttons, all at the same time.
   D. Press the Power button, and then press the Command and Control keys.

7. Which of these is most important in reading to perform the task described in the selection?
   A. understanding the order of the steps
   B. memorizing the steps in order
   C. drawing a diagram of the steps
   D. skimming over the steps

8. Which paraphrase shows the steps described in the selection in the correct order?
   A. Unplug the power adapter. Recharge the battery to ten percent. Then hold down the Command and Control keys. Press the Power button to restart your computer.
   B. Plug in external devices to the computer. Then hold down the Command, Control, and Power buttons to turn off the computer. Let the battery recharge to ten percent.
   C. Unplug all devices except the power adapter. Then restart the computer by holding down the Command, Control, and Power keys all at once. Let the battery charge to ten percent before plugging in externals.
   D. Hold down the Command and Control keys to shut down the computer. Then recharge the battery to ten percent. Restart the computer by pressing the Power key.

Literary Analysis *Read the selections, and answer the questions that follow.*

Shall I compare thee to a summer's day?
Thou art more lovely and more temperate.
Rough winds do shake the darling buds of May,
And summer's lease hath all too short a date.

—from "Sonnet 18" by William Shakespeare

The tide rises, the tide falls,
The twilight darkens, the curfew calls;
Along the sea-sands damp and brown
The traveller hastens toward the town,
And the tide rises, the tide falls.

—from "The Tide Rises, the Tide Falls" by Henry Wadsworth Longfellow

9. What form of poetry are the lines by William Shakespeare?
   A. lyric poetry
   B. humorous poetry
   C. concrete poetry
   D. narrative poetry

10. Which of these best describes the overall impression of Shakespeare's sonnet?
    A. The speaker loves summer more than autumn.
    B. The speaker is expressing tender love for someone.
    C. The speaker appreciates the different moods of summer.
    D. The speaker feels that summer days pass too quickly.

11. Which of these best expresses the setting of Longfellow's poem?
    A. a boat in the ocean
    B. a town near the sea
    C. a seashore near a town
    D. a lonely road near town

12. What is the main purpose of a narrative poem?
    A. to express a feeling
    B. to tell a story
    C. to describe a character
    D. to describe a setting

13. Which imagery from Longfellow's poem appeals to the senses of touch and sight?
    A. the tide rises, the tide falls
    B. the twilight darkens
    C. the traveller hastens
    D. the sea-sands damp and brown

14. Which of these best defines imagery in poetry?
    A. pictures that accompany poetry
    B. comparison of one thing to another
    C. language that appeals to the senses
    D. imagination in poetry

15. Which of these is an example of the use of imagery?
    A. The icy snow crunched underfoot.
    B. Jack filled his plate with food.
    C. Two chimneys rose from the house.
    D. His mind was busily at work.

16. Which of these reflects the actual meaning of words?
    A. a description using metaphor
    B. a description using analogy
    C. a figurative description
    D. a literal description

17. Which of these best shows the use of analogy in a poem?
    A. a description of a candle flame that can be compared to a life
    B. a description of a storm using images that appeal to the senses
    C. a description of a character who undergoes changes
    D. a description of sights and sounds found in nature

Vocabulary: Word Origins

18. In which of these will you most likely find word origins?
    A. a thesaurus
    B. a dictionary
    C. a history book
    D. an almanac

19. If *aquatic* comes from the Latin word *aqua,* meaning "water," which word probably shares the same origin as *aquatic*?
    A. aquarium
    B. acquire
    C. quart
    D. quality

20. If *receive* comes from the Latin word *recipere,* meaning "to take," which word probably shares the same origin as *receive*?
    A. reception
    B. recipe
    C. recite
    D. respite

21. If *gratify* comes from the Latin word *gratus*, meaning "pleasing," which word probably shares the same origin as *gratify*?
   A. graduate
   B. congratulate
   C. migrate
   D. grating

Grammar

22. What is the preposition in the following sentence?

   The poet drew inspiration from nature.

   A. poet
   B. drew
   C. from
   D. nature

23. What is the prepositional phrase in the following sentence?

   Each day, White created both humorous and touching poetry in his attic room.

   A. in his attic room
   B. both humorous and touching poetry
   C. each day
   D. his attic room

24. What is the infinitive in the following sentence?

   Elsa likes to read poetry that is composed by children.

   A. likes
   B. to
   C. read
   D. by

25. Which sentence contains an infinitive phrase?
   A. To Jenny, the poem sounded false.
   B. Eduardo recited the lines to me.
   C. We hope to visit the poet's birthplace.
   D. The writer paid tribute to his parents.

26. Which is the best way to vary the dull pattern in the following sentence?

   The cyclists pedaled to the top of the hill.

   A. The cyclists pedaled quickly to the top of the hill.
   B. The three cyclists pedaled to the top of the steep hill.
   C. Huffing and chuffing, the cyclists pedaled slowly up the steep hill.
   D. Several cyclists rode slowly up the steep hill.

27. Which of these best defines an appositive phrase?
   A. a phrase that begins with a preposition and ends with a noun
   B. a noun phrase that defines other words in a sentence
   C. an infinitive with a modifier that acts as a single part of speech
   D. a form of verb that follows the word *to* and acts as a noun, adjective, or adverb

Spelling

28. In which sentence is the underlined word spelled correctly?
   A. Phil's <u>absince</u> affected the project.
   B. Her argument seemed <u>ilogical</u>.
   C. We found an <u>affordable</u> vacation.
   D. There was <u>resistence</u> to my idea.

29. Which word would correctly complete the following sentence?

   Who is _____ for notifying the newspaper of our book sale?

   A. responsable
   B. responsible
   C. responssible
   D. responseable

30. Which word would correctly complete the following sentence?

   An additional _____ of the play is scheduled for Sunday afternoon.

   A. performance
   B. performence
   C. performmence
   D. performince

ESSAY

Writing

31. Imagine that you want to write either a lyric or a narrative poem about a river. Decide whether you want to describe your impressions of the river or tell a story about it. Write the first line of a poem you might write. If you are writing a lyric poem, make sure to include at least two details about the river's qualities; if you are writing a narrative poem, include information about the setting and a character in the poem.

32. Choose one of the poems from this test and imagine that you have been asked to write a review of it. Write the headings "Word Choice" and "Imagery." Then write an example of each from the poem and tell whether you think the poet uses the word or words and images effectively. Give reasons for your opinions.

33. You are planning a summer trip to another state, far away from your home state. Should you travel by plane or by car. Write a comparison-and contrast essay in which you examine the similarities and differences between the two methods of travel.

ANSWERS

Poetry by Jacqueline Woodson

Vocabulary Warm-up Exercises, p. 2

A. 1. upstate
2. awhile
3. dabbing
4. regular
5. squints
6. grins

B. Sample Answers
1. When *lava* and ash shoot out of a *volcano*, tourists are urged to stay far away from the dangerous site.
2. Planting a *maple* in the front yard of a house in Vermont is a wise choice.
3. The *preacher* addresses his congregation each Sunday to talk about religious ideas.
4. When creating *superheroes*, the artists try to make them look unusual and give them extraordinary powers.
5. The most amazing *moment* of the year was the stroke of midnight on New Year's Eve, when confetti poured down from the ceiling.

Reading Warm-up A, p. 3

Sample Answers
1. (everyday); My regular morning routine begins with waking up at 6:00 A.M., eating a quick breakfast, taking a fast shower, and running out the door.
2. a brief time; I played video games for awhile yesterday.
3. (farther south); Upstate is the area in the northern part of a state.
4. (frowns); smiles
5. (a tear away); someone might be dabbing spilled soda off of a table.
6. peers; When someone squints, they narrow their eyes to help them to see better.

Reading Warm-up B, p. 4

Sample Answers
1. Leaving her friends in Chicago would be the most horrible moment for Tonya.; A *moment* is "a particular point in time."
2. favorite climbing tree; A *maple* is a big tree of hard wood that has pretty leaves and produces sweet sap.
3. (Her ten-year-old brother); A *preacher* talks about religious ideas, and paradise is a place people associate with religion.
4. an island; A *volcano* is a mountain with a large hole in the top that can explode and send hot, melted rock called *lava* into the air.
5. (fairy-tale endings; the ease of change); One of my favorite *superheroes* was a woman who could fly through the air and see through walls.

Jacqueline Woodson

Listening and Viewing, p. 5

Segment 1. Jacqueline Woodson's interest in writing began when she learned to write her name and understood that letters made words and words made sentences. She then understood that the world is moved through words, and realized what great power words, therefore, hold. Students may suggest that because Woodson tries to begin from a place that is real to her, her stories are valid and appealing to her audience. Being honest in her writing enables her to develop realistic characters who deal with universal issues.

Segment 2. Jacqueline Woodson thinks the white space on the page surrounding a poem is important because it offers a break from stimuli or distraction; the white space around the poem is like air that allows the words to sink in.

Segment 3. Jacqueline Woodson first hears a voice in her head; the voice is usually a character telling her a story. She then develops details about the character. Students may suggest that they would not outline or envision the ending of a story, but would pull bits and pieces of the story together over time and might work on several different types of writing at once.

Segment 4. Jacqueline Woodson is rewarded when she knows that she has written a good, complete story that can impact the world somehow. Students may suggest that self-expression is so important that a writer should not fear the reaction from a reader but embrace it. Alternatively, students may say that a writer must consider readers in order to appeal to them.

Learning About Poetry, p. 6

1. C; 2. B; 3. B; 4. B; 5. B; 6. C

The Poetry of Jacqueline Woodson

Model Selection: Poetry, p. 7

1. alliteration ("Ms. Marcus"); assonance ("little bit skinny")
2. simile; Eric's voice with an angel's voice
3. personification (Some students may say that *like* in the second line introduces a simile. Explain that the simile involves personification.)
4. assonance: "leaves . . . reaching"; alliteration: "like . . . like . . . leaves"

Selection Test A, p. 8

Learning About Poetry

1. ANS: A	DIF: Easy	OBJ: Literary Analysis
2. ANS: D	DIF: Easy	OBJ: Literary Analysis

3. ANS: C	DIF: Easy	OBJ: Literary Analysis	3. ANS: C	DIF: Average	OBJ: Literary Analysis
4. ANS: D	DIF: Easy	OBJ: Literary Analysis	4. ANS: C	DIF: Challenging	OBJ: Literary Analysis
5. ANS: D	DIF: Easy	OBJ: Literary Analysis	5. ANS: D	DIF: Average	OBJ: Literary Analysis
			6. ANS: A	DIF: Average	OBJ: Literary Analysis
			7. ANS: D	DIF: Average	OBJ: Literary Analysis

Critical Reading

6. ANS: D	DIF: Easy	OBJ: Comprehension
7. ANS: C	DIF: Easy	OBJ: Comprehension
8. ANS: C	DIF: Easy	OBJ: Interpretation
9. ANS: C	DIF: Easy	OBJ: Comprehension
10. ANS: B	DIF: Easy	OBJ: Interpretation
11. ANS: C	DIF: Easy	OBJ: Comprehension
12. ANS: A	DIF: Easy	OBJ: Comprehension
13. ANS: B	DIF: Easy	OBJ: Literary Analysis
14. ANS: C	DIF: Easy	OBJ: Comprehension
15. ANS: C	DIF: Easy	OBJ: Interpretation

Critical Reading

8. ANS: B	DIF: Average	OBJ: Comprehension
9. ANS: B	DIF: Challenging	OBJ: Comprehension
10. ANS: C	DIF: Average	OBJ: Comprehension
11. ANS: A	DIF: Average	OBJ: Literary Analysis
12. ANS: A	DIF: Average	OBJ: Interpretation
13. ANS: B	DIF: Average	OBJ: Interpretation
14. ANS: C	DIF: Average	OBJ: Comprehension
15. ANS: B	DIF: Average	OBJ: Interpretation
16. ANS: B	DIF: Average	OBJ: Literary Analysis
17. ANS: B	DIF: Challenging	OBJ: Interpretation
18. ANS: D	DIF: Challenging	OBJ: Interpretation

Essay

16. Students should point out that Lonnie is warm, observant, positive, and appreciative. Lonnie is quick to see the good in others, and he appreciates the support given him by figures such as Ms. Marcus, the teacher, and Rodney, Miss Edna's son, who fills the role of older foster brother and mentor to Lonnie. At the same time, Lonnie is portrayed as timid. For example, in "Describe Somebody," he fears Eric's anger; and in "Almost a Summer Sky," he claims he understands why Rodney had to live upstate with the trees for a while, even though he does *not* understand why. Students should explain why they would like to know Lonnie personally or not.

    Difficulty: *Easy*

    Objective: *Essay*

17. A possible theme statement for "Describe Somebody" might be "Everyone around us, including those who may appear mean or unlikable, possesses a talent or an ability." The theme is supported by the speaker's revelation that Eric is in a choir and sings beautifully and by the speaker's comments about Angel's ability at science and Lamont's talent for drawing. In "Almost a Summer Sky," the theme might be stated as follows: "Just as families offer their members protection, shelter, and comfort, nature offers shade and protection to those who live in harmony with their environment." This theme is supported by Rodney's description of the trees upstate as well as by Lonnie's comfort in living with Miss Edna and her family.

    Difficulty: *Easy*

    Objective: *Essay*

Essay

19. Students' choice of details will vary. In "Describe Somebody," for example, they may cite Ms. Marcus's smile, Angel's volcano exhibit for science fair, and Eric's voice like an angel. These details create a mood of pleasure and point to the central message: everyone has a strength and capacity for achievement. In "Almost a Summer Sky," students might single out the light, warm rain, the blue patch in the sky, the upstate trees as big as three men, Lily's big smile, and Rodney's comparison of the leaves to hands that offer shade. These details also create a mood of pleasure, and they point to the overall message of harmony with one's surroundings.

    Difficulty: *Average*

    Objective: *Essay*

20. In their essays, students should point out that the poem they choose qualifies as a lyric because it expresses the thoughts and feelings of a single speaker, Lonnie. If students opt to offer an example of figurative language from the poem they have selected, they might cite the simile comparing Eric's voice to an angel's in "Describe Somebody" or the personification comparing the trees' leaves to hands reaching out in "Almost a Summer Sky." Sensory images abound in both poems: for example, Ms. Marcus's long, shiny, brown hair in "Describe Somebody" and the light, warm rain in "Almost a Summer Sky." Repetition includes the expression "real good" in "Describe Somebody" and "a poet's heart," "brother," and "trees" in "Almost a Summer Sky."

    Difficulty: *Average*

    Objective: *Essay*

Selection Test B, p. 11

Learning About Poetry

1. ANS: B	DIF: Average	OBJ: Literary Analysis
2. ANS: D	DIF: Average	OBJ: Literary Analysis

Diagnostic Test 7, p. 15

MULTIPLE CHOICE

1. ANS: C
2. ANS: A
3. ANS: D
4. ANS: B
5. ANS: D
6. ANS: A
7. ANS: D
8. ANS: C
9. ANS: A
10. ANS: C
11. ANS: B
12. ANS: A
13. ANS: C
14. ANS: D
15. ANS: D

Poetry Collection: Eleanor Farjeon, Walter de la Mare, Georgia Douglas Johnson

Vocabulary Warm-up Exercises, p. 19

A.
1. gleam
2. horizon
3. peers
4. throbbed
5. scampering
6. scatter

B. Sample Answers

1. *Casements* allow windows to open by swinging out to the sides instead of having to be pulled up.
2. I'd rather sleep on a cotton mattress than on a *thatch* one because the straw would be hard and scratchy.
3. I think Florida would be the state with the city at the *uttermost* point from an Alaskan city.
4. If the coast were constantly *battered*, then waves and wind would be hitting the rocky shores.
5. Since everything appears huge to a small child, even a small lake would seem to have *immensity*.
6. I would describe gelatin as *slithery*.

Reading Warm-up A, p. 20

Sample Answers

1. the sun sinks slowly; The *horizon* is the place where land or water seems to meet the sky.
2. (into the growing gloom); Since *peers* is used to describe how a person looks hard at something that is difficult to

see, it is a good word to use when talking about how someone can't see very well as darkness comes.
3. hustles home before nightfall; *Scampering* means "the act of running with short, quick steps."
4. (moon); Stars also *gleam* at night.
5. They are afraid of becoming the mighty bird's evening meal; *Scatter* means "to toss around or cause to go here and there."
6. (activity and excitement); *Throbbed* means "beat quickly, as a heart."

Reading Warm-up B, p. 21

Sample Answers

1. the tops of makeshift shelters; *Thatch* is dried straw used to make roofs.
2. (are thrown open); Every night across the planet, windows are opened wide so people can lean out of them and gaze up at the skies.
3. universe; If you were traveling in space and got lost, you might never find your way back to Earth because of its *immensity*.
4. (sticks together); *Slithery* surfaces, like wet floors, can cause people to fall, and that is disastrous.
5. (smooth); Forces such as wind, meteors, and other flying objects might have *battered* space vehicles and space stations.
6. (universe); People want to explore *uttermost* places of our universe because they want to discover new things and have always been curious about the unknown.

Poetry Collection: Eleanor Farjeon, Walter de la Mare, Georgia Douglas Johnson

Reading: Preview to Determine Meanings From Context, p. 22

1. catch (line 13)
2. A. It is a tree.
   B. bark (line 26)
3. sees
4. "Where the sky-line encircled the sea"
5. A. It is a noun.
   B. distant corner; places that are hard to get to

Literary Analysis: Sound Devices, p. 23

"Cat!"

Rhythm—The poem captures the chase by using very short lines that open on a strong beat: good examples include lines 3, 11, and 13. *Rhyme*—While there is no real pattern of end rhyme, there is frequent use of the same few sounds—for instance, lines 1, 2, and 7 (*cat/scat/mat*) and lines 3–6 (*after her/flatterer/chatterer/scatter her*). *Alliteration*—The many *s* sounds, echoing the cat's hiss or scratch, include those in lines 4–6 (*sleeky, spitfire, scatter*) and the *sl* sounds in lines 15–16 (*slathery, slithery*). *Onomatopoeia*—Among the many examples (some of which are invented by the poet) are *wuff, scratcher, hisser, pffts,* and *scritching.*

"Silver"

Rhythm—The poem captures the steady movement of the moonlight in lines that contain four beats and often open on a beat; good examples include the first four lines. *Rhyme*—The end rhymes form a pattern in which each pair of lines rhyme (*moon/shoon* in lines 1–2, *sees/trees* in lines 3–4, and so on). *Alliteration*—Examples include the *th* in line 3 (*this, that*) and the *k* sounds in line 5 (*casements, catch*). *Onomatopoiea—scampering*

"Your World"

Rhythm—Each line has three beats, but the odd-numbered lines have an extra syllable at the end. Two unstressed syllables often precede a stressed syllable, as in line 5: "But I SIGHTed the DIStant hoRIzon." The steady da-da-DUM of the rhythm beats home the poem's advice. *Rhyme*—The even-numbered lines rhyme (*abide/side* in lines 2 and 4 and so on). *Alliteration*—Examples include the *n* sounds in line 3 (*narrowest, nest*). *Onomatopoeia—throbbed, battered,* perhaps *soared.*

Vocabulary Builder, p. 24

A. 1. F; 2. F; 3. T

B. 1. A <u>flatterer</u> lavishly praises someone else.

2. You might keep a pet dog in a <u>kennel</u>.

3. A person who is feeling absolutely wonderful might say he or she is in a state of <u>rapture</u>.

C. 1. B; 2. A; 3. D

Enrichment: Phases of the Moon, p. 27

1. It takes about a month for the moon to complete its phases and orbit around Earth.

2. They traveled when the moon was full because the nights were the least dark then.

3. They probably tried to commit them during a new moon because the nights were darkest then, and it was easier to go unnoticed and escape capture.

4. *Wax* means "to grow in size"; *wane* means "to get smaller." *Sample sentence:* His interest in the film began to *wane* until finally he dozed off.

Selection Test A, p. 28

Critical Reading

1. ANS: A	DIF: Easy	OBJ: Comprehension
2. ANS: B	DIF: Easy	OBJ: Literary Analysis
3. ANS: C	DIF: Easy	OBJ: Interpretation
4. ANS: A	DIF: Easy	OBJ: Reading
5. ANS: D	DIF: Easy	OBJ: Comprehension
6. ANS: B	DIF: Easy	OBJ: Literary Analysis
7. ANS: B	DIF: Easy	OBJ: Reading
8. ANS: C	DIF: Easy	OBJ: Comprehension
9. ANS: B	DIF: Easy	OBJ: Interpretation
10. ANS: A	DIF: Easy	OBJ: Comprehension
11. ANS: C	DIF: Easy	OBJ: Reading
12. ANS: B	DIF: Easy	OBJ: Literary Analysis
13. ANS: A	DIF: Easy	OBJ: Literary Analysis

Vocabulary and Grammar

14. ANS: A	DIF: Easy	OBJ: Grammar
15. ANS: D	DIF: Easy	OBJ: Vocabulary

Essay

16. Students should recognize that the speaker is chasing the cat. The speaker does not seem to like the cat. Students should cite details to support their inferences. They may speculate that the speaker is a dog and should cite details to support that inference, including the "Wuff!" lines and/or the speaker's actions and negative remarks about the cat.

Difficulty: *Easy*

Objective: *Essay*

17. Students should choose one poem, state their opinion about it, and cite examples of at least two sound devices. For "Cat!" they could cite examples of onomatopoeia and rhythm and recognize that the poem also uses a great deal of rhyme, even though the end-of-line rhymes do not form a regular pattern. For "Silver" and "Your World," they could cite examples of rhythm, rhyme, alliteration, or onomatopoeia.

Difficulty: *Easy*

Objective: *Essay*

Selection Test B, p. 31

Critical Reading

1. ANS: B	DIF: Average	OBJ: Interpretation
2. ANS: D	DIF: Average	OBJ: Interpretation
3. ANS: A	DIF: Average	OBJ: Literary Analysis
4. ANS: A	DIF: Challenging	OBJ: Literary Analysis
5. ANS: A	DIF: Average	OBJ: Interpretation
6. ANS: B	DIF: Average	OBJ: Reading
7. ANS: A	DIF: Challenging	OBJ: Literary Analysis
8. ANS: D	DIF: Average	OBJ: Literary Analysis
9. ANS: C	DIF: Average	OBJ: Comprehension
10. ANS: D	DIF: Challenging	OBJ: Reading
11. ANS: C	DIF: Average	OBJ: Literary Analysis
12. ANS: C	DIF: Challenging	OBJ: Literary Analysis
13. ANS: A	DIF: Average	OBJ: Literary Analysis

Vocabulary and Grammar

14. **ANS:** D   **DIF:** Average   **OBJ:** Vocabulary
15. **ANS:** D   **DIF:** Average   **OBJ:** Vocabulary
16. **ANS:** B   **DIF:** Average   **OBJ:** Grammar
17. **ANS:** A   **DIF:** Average   **OBJ:** Grammar

Essay

18. Students should recognize that the poem describes a moonlit night with a peaceful, magical mood, or atmosphere. They should cite images and word choices as well as sound devices that contribute to the mood. Among the images they may mention are the opening image of the moon silently walking through the night in silver shoes, the moonbeams on the sleeping dog, and the fish gleaming in a silver stream of silver reeds. Among the word choices they may mention are the old-fashioned word *shoon* and the repetition of *silver*. In discussing the sound devices, they should mention that alliteration contributes to the poem's magical music, citing examples such as the *s* sounds in *slowly* and *silently* in line 1, the *b* sounds in *beams beneath* in line 6, and the *k* sounds in *casements catch* in line 5 and in *couched* and *kennel* in line 7. They should also recognize that each pair of lines rhymes and that the rhythm is also regular, contributing to the slow music of the poem.
    Difficulty: *Average*
    Objective: *Essay*

19. Students should recognize the poem's central message that our world, or life experience, can be as broad and open as we want to make it. They should cite details from the poem that express that view, literally (as in the first line) or figuratively (in the bird imagery, for example). They should then react to that view, giving reasons and examples why they agree or disagree. Those who agree will likely put the stress on individual experience and personal perceptions, while those who disagree may mention social, political, and economic factors or may criticize the worldview as self-indulgent for not taking into account family or social responsibilities that have to be met.
    Difficulty: *Challenging*
    Objective: *Essay*

Poetry Collection: Eve Merriam; Nikki Giovanni; Alfred, Lord Tennyson

Vocabulary Warm-up Exercises, p. 35

A. 1. ancient
   2. funeral
   3. captured
   4. triumph
   5. foul
   6. interior

B. Sample Answers

1. Both my *signature* and the *whorls* on my fingertips are unique only to me.
2. Since an *atom* is so small, you would need a powerful microscope to see it.
3. I would like to *imprint* on people's minds that every human being deserves to be loved.
4. People take others to court for *slander* because a bad reputation can ruin your life.
5. When I read about earthquakes and other natural disasters, I feel *mournful* for the victims.

Reading Warm-up A, p. 36
Sample Answers

1. <u>actions</u>; One example of *foul* behavior would be physically hurting someone else.
2. <u>gaining equal rights</u>; I felt *triumph* when I finally made the honor roll.
3. <u>he staged boycotts and marches to speak out against injustices in America</u>; *Captured* means "taken by force."
4. (extraordinary); A very smart person would have an interesting *interior* life because his or her mind would always be full of new and thoughtful ideas.
5. <u>modern</u>; *Ancient* times are days of long ago. The days of the Egyptians and Romans are *ancient* times.
6. (at his home church in Atlanta, at his college); I think King's *funeral* service in Atlanta included many political figures and many, many tearful African Americans.

Reading Warm-up B, p. 37
Sample Answers

1. <u>handwriting</u>; A *signature* is the unique way you write your own name.
2. <u>on the pads of your fingers</u>; The *whorls* on my fingers are different from everyone else's.
3. (others' faces); I would like to *imprint* on others' minds that using violence is not the way to go about bringing change.
4. <u>these new developments</u>; Many people are *unhappy* about these new developments.
5. <u>Imagine accusing the true cardholder of a crime committed by the identity thief!</u>; If you wrongly accuse someone of something, you are damaging his or her reputation and that is *slander*.
6. (split); Since an *atom* is so tiny, splitting it would have been really hard.

Poetry Collection: Eve Merriam; Nikki Giovanni; Alfred, Lord Tennyson

Reading: Preview to Determine Meanings From Context, p. 38

unique: context clues—"mine alone"; likely meaning—one and only

kettles: context clues—"big bass drums," "roar," "resounding against the wood"; likely meaning—large drums

slander: context clues—"spite"; "love of truth and right" (contrast); likely meaning—dishonest insult; spiteful lies

Literary Analysis: Sound Devices, p. 39

1. Examples include the aspirated *w* sounds in line 2 *(whorls, whirls, wheels)* and the repeated *m* sounds in line 19 *(my mark).*
2. Examples include *Pa-Rum* and *rat-tat-tat.* The two words imitate the sound of a drum.
3. Examples of alliteration: *Ring-rich-redress* (lines 11–12), *modes-manners* (lines 15–16), *care-coldness* (lines 17–18), *mournful-minstrel* (lines 19–20). An example of onomatopoeia is the word *ring,* used throughout the poem. *Ring* imitates the sound of a bell.
4. "Ring Out, Wild Bells" follows an *abba* pattern of rhymes in which the first and fourth lines of each stanza rhyme with each other and the second and third lines rhyme with each other.
5. The poet is trying to imitate the rhythm of drumbeats.
6. It is about ringing bells, which are musical.

Vocabulary Builder, p. 40

A. 1. F; 2. T; 3. F
B. Sample Responses
1. Yes, the twentieth century saw a lot of <u>strife</u>.
2. An independent person might display <u>singularity</u> in his or her personality or interests.
3. At a loud concert you might hear <u>resounding</u> music.
C. 1. C; 2. B; 3. A

Enrichment: Fingerprints, p. 43

A. 1. The same fingerprints at different crime scenes would prove that the same criminal is responsible for each of the crimes.
2. Smooth, clean surfaces or very sticky surfaces would probably provide the clearest fingerprints.
3. Rain or snow might spoil fingerprints left at crime scenes. Any disturbance to the fingerprints, such as touching them, would also destroy prints.
4. He or she might wear gloves.
5. They might be used to identify people for other reasons—to make sure people do not vote twice, for example.
B. Students' descriptions will vary.

Poetry Collections: Eleanor Farjeon, Walter de la Mare, Georgia Douglas Johnson; Eve Merriam; Nikki Giovanni; Alfred, Lord Tennyson

Build Language Skills: Vocabulary, p. 44

The Suffix *-ous*
A. Sample Sentences
1. Do not eat wild berries unless you know they are not <u>poisonous</u>.
2. Good comedies are very <u>humorous</u>.
3. The Internet is a <u>marvelous</u> invention.
4. The fine performance received <u>thunderous</u> applause.
5. The military victory was a <u>glorious</u> occasion.
B. 1. F; 2. F; 3. T; 4. T; 5. F

Build Language Skills: Grammar, p. 45

Subject Complements
A. 1. musical, PA; 2. example, PN; 3. I, PP; 4. familiar, PA; 5. none (*Sounded* in this sentence is not a linking verb.)
B. Sample Sentences
1. The cat is a good <u>hunter</u>. PN
2. Martin Luther King, Jr., was a very influential <u>person</u>. PN
3. The fingerprint seemed <u>unclear</u> to me. PA
4. The bravest person is <u>she</u>. PP
5. The bells are very <u>melodious</u>. PA

Selection Test A, p. 46

Critical Reading

1. ANS: D	DIF: Easy	OBJ: Interpretation
2. ANS: A	DIF: Easy	OBJ: Comprehension
3. ANS: A	DIF: Easy	OBJ: Literary Analysis
4. ANS: B	DIF: Easy	OBJ: Reading
5. ANS: D	DIF: Easy	OBJ: Comprehension
6. ANS: D	DIF: Easy	OBJ: Comprehension
7. ANS: A	DIF: Easy	OBJ: Literary Analysis
8. ANS: B	DIF: Easy	OBJ: Interpretation
9. ANS: C	DIF: Easy	OBJ: Comprehension
10. ANS: D	DIF: Easy	OBJ: Reading
11. ANS: B	DIF: Easy	OBJ: Reading
12. ANS: A	DIF: Easy	OBJ: Literary Analysis
13. ANS: C	DIF: Easy	OBJ: Literary Analysis

Vocabulary and Grammar

14. ANS: A	DIF: Easy	OBJ: Vocabulary
15. ANS: C	DIF: Easy	OBJ: Grammar

Essay

16. Students should recognize that the speaker values her thumbprint and sees it as a sign of her individuality, or uniqueness. They should cite details—such as "mine alone," "What a treasure," and "my universe key"—from the poem to support their observations about the thumbprint.
    Difficulty: *Easy*
    Objective: *Essay*

17. Students should choose one poem, state their opinion about it, and illustrate its musicality by citing examples of sound devices. For "The Drum," they should cite the strong rhythm and onomatopoeia, and recognize that these devices help capture the sound a drum beating. For "Ring Out, Wild Bells," they should cite rhythm and rhyme, recognizing that these form a regular pattern; and onomatopoeia, mentioning the word *ring* and recognizing how the repetition of this word helps captures the sound of the bells. Students also may include examples of alliteration from the poem, such as *mind* and *more, ring* and *redress, mournful* and *minstrel.* In the unlikely event students name "Thumbprint!" as the most musical of the three poems, they should cite the poem's rhythm and also may mention the occasional instances of alliteration (as in *whorls, whirls, wheels*) and onomatopoeia (as in *whirls* and *wheels*).
    Difficulty: *Easy*
    Objective: *Essay*

Essay

18. Students may cite the strong rhythm created by the pauses in each line and the onomatopoeia in which *pa-rum* and *rat-tat-tat* are repeated periodically throughout the poem. They might recognize that the rhythm and onomatopoeia capture the sound of a beating drum. Some students may mention examples of alliteration, such as *big* and *bass* in the second stanza and *different drum* in the third, and suggest that the alliteration contributes to the poem's steady music.
    Difficulty: *Average*
    Objective: *Essay*

19. Students should recognize that the poem describes the poet's hope that the new year will bring a better world. They should point to the many unjust or unpleasant details that the poet hopes the New Year's bells will ring out and the many good things he hopes the bells will ring in. Students should recognize that the strong pattern of rhythm and rhyme, as well as the repetition of the onomatopoeic word *ring*, not only stresses the ringing that the poem describes but also underscores the theme of change and hope.
    Difficulty: *Challenging*
    Objective: *Essay*

Poetry Collection: Patricia Hubbell, Richard García, Langston Hughes

Vocabulary Warm-up Exercises, p. 53

A. 1. dew
2. bulging
3. hose
4. perch
5. muck
6. direct

B. Sample Answers

1. The *elevator* doors closed and we began to move up and up, from the shoe department to sporting goods.
2. We mixed cement in the *trough* while the vegetables drained in the sink.
3. The coal *tenders* did not let the supply of fuel run out.
4. *Urban* shopping centers are always in cities.
5. The farmer is *raising* the barn with the help of his neighbors and it will take a week or so.
6. A floor of *concrete* is much less likely to catch fire than one made of wood.

Selection Test B, p. 49

Critical Reading

1. ANS: D	DIF: Average	OBJ: Interpretation
2. ANS: A	DIF: Challenging	OBJ: Literary Analysis
3. ANS: A	DIF: Average	OBJ: Interpretation
4. ANS: B	DIF: Challenging	OBJ: Reading
5. ANS: B	DIF: Average	OBJ: Reading
6. ANS: C	DIF: Average	OBJ: Literary Analysis
7. ANS: D	DIF: Average	OBJ: Reading
8. ANS: A	DIF: Average	OBJ: Interpretation
9. ANS: A	DIF: Average	OBJ: Interpretation
10. ANS: D	DIF: Average	OBJ: Interpretation
11. ANS: A	DIF: Challenging	OBJ: Comprehension
12. ANS: A	DIF: Average	OBJ: Literary Analysis
13. ANS: D	DIF: Challenging	OBJ: Literary Analysis

Vocabulary and Grammar

14. ANS: A	DIF: Average	OBJ: Vocabulary
15. ANS: C	DIF: Average	OBJ: Vocabulary
16. ANS: B	DIF: Average	OBJ: Grammar
17. ANS: A	DIF: Average	OBJ: Grammar

Reading Warm-up A, p. 54

Sample Answers

1. (The sun has risen just enough for us to walk safely without a flashlight.); *Dew* is small drops of liquid that are sometimes on things outdoors in the early morning.
2. on a high branch; I like to *perch* on top of the car and watch the fireworks on the Fourth of July.
3. (bucket, brush, shampoo bottle); I fell in a big mud puddle in the park and got covered in *muck*.
4. (the stream of water); He attempts to *aim* the stream of water at Terry.
5. (garden hose, turns on the faucet, stream of water); It's probably best not to try to *hose* down things indoors because the water will spread all over the floor and ruin everything in the house.
6. pocket; I think some big, delicious doggie treats were in the *bulging* pocket.

Reading Warm-up B, p. 55

Sample Answers

1. big, city; I live in Chicago, which is a big *urban* area where lots of people live and work.
2. tall buildings; Workers are *raising* a new high-rise apartment building in my town.
3. cement, water, and other things; Sidewalks are made of *concrete.*
4. (mixing cement, water, and other things); A *trough* might also be used to mix large amounts of dough or to feed and water animals.
5. (watch over bulldozers, cement mixers, cranes, and other heavy machinery); I was a *tender* when my dad asked me to watch the pot of soup that was cooking on the stove.
6. rise to new heights; I once rode in an *elevator* car to the observation deck of the Empire State Building. I thought we would never get to the top.

Poetry Collection: Patricia Hubbell, Richard García, Langston Hughes

Reading: Reread and Read Ahead to Determine Meanings From Context, p. 56

1. Likely meaning of hose in line 2: water (something) by training a hose on it
   Clue: "drivers are washing"
2. Likely meaning of muck in line 5: a wet and sticky substance; goop
   Clue: "standing in"

3. Likely meaning of perch in line 7: sitting on top
   Clue: "on their backs"
4. Likely meaning of bellow in line 14: cry out, scream
   Clue: none
5. Likely meaning of urban in line 16: relating to a city
   Clue: "raising a city"

Literary Analysis: Figurative Language, p. 57

1. Similes in "Concrete Mixers": lines 1–2, drivers of concrete mixers and elephant tenders; lines 4–6, rows of concrete mixers and rows of elephants; line 7, drivers and mahouts (Asian elephant drivers, or keepers); line 9, trough on concrete mixer and elephant trunk; lines 14–16, concrete mixers and elephants,
2. Metaphor in "Concrete Mixers": line 3, concrete mixers and monsters
3. Personification in "Concrete Mixers": line 16, concrete mixers and human beings raising a city
4. Personification in "The City Is So Big": line 2, bridges and human being quaking with fear; line 7, machines and people eating; line 8, stairways (escalators) and people walking

Vocabulary Builder, p. 58

A. 1. F; 2. T

B. Sample Answers

1. The owner of a suitcase with lots of travel labels probably likes to roam around the world.
2. A ponderous suitcase would be hard to carry.

C. 1. C; 2. C

Enrichment: Concrete, p. 61

A. 1. *concrete:* a substance used in construction; made from a mixture of cement, water, and inert materials
2. *inert:* not participating in a chemical reaction
3. *aggregate:* any of the substances, such as gravel or sand, mixed with water and cement to form concrete
4. *hydration:* a chemical reaction in which a substance mixes with water
5. *water/cement ratio:* the amount of water compared with the amount of cement in concrete
6. *portland cement:* a type of cement developed in 1824 and used in making concrete today

B. Sample Questions

1. What sort of aggregate should I use?
2. What water/cement ratio should I use?
3. At what temperature should the concrete be mixed?

Selection Test A, p. 62

Critical Reading

1. ANS: C	DIF: Easy	OBJ: Comprehension
2. ANS: B	DIF: Easy	OBJ: Literary Analysis
3. ANS: A	DIF: Easy	OBJ: Literary Analysis
4. ANS: D	DIF: Easy	OBJ: Reading
5. ANS: B	DIF: Easy	OBJ: Comprehension
6. ANS: D	DIF: Easy	OBJ: Interpretation
7. ANS: B	DIF: Easy	OBJ: Literary Analysis
8. ANS: C	DIF: Easy	OBJ: Reading
9. ANS: D	DIF: Easy	OBJ: Interpretation
10. ANS: A	DIF: Easy	OBJ: Comprehension
11. ANS: B	DIF: Easy	OBJ: Reading
12. ANS: C	DIF: Easy	OBJ: Literary Analysis
13. ANS: A	DIF: Easy	OBJ: Literary Analysis

Vocabulary and Grammar

14. ANS: A	DIF: Easy	OBJ: Vocabulary
15. ANS: B	DIF: Easy	OBJ: Grammar

Essay

16. Students should recognize that all three poets make cities seem like vibrant, poetic places, although some students may feel that García also makes cities seem a little scary. Some students may have the poets discuss the use of figurative language, especially in "Concrete Mixers" and "The City Is So Big."

Difficulty: *Easy*

Objective: *Essay*

17. Students should choose one poem, state their opinion about it, and cite examples from the poem to explain their opinions. They should consider figurative language as well as other aspects of the poem, such as whether they can relate to it or whether they find it musical.

Difficulty: *Easy*

Objective: *Essay*

Selection Test B, p. 65

Critical Reading

1. ANS: A	DIF: Challenging	OBJ: Literary Analysis
2. ANS: B	DIF: Average	OBJ: Interpretation
3. ANS: C	DIF: Average	OBJ: Literary Analysis
4. ANS: D	DIF: Average	OBJ: Reading
5. ANS: D	DIF: Challenging	OBJ: Reading
6. ANS: B	DIF: Average	OBJ: Comprehension
7. ANS: C	DIF: Average	OBJ: Interpretation
8. ANS: A	DIF: Average	OBJ: Interpretation
9. ANS: D	DIF: Average	OBJ: Literary Analysis
10. ANS: D	DIF: Average	OBJ: Interpretation

11. ANS: B	DIF: Challenging	OBJ: Literary Analysis
12. ANS: C	DIF: Average	OBJ: Interpretation
13. ANS: B	DIF: Average	OBJ: Comprehension
14. ANS: D	DIF: Challenging	OBJ: Literary Analysis

Vocabulary and Grammar

15. ANS: A	DIF: Average	OBJ: Vocabulary
16. ANS: B	DIF: Average	OBJ: Grammar
17. ANS: D	DIF: Average	OBJ: Grammar

Essay

18. Students should recognize that the poem compares concrete mixers to elephants and their drivers to elephant tenders, or mahouts. They should also recognize that the comparison is extended with more specific details, such as the rows of mixers compared to elephants lined up tail to trunk, the movement of the mixers to the movement of elephants, the sound of the mixers to the bellow of elephants, and the spray of the mixers to the spray of elephants.

Difficulty: *Average*

Objective: *Essay*

19. Students should recognize that the three poems celebrate cities as vibrant, poetic places and should cite examples from the poems that illustrate the poets' views. The three impressions contrast in that Hubbell focuses on the playfulness of the city, Hughes on the romance and music of the city, and García on the mystery of the city. Students should then give their own views, defending them with sufficient examples and other details.

Difficulty: *Challenging*

Objective: *Essay*

Poetry Collection: Pablo Neruda, Elizabeth Bishop, Emily Dickinson

Vocabulary Warm-up Exercises, p. 69

A. 1. limp
   2. cicada
   3. sawing
   4. drifting
   5. relieved
   6. rut

B. Sample Answers

1. F. A *boulevard* is a wide street.
2. T. A farmer would be unlikely to own a crown, or *diadem*, because it would take a lot of money to buy one.
3. F. The *mangrove* tree grows along the shore.
4. F. *Keys* are small, low islands.

5. F. In *latticework*, half the strips run in one direction and half in the other.
6. F. The *heron* is a bird that lives near the shore and wades in water.

Reading Warm-up A, p. 70

Sample Answers

1. (wind); I might see a balloon *drifting* with the wind.
2. in every road was filled with water or mud; A deep *rut* in a road can damage the underside of a car or its tires if you drive through it too fast.
3. (insect; loud sawing noise); Katydids make a loud *sawing* noise on summer nights.
4. the weather grew hot and muggy; A *limp* handshake would be one in which someone did not grasp your hand very firmly.
5. (cool breeze); I had a bad scrape on my leg and I was *relieved* from the pain once I put on antibiotic cream and a bandage.

Reading Warm-up B, p. 71

Sample Answers

1. an unusual kind of tree; A *mangrove* would not grow where I live because it is too cold and there is no coast.
2. (twisted stilts); A pie's *latticework* top crust would be strips of dough that crisscross.
3. low-lying islands; We took a boat ride around several of the *keys* and saw lots of birds and other wildlife.
4. watery; The *boulevard* near my house is eight lanes wide and has a grassy center strip with trees and benches.
5. (wading birds); Since a *heron* must dip its beak in water to get its dinner, a heron most likely eats fish.
6. (crown); I saw the winner of Miss Teen America wearing a *diadem*.

Poetry Collection: Pablo Neruda, Elizabeth Bishop, Emily Dickinson

Reading: Reread and Read Ahead to Determine Meanings From Context, p. 72

latticework: context clues—"Under the trees light / has dropped," "light / like a green / latticework of branches"; likely meaning—crossing; dictionary meaning: a lacy cross pattern

heron: context clues—"the mangrove keys . . . / where occasionally a heron may undo his head, / shake up his feathers"; likely meaning—a type of bird; dictionary meaning: wading bird with a long neck, long legs, and a long, tapered bill, living along marshes and river banks

uninjured: context clue—"someone sleeping . . . barely disturbed"; likely meaning—safe; dictionary meaning: not harmed

Literary Analysis: Figurative Language, p. 73

1. "like a green / latticework of branches," "like clean / white sand"
2. Students' opinions will vary, but many students are likely to say that "like clean / white sand" captures some of the beauty and enchantment the poet wants to convey.
3. The cicada is said to be creating a song, a human activity.
4. "The world is / a glass overflowing / with water."
5. It helps convey a sense of wonder, beauty, abundance, and satisfaction.

Vocabulary Builder, p. 74

A. 1. T; 2. T; 3. F; 4. F
B. Sample Answers

1. A doctor might conclude that someone is in a coma if the person is <u>unresponsive</u>.
2. A person usually <u>debates</u> the benefits and drawbacks before making a big decision.
3. Some people sleep <u>uneasily</u> when they are worried about a great danger.
4. A heavy-wheeled vehicle might leave a <u>rut</u> on a dirt road.

Enrichment: Wind Force, p. 77

Students' descriptions should show a convincing progression from calm air to the conditions present anywhere along the Beaufort scale from "moderate gale" to "hurricane."

Poetry Collections: Patricia Hubbell, Richard García, Langston Hughes; Pablo Neruda, Elizabeth Bishop, Emily Dickinson

Build Language Skills: Vocabulary, p. 78

The Suffix -*ment*
A. Sample Answers

1. Knowing math is a <u>requirement</u> for being an engineer.
2. His <u>involvement</u> in the environmental movement goes back many years.
3. There was a new <u>development</u> in the scandal today.
4. He felt all the <u>excitement</u> of a child opening a gift for the first time.
5. Jane and her brother got into an <u>argument</u> over which team was the best in baseball.

B. 1. context; 2. synonymous; 3. restatement; 4. clarify; 5. confirm

Build Language Skills: Grammar, p. 79

Direct and Indirect Objects

A. 1. direct object: role

2. indirect object: us; direct object: advice

3. direct object: Nancy and me (corrected from *Nancy and I*)

4. indirect object: readers; direct object: feelings

5. none

B. Sample Sentences (4 and 5 include indirect objects)

1. The heavy machinery tore holes in the ground.

2. Great poets enrich our lives.

3. My thoughts scared me to death.

4. The glowing light showed us the way home.

5. The islanders taught me songs.

Poetry Collection: Pablo Neruda, Elizabeth Bishop, Emily Dickinson

Selection Test A, p. 80

Critical Reading

1. ANS: A	DIF: Easy	OBJ: Comprehension
2. ANS: B	DIF: Easy	OBJ: Interpretation
3. ANS: C	DIF: Easy	OBJ: Literary Analysis
4. ANS: C	DIF: Easy	OBJ: Literary Analysis
5. ANS: B	DIF: Easy	OBJ: Comprehension
6. ANS: A	DIF: Easy	OBJ: Literary Analysis
7. ANS: D	DIF: Easy	OBJ: Reading
8. ANS: D	DIF: Easy	OBJ: Comprehension
9. ANS: B	DIF: Easy	OBJ: Comprehension
10. ANS: C	DIF: Easy	OBJ: Literary Analysis
11. ANS: C	DIF: Easy	OBJ: Reading
12. ANS: A	DIF: Easy	OBJ: Literary Analysis

Vocabulary and Grammar

13. ANS: A	DIF: Easy	OBJ: Vocabulary
14. ANS: B	DIF: Easy	OBJ: Grammar
15. ANS: A	DIF: Easy	OBJ: Vocabulary

Essay

16. Students should explain that "Ode to Enchanted Light" describes a peaceful, wonderful scene and that "The Sky Is Low, the Clouds Are Mean" describes an unpleasant, uncomfortable scene. Students should cite figures of speech and other details that contribute to the scene they describe—for example, the comparison to "clean white sand" or the cicadas singing in "Ode to Enchanted Light," or the mean clouds and complaining wind in "The Sky Is Low, the Clouds Are Mean."

Difficulty: *Easy*

Objective: *Essay*

17. Students should relate that a storm hits a coastal area on or near mangrove keys (little islands where tropical trees called mangroves grow). One little boulevard with rows of palm trees is hit. The rain pours. Then, the storm goes away. One person has slept through it in the bottom of his rowboat.

Difficulty: *Easy*

Objective: *Essay*

Selection Test B, p. 83

Critical Reading

1. ANS: A	DIF: Average	OBJ: Comprehension
2. ANS: C	DIF: Average	OBJ: Interpretation
3. ANS: D	DIF: Average	OBJ: Literary Analysis
4. ANS: C	DIF: Average	OBJ: Reading
5. ANS: A	DIF: Average	OBJ: Interpretation
6. ANS: C	DIF: Challenging	OBJ: Literary Analysis
7. ANS: A	DIF: Average	OBJ: Comprehension
8. ANS: D	DIF: Average	OBJ: Literary Analysis
9. ANS: B	DIF: Average	OBJ: Reading
10. ANS: A	DIF: Average	OBJ: Literary Analysis
11. ANS: B	DIF: Average	OBJ: Literary Analysis
12. ANS: B	DIF: Challenging	OBJ: Literary Analysis

Vocabulary and Grammar

13. ANS: A	DIF: Average	OBJ: Vocabulary
14. ANS: B	DIF: Average	OBJ: Vocabulary
15. ANS: B	DIF: Average	OBJ: Grammar
16. ANS: C	DIF: Average	OBJ: Grammar
17. ANS: D	DIF: Average	OBJ: Grammar

Essay

18. Students should discuss the sense of wonder that the poem conveys about nature and should indicate that the word *enchanted* helps convey that sense of wonder. A good essay might provide a definition of *enchanted* that recognizes its association with magic. Students should then discuss how the poem's figurative language and other imagery, particularly the final metaphor of the overlowing glass, convey that sense of wonder or enchantment.

Difficulty: *Average*

Objective: *Essay*

19. Students should note that the final two lines of the poem state the central theme figuratively, and they should restate it literally: Nature, like people, sometimes has its bad days. They may expand this idea to a recognition that Dickinson uses the poem to try to help us understand nature and that she attributes no malice to nature for the cold, nasty day but instead implies that we should forgive nature as we do a friend or relative having a bad day. Students should explain that all the personification in the poem reinforces the central idea of nature's similarity to human beings. Among the examples of personification they may mention are the clouds being mean, the flake of snow debating whether it will cross the barn or go through a rut, the narrow wind complaining about maltreatment, and the idea of nature being capable of wearing a diadem, or crown.

Difficulty: *Challenging*

Objective: *Essay*

Poetry Collection: May Swenson, Billy Collins, Dorothy Parker

Vocabulary Warm-up Exercises, p. 87

A. 1. winding
2. frosty
3. glimmered
4. inhabitants
5. unlikely
6. wonderment

B. Sample Answers

1. Yes, I'd like to learn about the *ancient* Egyptians.
2. I could light a candle or match to create a *flare.*
3. I think the mayor should be the *torchbearer* in the nighttime parade.
4. One *ritual* that Americans practice in the United States is celebrating Thanksgiving.
5. Yes, fireworks were *illuminating* our block and the surrounding neighborhood.
6. No, the *Druids* lived in Europe, not what is now the United States.

Reading Warm-up A, p. 88

Sample Answers

1. (light coating of snow, the holiday decorations, and the crowds of people scurrying about); Her eyes popped open with *amazement* at the light coating of snow, the holiday decorations, and the crowds of people scurrying about.
2. people; The *inhabitants* in my town represent many different ethnic groups and they participate in the annual fairs and holiday parades.
3. (Silver and white glitter); I like a drinking glass that is made to look *frosty.*

4. crowded; *Winding* means "twisting and turning."
5. (Tiny lights, like stars); When we were coming back from the country, the lights of the city *glimmered* in the distance.
6. probably; An *unlikely* event is aliens landing on my front lawn.

Reading Warm-up B, p. 89

Sample Answers

1. long ago; Another *ancient* people is the Romans.
2. (member of the educated class of the Celts); The word *druid* means "knowing the oak tree" and since the Druids spent so much time in oak forests, it makes sense that they would be called "Druids."
3. Each year, each festival; A *ritual* on Flag Day is to fly the American flag in our yards.
4. (lighting the sticks of his companions); A *torchbearer* carries the Olympic torch from one city to another before the Olympic Games start.
5. whole circle of flames; A halogen light bulb is *illuminating* my desk.
6. shooting star; If fat drips onto the fire in the grill, a *flare* of light shoots up from the fire.

Literary Analysis: Comparing Humorous Imagery, p. 90

"Southbound on the Freeway":

sight: "metal and glass," "transparent parts," "see their guts," "feet are round and roll," "diagrams—or long measuring tapes, dark with white lines," "four eyes, two in the back are red," "five-eyed one," "red eye turning on top of his head, winding among them from behind," "soft shapes, shadowy inside—hard bodies"

sound: "they all hiss"

touch/motion: "red eye turning," "winding among them"

"The Country":

sight: "box of wooden, strike-anywhere matches," "face was absolutely straight," "round tin," "behind the floral wallpaper," "between the needles of his teeth," "the sudden flare," "one bright, shining moment," "a torchbearer," "little brown druid illuminating some ancient night," "lit up in the blazing insulation," "tiny looks of wonderment on the faces," "house in the country"

sound: "the blue tip scratching"

touch: "twisted the lid down," "whisk away the thought," "padding along a cold water pipe," "gripping a single wooden match," "against a rough-hewn beam"

"The Choice":

sight: "rolling lands," "houses of marble," "billowing farms," "smoldering rubies," "laces rare," "dresses that glimmered with frosty sheen," "shining ribbons"

sound: "a lilting song," "a melody, happy and high," "to whistle low"

smell: "smoldering rubies"

touch: "pearls to trickle between my hands," "to circle my arms," "you were sudden and swift and strong," "horses to draw me"

Vocabulary Builder, p. 91

A. Sample Answers

1. I remember sheets, <u>billowing</u> in the wind, that my mother hung out on the clothesline.
2. The windows in my house are <u>transparent</u>.
3. The <u>inhabitants</u> of my community like to go to the shore on vacation.
4. I think that folk singers have <u>lilting</u> voices.
5. When I went camping with my family, I sat and watched the <u>smoldering</u> fire.

B. 1. A; 2. C; 3. D; 4. B

Selection Test A, p. 93

Critical Reading

1. ANS: A	DIF: Easy	OBJ: Literary Analysis
2. ANS: C	DIF: Easy	OBJ: Comprehension
3. ANS: A	DIF: Easy	OBJ: Interpretation
4. ANS: B	DIF: Easy	OBJ: Literary Analysis
5. ANS: D	DIF: Easy	OBJ: Comprehension
6. ANS: B	DIF: Easy	OBJ: Interpretation
7. ANS: A	DIF: Easy	OBJ: Interpretation
8. ANS: C	DIF: Easy	OBJ: Literary Analysis
9. ANS: B	DIF: Easy	OBJ: Comprehension
10. ANS: D	DIF: Easy	OBJ: Literary Analysis
11. ANS: D	DIF: Easy	OBJ: Literary Analysis

Vocabulary

12. ANS: A	DIF: Easy	OBJ: Vocabulary
13. ANS: C	DIF: Easy	OBJ: Vocabulary
14. ANS: B	DIF: Easy	OBJ: Vocabulary

Essay

15. "Southbound on the Freeway" describes an everyday occurrence told from an unusual perspective. The description is funny because the cars on the highways are seen and commented on by an alien. "The Choice" compares two men—one rich and the other happy. The description isn't really funny until the last line of the poem, when the narrator says that someone needs to examine her head because she chose the happy man over the rich man.
    Difficulty: *Easy*
    Objective: *Essay*

16. "Southbound on the Freeway" describes a normal occurrence from an unusual perspective. It is funny because the cars on the highways are seen and described by an alien. "The Country" creates a picture of a mouse lighting a match inside the wall of a house—a pretty unlikely and ridiculous idea.
    Difficulty: *Easy*
    Objective: *Essay*

Selection Test B, p. 96

Critical Reading

1. ANS: B	DIF: Average	OBJ: Comprehension
2. ANS: A	DIF: Average	OBJ: Interpretation
3. ANS: B	DIF: Average	OBJ: Interpretation
4. ANS: B	DIF: Average	OBJ: Literary Analysis
5. ANS: C	DIF: Average	OBJ: Comprehension
6. ANS: D	DIF: Average	OBJ: Comprehension
7. ANS: D	DIF: Average	OBJ: Literary Analysis
8. ANS: A	DIF: Average	OBJ: Interpretation
9. ANS: D	DIF: Average	OBJ: Interpretation
10. ANS: D	DIF: Average	OBJ: Literary Analysis
11. ANS: D	DIF: Average	OBJ: Literary Analysis
12. ANS: C	DIF: Average	OBJ: Literary Analysis
13. ANS: A	DIF: Challenging	OBJ: Comprehension

Vocabulary

14. ANS: D	DIF: Average	OBJ: Vocabulary
15. ANS: B	DIF: Average	OBJ: Vocabulary
16. ANS: C	DIF: Average	OBJ: Vocabulary
17. ANS: A	DIF: Average	OBJ: Vocabulary

Essay

18. Students should mention that "Southbound on the Freeway" includes details that describe how cars would look from the point of view of a space alien. "The Country" takes two ordinary things—a mouse and a match—and combines them imaginatively to create a fantasy.
    Difficulty: *Average*
    Objective: *Essay*

19. Students may say that the speaker in "The Choice" sees a rich man she gave up compared with a seemingly happy man she stayed with. Students may suggest that the speaker is possibly joking about being sorry she gave up the rich man, though she may have real regrets, or that the speaker is no longer with the man she chose, so she is sorry for what she lost. Students may suggest that the speaker is not at peace or content with her past

decisions. Students may say that the speaker in "South-bound on the Freeway" is looking at cars on roads and mistakenly believing that these cars are the creatures that inhabit the planet. The speaker does not really understand what he or she is looking at, but some truths are realized in that the creatures slow down for the creature with the red light on top.

Difficulty: *Average*

Objective: *Essay*

Writing Workshop—Unit 4, Part 1

Writing for Assessment: Integrating Grammar Skills, p. 100

A 1. active; 2. passive; 3. active; 4. passive
B 1. A flash of lightning releases energy.
   2. Rapid heating of the air produces thunder.
   3. Owners of buildings use lightning rods.
   4. The metal in umbrellas attracts lightning.

Unit 4, Part 1 Answers

Benchmark Test 7, p. 101

MULTIPLE CHOICE
1. ANS: D
2. ANS: D
3. ANS: A
4. ANS: A
5. ANS: C
6. ANS: A
7. ANS: C
8. ANS: A
9. ANS: B
10. ANS: D
11. ANS: A
12. ANS: B
13. ANS: C
14. ANS: B
15. ANS: D
16. ANS: A
17. ANS: C
18. ANS: D
19. ANS: A
20. ANS: D
21. ANS: D
22. ANS: A
23. ANS: A
24. ANS: C
25. ANS: D

26. ANS: B
27. ANS: B
28. ANS: C
29. ANS: B
30. ANS: A
31. ANS: C

ESSAY

32. Students' ideas should clearly give supporting reasons why the song is important and should cite one or more examples of the use of sound devices in the song.

33. Students' notes should include things that appeal to the senses. For three of the items on the list, students should show examples of comparisons using figurative languages, demonstrating an understanding of and distinctions among simile, metaphor, and personification.

34. Students should list three ways that poetry helps us connect with others, such as by expressing feelings that we might share about the power of nature, about the difficulties of growing up, or about the satisfaction of doing a job well.

Unit 4, Part 2 Answers

Diagnostic Test 8, p. 108

MULTIPLE CHOICE
1. ANS: B
2. ANS: D
3. ANS: C
4. ANS: D
5. ANS: B
6. ANS: B
7. ANS: C
8. ANS: B
9. ANS: C
10. ANS: A
11. ANS: D
12. ANS: D
13. ANS: D
14. ANS: B
15. ANS: C

Poetry Collection: Robert Hayden, William Shakespeare, Ricardo Sánchez

Vocabulary Warm-up Exercises, p. 112

A. 1. resolution
   2. familial
   3. benefits

4. thicketed

5. aromas

6. brethren

B. Sample Answers

1. The *bonanza* find produced a lot of gold.

2. If it begins to rain at the party, you can *dart* underneath the canopy.

3. In modern times, believing that the earth is flat is sheer *folly*.

4. Wearing *shackles*, the animals could hardly move at all across the field.

5. The awards assembly began with the *summoning* of all winners to the stage.

6. Pick peaches from *yonder* tree, the one on this side of the hill.

Reading Warm-up A, p. 113

Sample Answers

1. (all of us were related); A synonym for brethren is brothers.

2. Low shrubs and berry bushes. There is a thicketed area of forsythia bushes behind my house where the rabbits hide.

3. (they were relatives); Everyone in my family has the same shape nose.

4. grilling meats and vegetables; My favorite aromas are roses and baking brownies.

5. advantage; To me, the benefits of being on the swim team are making good friends and getting lots of exercise.

6. (determination); I studied for my midterm exams with complete resolution, and I got all As.

Reading Warm-up B, p. 114

Sample Answers

1. freed from, slavery, better lives; *Shackles* means "metals rings and chains around a person's wrists or ankles" and "the lack of freedom caused by slavery."

2. (gold, rich); *Bonanza* means "relating to suddenly finding a lot of money or having a lot of good luck."

3. (hundreds of miles away); While I wait in the car, would you go into *yonder* convenience store and get me a quart of milk?

4. Some freed slaves heeded the army's calling of soldiers to fight Indians on the Great Plains.; I heeded the coach's *summoning* of all students interested in playing soccer.

5. this way and that, trying to avoid being caught; The fish in my dentist's aquarium *dart* in and out of the rocks and plants.

6. She was always ready with her fists; I think it is *folly* to make children play a musical instrument that they are not at all interested in.

Poetry Collection: Robert Hayden, William Shakespeare, Ricardo Sánchez

Reading: Reread to Paraphrase, p. 115

Sample paraphrase of "Blow, Blow, Thou Winter Wind": Blow, winter wind. Your cold is not as harsh as that of humans who don't give thanks. Your bite isn't as sharp even though you make the air rough. Under the holly, sing that most friends are false and most love is foolish. Life is jolly nevertheless. Make us cold, winter sky. You don't pain as much as people who forget favors we do for them. Although you freeze waters, your sting is not as sharp as the pain someone feels when forgotten by a friend.

Sample paraphrase of "Old Man": The old man (the speaker's grandfather) was wise. He had a face of wrinkles from the life he'd lived. Long ago, during nights at family get-togethers in Albuquerque, he told me, "You are of Indian blood, among other things." The old man, loved and respected, used to talk about Indian villages, where the family came from. That blood predates the arrival of Spaniards, from whom our blood also comes. The mixed blood was rich but caused a lot of pain. The old man was in touch with the earth and is now gone in body but alive in spirit.

Literary Analysis: Lyric and Narrative Poetry, p. 116

A. *Lyric poem title:* "Blow . . ." or "Old Man"

1. It has one speaker who expresses his or her feelings and thoughts.

2. Among the emotions students may identify for "Blow . . ." are anger toward humans, hostile challenge to the wind. Among the emotions for "Old Man" are love, respect, honor, the pang of memory.

3. *Images in "Blow . . .":* keen tooth, rude breath to express negatives in man; *Images in "Old Man":* running rivulets . . . rich furrows to express marks life left on him; "who felt the heated sweetness of chile verde" to express old man's closeness to the basic things in life.

4. *Main impression of "Blow . . .":* Disappointment in humans; *Main impression of "Old Man":* love for grandfather

B. *Narrative poem title:* "Runagate Runagate"

1. It's a narrative poem because it tells a series of events—a story.

2. The first stanza tells about a general uprising of slaves—how they could not turn back—and indicates how slave owners identified people as their property. The second stanza introduces Harriet Tubman and her role in leading slaves to freedom.

3. The main conflict is between escaping slaves and slave owners. In the end, the slaves maintain their commitment to escape.

4. The main setting is the woods that the slaves traveled through on their way to freedom.

5. In the first stanza, unnamed slaves are the main characters. The second stanza focuses on Harriet Tubman, leader of the escaped slaves. The slave owners, although intimidating, might be considered minor characters.

Vocabulary Builder, p. 117

A. 1. A rich relative might leave someone a *legacy* when he or she dies.

2. A person who fails to give thanks to those who help him or her shows *ingratitude*.

3. Some students feel *anguish* on the night before a big test.

4. *Beckoning* smells may tempt me to visit a kitchen.

B. 1. B; 2. B; 3. D; 4. A

Enrichment: Old Age and Harriet Tubman, p. 120

A. Responses will vary, depending on the ads students find.

B. Tubman's achievements later in life include assisting the writer of Tubman's biography, speaking out for the rights of women and African Americans, helping to organize the African Methodist Episcopal (AME) Church, and setting up a home for elderly African Americans.

Selection Test A, p. 121

Critical Reading

1. ANS: C	DIF: Easy	OBJ: Comprehension
2. ANS: A	DIF: Easy	OBJ: Reading
3. ANS: D	DIF: Easy	OBJ: Literary Analysis
4. ANS: D	DIF: Easy	OBJ: Interpretation
5. ANS: B	DIF: Easy	OBJ: Comprehension
6. ANS: C	DIF: Easy	OBJ: Literary Analysis
7. ANS: A	DIF: Easy	OBJ: Interpretation
8. ANS: B	DIF: Easy	OBJ: Reading
9. ANS: C	DIF: Easy	OBJ: Literary Analysis
10. ANS: A	DIF: Easy	OBJ: Interpretation
11. ANS: D	DIF: Easy	OBJ: Comprehension
12. ANS: B	DIF: Easy	OBJ: Reading

Vocabulary and Grammar

13. ANS: D	DIF: Easy	OBJ: Vocabulary
14. ANS: D	DIF: Easy	OBJ: Vocabulary
15. ANS: B	DIF: Easy	OBJ: Grammar

Essay

16. *Sample paraphrase of first stanza of "Blow, Blow, Thou Winter Wind":* Blow, winter wind. You are not as mean as people who do not show gratitude when they should. Even though you are harsh and unseen, your bite is not as sharp as that of those unkind, ungrateful people. Sing heigh-ho under the green holly. Most friendship is false, and most love is foolishness. Still, life is happy.

Difficulty: *Easy*

Objective: *Essay*

17. Students should recognize that the grandfather is a proud old man who lived a traditional life close to the earth. They should recognize that he teaches the speaker about his dual Indian (or Native American) and Spanish heritage and that the speaker admires and respects him very much.

Difficulty: *Easy*

Objective: *Essay*

Selection Test B, p. 124

Critical Reading

1. ANS: B	DIF: Average	OBJ: Interpretation
2. ANS: A	DIF: Average	OBJ: Interpretation
3. ANS: A	DIF: Average	OBJ: Reading
4. ANS: D	DIF: Average	OBJ: Literary Analysis
5. ANS: C	DIF: Average	OBJ: Literary Analysis
6. ANS: B	DIF: Challenging	OBJ: Comprehension
7. ANS: A	DIF: Average	OBJ: Interpretation
8. ANS: C	DIF: Average	OBJ: Reading
9. ANS: C	DIF: Average	OBJ: Literary Analysis
10. ANS: B	DIF: Average	OBJ: Literary Analysis
11. ANS: B	DIF: Challenging	OBJ: Interpretation
12. ANS: C	DIF: Average	OBJ: Comprehension
13. ANS: B	DIF: Challenging	OBJ: Reading

Vocabulary and Grammar

14. ANS: D	DIF: Average	OBJ: Vocabulary
15. ANS: D	DIF: Average	OBJ: Vocabulary
16. ANS: A	DIF: Average	OBJ: Grammar
17. ANS: B	DIF: Average	OBJ: Grammar

Essay

18. Students' definitions should recognize that a lyric poem is one in which the speaker expresses his or her thoughts and feelings. Students should then prove that either poem is a lyric poem by citing examples of thoughts and feelings expressed by the poem's speaker.

Difficulty: *Average*

Objective: *Essay*

19. Students should note details in the poem that contribute to the suspense, such as the darkness, the shapes of terror in the opening lines, the description of "no place to hide" (line 45), the hounds in the opening lines and in the second part of the poem (line 47), the escaping slaves' expressions of doubt and the conductor's leveled pistol and threats in response, the quotations from "wanted" posters, and the details about hoot owls, ghosted air, "hants," scary leaves, and the ghost-story train. Some students may also discuss the rhythm as a tool adding to the suspense, noting particularly that in the opening lines the poet captures the sound of fearful running.

Difficulty: *Challenging*

Objective: *Essay*

Poetry Collection: Emma Lazarus, Henry Wadsworth Longfellow, Paul Laurence Dunbar

Vocabulary Warm-up Exercises, p. 128

A. 1. defiance

2. hovel

3. huddled

4. cruelties

5. refuse

6. peril

B. Sample Answers

1. Going to the dentist doesn't fill me with *dread* because he uses a painless drill.

2. I would not buy a *steed* for a young child learning to ride because the horse would not be gentle enough for a learner.

3. Some people who have long vacations look *transfigured* because they are relaxed and rested.

4. I would want to avoid *teeming* highways during rush hours when a lot of cars are on the road.

5. It is important for the *masses* to vote in elections so they have a say in the government.

6. When people don't listen to their *consciences*, they often regret their actions.

Reading Warm-up A, p. 129

Sample Answers

1. Americans were not going to stand for any laws being forced on them!; I was once in *defiance* of my older sister when she blamed me for breaking something, and I said I did not do it, and therefore, would not pay for it.

2. (together); During rush hour, I had to stand *huddled* in the corner of a bus because there was not much room.

3. (beat, sold); Some *cruelties* people do today include torturing prisoners of war and harming innocent animals for no reason.

4. fine home; A *hovel* might be one small room with a dirt floor and only mats to sleep on.

5. a cruel ruler's soldiers who knocked down your door and attacked you; My uncle was in a bad car accident and he was in *peril* of dying, but he pulled through.

6. (garbage); Please place all *refuse* in the trashcan.

Reading Warm-up B, p. 130

Sample Answers

1. sitting atop, ride; His *steed* would be strong and fast, and it might be all white with a black diamond on its forehead.

2. (leaders); Egyptian pharaohs made the *masses* build huge pyramids for them.

3. (much stronger British army); I had a feeling of *dread* when I had to give a speech in front of the school assembly.

4. New buildings began rising up everywhere. Docks for ships, stretched out into the sea; Our basement was *transfigured* into a family room and playroom after the renovation.

5. (people, industry); In a *teeming* city, lots of people would be going into and coming out of buildings, jamming the sidewalks, and crowding into the buses and subways.

6. freedom should extend to all; My friends and I followed our *consciences* when we decided not to join some other groups making mischief after the football game.

Poetry Collection: Emma Lazarus, Henry Wadsworth Longfellow, Paul Laurence Dunbar

Reading: Reread to Paraphrase, p. 131

Sample paraphrase of "The New Colossus": Unlike the giant bronze statue on the Greek island of Rhodes, with its image of conquest, the statue on our shores is a mighty but motherly woman. As she looks out at the harbor between two cities, she holds a torch that welcomes immigrants. She seems to tell the nations of the Old World to keep their stuffy ceremony. This statue instead asks for poor outcasts who yearn to live more freely.

Sample paraphrase of "Harriet Beecher Stowe": Stowe's courageous book *Uncle Tom's Cabin* helped many people emotionally understand the cruelty of slavery. With her book, she awakened their consciences. The book's message of freedom affected both black and white Americans at all economic levels. Her book told people what to do and foretold events. The conflict between blacks and whites changed both. Blessed be this daring woman. She brought both freedom to blacks and fame to herself.

Literary Analysis: Lyric and Narrative Poetry, p. 132

A. Lyric Poem Title: "Harriet Beecher Stowe" or "The New Colossus"

1. It has one speaker who expresses his or her feelings and thoughts.

2. Among the emotions students may identify for "The New Colossus" are patriotism, sympathy for the oppressed, admiration for the statue, and contempt for Old World pomp and snobbery; for "Harriet Beecher Stowe," admiration for Stowe, love of freedom, sympathy for the oppressed, and brotherhood toward people of all races.

3. *Images in "The New Colossus" and their ideas:* conquering limbs astride from land to land to describe the Colossus of Rhodes as pompous; golden door as an image of America as a welcoming place; *Images in "Harriet Beecher Stowe" and their ideas:* freedom's clear reveille sweeping from hovels to thrones to summarize the book's effects on the powerful and powerless alike; justice depicted as a sword coming from its sheath to conquer injustice; two peoples in the fiery wave to describe the book's effects on both white and black Americans.

4. *Main impression of "The New Colossus":* The Statue of Liberty represents America's welcome to those who must leave their homelands; *Main impression of "Harriet Beecher Stowe":* In writing *Uncle Tom's Cabin,* Stowe had a revolutionary effect on American history.

B. Narrative Poem Title: "Paul Revere's Ride"

1. It tells a story.

2. Paul Revere learns when and where the British troops are coming and rides through the night to warn the colonists in the villages and farms of Massachusetts.

3. The conflict is Revere's efforts in fighting the British (during the American Revolution). He succeeds in warning the colonists before the British advance.

4. the Massachusetts colony on the night of April 18, 1775

5. Paul Revere is the main character. Minor characters include his friend, the people he warns, and the British troops.

Vocabulary Builder, p. 133

A. 1. The mood at a funeral is usually *somber.*

2. A powerful person might feel *complacent* about his or her future.

3. A shocking accident may leave someone *aghast.*

4. The adjective *yearning* describes a person who craves a piece of candy.

B. 1. A; 2. C; 3. D; 4. D

Enrichment: American Heroes, p. 136

A. 1. Among the many possible traits students may name are perseverance, self-reliance, ambition, desire to help others, and patriotism.

2. Students should recognize that in times past, women had fewer opportunities outside the home.

3. Students should support their opinions with concrete examples.

4. Students are likely to feel that it is important to have heroes to knit together a society, instill pride, serve as role models for youngsters, and embody the values and achievements of that society.

5. Students who think our idea of heroism will change may suggest that valued achievements do change over time as science advances and new needs or dangers are faced. Students who think our idea of heroism will not change are likely to focus on the enduring values that heroes embody rather than on the specific achievements they attain.

B. Responses will vary, but students should offer support for calling the person heroic.

Poetry Collections: Robert Hayden, William Shakespeare, Ricardo Sánchez; Emma Lazarus, Henry Wadsworth Longfellow, Paul Laurence Dunbar

Build Language Skills: Vocabulary, p. 137

Word Origins

A. 1. It makes clear that a corral is often circular.

2. Lyric poetry is often musical.

3. A television pundit should display in-depth knowledge of the subject he or she discusses.

4. It suggests that the fascinating thing works in an almost magical way to absorb your attention.

B. 1. T; 2. F; 3. T; 4. F; 5. F

Build Language Skills: Grammar, p. 138

Prepositions and Prepositional Phrases

A. 1. preposition: of; object: poetry; phrase: of poetry; modifies *study;* adjective

2. preposition: between; object: lines; phrase: between the lines; modifies *read;* adverb

3. preposition: by; object: poet; phrase: by an African American poet; modifies *poem;* adjective

4. preposition: after; object: Civil War; phrase: after the Civil War; modifies *wrote;* adverb

5. preposition: with; object: me; phrase: with me; modifies *read;* adverb

B. Sample expanded sentences:

1. The dog with black spots barked all night.
2. The moonlight streamed through the garden.
3. We sat together on an old stone bench.

Poetry Collection: Emma Lazarus, Henry Wadsworth Longfellow, Paul Laurence Dunbar

Selection Test A, p. 139

Critical Reading

1. ANS: B	DIF: Easy	OBJ: Comprehension
2. ANS: A	DIF: Easy	OBJ: Reading
3. ANS: B	DIF: Easy	OBJ: Interpretation
4. ANS: D	DIF: Easy	OBJ: Literary Analysis
5. ANS: C	DIF: Easy	OBJ: Interpretation
6. ANS: B	DIF: Easy	OBJ: Reading
7. ANS: B	DIF: Easy	OBJ: Comprehension
8. ANS: A	DIF: Easy	OBJ: Literary Analysis
9. ANS: A	DIF: Easy	OBJ: Literary Analysis
10. ANS: D	DIF: Easy	OBJ: Comprehension
11. ANS: B	DIF: Easy	OBJ: Interpretation
12. ANS: C	DIF: Easy	OBJ: Reading

Vocabulary and Grammar

13. ANS: A	DIF: Easy	OBJ: Vocabulary
14. ANS: A	DIF: Easy	OBJ: Vocabulary
15. ANS: B	DIF: Easy	OBJ: Grammar

Essay

16. Students should explain that "Paul Revere's Ride" takes place in New England one night at the start of the American Revolution. They should identify Paul Revere as the main character. They should explain the reason Revere makes his famous ride and sum up the route he took.

Difficulty: *Easy*
Objective: *Essay*

17. Students who discuss Revere should recognize that Revere's courage in warning his fellow colonists of the approaching British troops helped get the American Revolution off to a successful start. Those who discuss Stowe should recognize that her book *Uncle Tom's Cabin* helped sway public sympathy against slavery at the time of the Civil War. Students should cite specific details from the poems to support their ideas about the figure they discuss.

Difficulty: *Easy*
Objective: *Essay*

Selection Test B, p. 142

Critical Reading

1. ANS: D	DIF: Average	OBJ: Interpretation
2. ANS: C	DIF: Average	OBJ: Comprehension
3. ANS: A	DIF: Challenging	OBJ: Reading
4. ANS: A	DIF: Average	OBJ: Literary Analysis
5. ANS: B	DIF: Challenging	OBJ: Reading
6. ANS: A	DIF: Average	OBJ: Interpretation
7. ANS: C	DIF: Challenging	OBJ: Comprehension
8. ANS: A	DIF: Average	OBJ: Literary Analysis
9. ANS: D	DIF: Challenging	OBJ: Literary Analysis
10. ANS: A	DIF: Average	OBJ: Literary Analysis
11. ANS: D	DIF: Average	OBJ: Comprehension
12. ANS: D	DIF: Average	OBJ: Reading
13. ANS: C	DIF: Average	OBJ: Literary Analysis

Vocabulary and Grammar

14. ANS: C	DIF: Average	OBJ: Vocabulary
15. ANS: B	DIF: Average	OBJ: Grammar
16. ANS: A	DIF: Average	OBJ: Vocabulary
17. ANS: D	DIF: Average	OBJ: Grammar

Essay

18. Students' essays should recognize that a lyric poem is one in which the speaker expresses his or her thoughts and feelings. They should then prove that either "The New Colossus" or "Harriet Beecher Stowe" is a lyric poem by citing examples of thoughts and feelings expressed by the poem's speaker.

Difficulty: *Average*
Objective: *Essay*

19. Students who discuss Revere should recognize that his courage in warning his fellow colonists of the approaching British troops helped get the American Revolution off to a successful start. Those who discuss Stowe should recognize that her book *Uncle Tom's Cabin* helped sway public sympathy against slavery at the time of the Civil War. Those who discuss the Statue of Liberty should recognize the statue as a symbol of liberty as well as a welcome for newcomers to America's shores. Students should cite specific details from the poems to support their ideas about the two figures they discuss.

Difficulty: *Challenging*
Objective: *Essay*

Poetry Collection: John Updike, N. Scott Momaday, Alice Walker

Vocabulary Warm-up Exercises, p. 146

A. 1. continent
2. swarm
3. shimmer
4. dusk
5. withdraw
6. planes

B. Sample Answers

1. I would not use a *radiator* in a place that had ninety-degree temperatures because I would certainly not need to heat a room.
2. I think that a person might *stiffen* when feeling very afraid.
3. Athletes might wear *parkas* when snow skiing or doing any other sports outside in cold weather.
4. I would only use the word *behold* when I wanted to point out something very special.
5. I can recognize the *accents* of people from Boston, South Carolina, Brooklyn, and Minnesota.
6. Since *cedars* have sweet-smelling wood, it would be good for clothes chests because it would scent the stored clothes.

Reading Warm-up A, p. 147

Sample Answers

1. American; The names of each *continent* are as follows: Africa, Antarctica, Asia, Australia, Europe, North America, South America. (*Note:* some geographers call Europe and Asia, which are joined, Eurasia.)
2. (flashy jewelry); *Shimmer* means "to shine softly with a light that seems to shake."
3. good-looking; Cheekbones can look like *planes* because they can appear to be like flat surfaces.
4. (bees); I saw a *swarm* of people at the opening of last year's biggest movie.
5. as they aged; I had to *withdraw* from the library because I was laughing uncontrollably.
6. (on any summer day); *Dusk* is the beginning of night-time, so people are usually home from work and young children are inside, and listening to music is relaxing in the evening.

Reading Warm-up B, p. 148

Sample Answers

1. historical places; *Behold* means "to look at or observe."
2. (frozen); A person who would *stiffen* would stop moving or move as if it were very difficult to take a step.
3. in the woods behind our house; *Cedars* are tall ever-greens with needles and red-colored wood.

4. (snowshoes); They would wear *parkas*, which are thick, warm coats with hoods, so that they would stay warm in the cold, winter weather.
5. heated the room; I like to put my hands on the *radiator* to warm them.
6. (Bostonians); I have heard these three *accents:* German, Texan, and Brooklyn.

Poetry Collection: John Updike, N. Scott Momaday, Alice Walker

Reading: Read According to Punctuation to Paraphrase, p. 149

Lines 3–5: The earth shines with leaves.

Lines 6–8: The sky shines with rain.

Lines 9–15: Winds that moan as they blow on the mountains carry pollen in the air.

Lines 16–19: Cedars blacken the slopes, as do pines.

Lines 20–28: At dawn, eagles fly above the flat land where light gathers in patches.

Lines 29–31: Grasses shine with a waving light.

Lines 32–36: Shadows shrink and move away like smoke.

Literary Analysis: Imagery, p. 150

Sample imagery for "January": Sight—sun a spark hung thin between the dark and dark; fat snowy footsteps tracked on the floor; parkas piled up near the door; still, frozen river beneath the trees' black lace; low sky; gray air; radiator; *Sound*—radiator purring all day; *Touch*—fat footsteps tracked on the floor; frozen river held still; *Taste*—none; *Smell*—none

Sample imagery for "New World": Sight—earth glitters with leaves; sky glistens with rain; cedars blacken the slope; light gathers in pools; grasses shimmer and shine; *Sound*—winds that low; *Touch*—Pollen is borne on winds; winds that lean upon mountains; eagles hie and hover; shadows withdraw and lie away like smoke; *Smell*—shadows lie away like smoke; *Taste*—none

Sample imagery for "For My Sister Molly . . .": Sight—fairy rooster. . . ; on nights the fire was burning low; as bright [as flowers]; *Sound*—And coached me in my songs of Africa; spoke in accents never heard; *Touch*—a fairy rooster from Mashed potatoes; when the sun was hot; the children's questions . . . Pouring; braided Hair; Frowned on wasp bites; *Smell*—And smelled as good as [flowers]; *Taste*—a fairy rooster from Mashed potatoes; green onions were his tail; waking up the story buds Like fruit

Vocabulary Builder, p. 151

A. 1. T; 2. F; 3. T

B. 1. A; 2. A; 3. B

C. 1. B; 2. A; 3. C

Enrichment: The Pulitzer Prize, p. 154

1. Since he left money to make a positive impact, he must have felt grateful, proud, and patriotic.
2. He probably thought journalism was important and wanted to do something for the field in which he worked most of his life.
3. Winning a Pulitzer Prize would get a writer more attention and respect, which in turn would help sell his or her books.
4. No, Pulitzer Prizes are for American journalism, arts, and letters.

Selection Test A, p. 155

Critical Reading

1. ANS: A	DIF: Easy	OBJ: Comprehension
2. ANS: A	DIF: Easy	OBJ: Literary Analysis
3. ANS: C	DIF: Easy	OBJ: Reading
4. ANS: C	DIF: Easy	OBJ: Interpretation
5. ANS: B	DIF: Easy	OBJ: Comprehension
6. ANS: A	DIF: Easy	OBJ: Reading
7. ANS: B	DIF: Easy	OBJ: Literary Analysis
8. ANS: D	DIF: Easy	OBJ: Reading
9. ANS: C	DIF: Easy	OBJ: Interpretation
10. ANS: A	DIF: Easy	OBJ: Literary Analysis

Vocabulary and Grammar

11. ANS: A	DIF: Easy	OBJ: Vocabulary
12. ANS: D	DIF: Easy	OBJ: Vocabulary
13. ANS: B	DIF: Easy	OBJ: Grammar

Essay

14. Students will probably write a sentence or separate paragraph for each stanza of the poem they choose—for "New World," four sentences or paragraphs; for "For My Sister Molly Who . . . ," three. They should restate the basic content of the poem using simpler language and sentence structures. They should add words to elliptical structures and clarify figurative language—for example, adding *She* before "Knew all the written things" and restating "waking up the story buds" as something such as "interesting us in stories." They should also eliminate repetition, such as the repetition of *moon* in the final sentence of "New World."

Difficulty: *Easy*
Objective: *Essay*

15. Students should recognize that Updike's description features not only cold temperatures but also short days and a cessation of the growing season. Those who live in more northerly climate zones are likely to find more in

common with Updike's description, but even those in warmer, more southerly areas should recognize that days are shorter in winter.

Difficulty: *Easy*
Objective: *Essay*

Selection Test B, p. 158

Critical Reading

1. ANS: A	DIF: Average	OBJ: Comprehension
2. ANS: D	DIF: Average	OBJ: Interpretation
3. ANS: A	DIF: Challenging	OBJ: Literary Analysis
4. ANS: C	DIF: Average	OBJ: Literary Analysis
5. ANS: B	DIF: Average	OBJ: Reading
6. ANS: B	DIF: Average	OBJ: Interpretation
7. ANS: D	DIF: Average	OBJ: Comprehension
8. ANS: C	DIF: Average	OBJ: Literary Analysis
9. ANS: D	DIF: Average	OBJ: Reading
10. ANS: B	DIF: Average	OBJ: Interpretation
11. ANS: A	DIF: Average	OBJ: Reading
12. ANS: D	DIF: Average	OBJ: Interpretation
13. ANS: D	DIF: Challenging	OBJ: Reading

Vocabulary and Grammar

14. ANS: A	DIF: Average	OBJ: Vocabulary
15. ANS: C	DIF: Average	OBJ: Vocabulary
16. ANS: B	DIF: Average	OBJ: Grammar
17. ANS: D	DIF: Average	OBJ: Grammar

Essay

18. Students should recognize that Molly is a creative, kind, and entertaining older sister with a strong interest in literature and culture. They should cite details to support their conclusions, such as Molly's making the fairy rooster, Molly's never refusing to answer the speaker's many questions, Molly's knowing Hamlet well and loving to read "Sam McGee from Tennessee," and Molly's telling stories.

Difficulty: *Average*
Objective: *Essay*

19. Students who choose "January" should explain how particular images help convey the speaker's appreciation of the cold winter beauty and the cozy warmth inside. Those who choose "New World" should explain how particular images help convey the speaker's admiration for the lush landscape. Those who choose

"For My Sister Molly . . ." should explain how particular images help convey the gratitude and admiration that the speaker feels for Molly.

Difficulty: *Average*
Objective: *Essay*

Poetry Collection: Amy Ling, Wendy Rose,
E. E. Cummings

Vocabulary Warm-up Exercises, p. 162

A. 1. century
2. eldest
3. delicious
4. image
5. perch
6. twinkling

B. Sample Answers
1. F. A *woodpecker* will only live in areas with trees, since that is how it gets its food.
2. T. Because most people are at work or school on weekday mornings, you aren't as likely to experience *jostling* then.
3. F. *Slippered* feet are not appropriate for a hike, or even the outdoors, because feet in slippers would be wearing soft, light shoes instead of sturdy, hard-soled shoes.
4. F. Mother Nature does give us *exquisite* gifts, but earthquakes are not among them because they are disastrous, not enjoyable and delightful.
5. T. Since these things can all be bluish-green, you could use *aqua* to describe them.
6. T. A *humorous* line would be a funny line, which could make you laugh aloud.

Reading Warm-up A, p. 163

Sample Answers
1. to be so admired just for doing what a giant sea turtle does best; What is *delicious* to me is a long, hot shower.
2. (size); An *image* is a representation of something; in this case, it's what the people see when they look at the turtle.
3. flying; A good place for a bird to *perch* would be on a limb that is high off the ground.
4. (more than eighty years); The *eldest* member of our family is my ninety-year-old grandmother, who is still very active in her retirement home.
5. fireworks; I have seen the lights of airplanes that have been *twinkling* in the dark sky.
6. (year); The turtle saw the beginning of the twenty-first *century* (the year 2000).

Reading Warm-up B, p. 164
Sample Answers
1. smile; The most *exquisite* nonverbal communication I have seen was a father hugging his baby with a lot of tenderness.
2. (serious); I heard a very *humorous* opening act during a late-night television show last weekend.
3. ocean; *Aqua* means "bluish-green in color."
4. (mimes try to avoid creating any sounds); My *slippered* feet are covered in thick, black socks, with fur trim.
5. (a scene); Since *jostling* involves pushing and shoving, you can imagine that people might be speaking angrily. Also, you could hear things like backpacks and purses bumping around.
6. watching a mime perform; The work of a *woodpecker* is noisily drilling holes into trees with its beak to get its food (insects).

Poetry Collection: Amy Ling, Wendy Rose,
E. E. Cummings

Reading: Read According to Punctuation to Paraphrase, p. 165

Lines 3–4: I suddenly felt dizzy.

Lines 5–9: Colorful flowers were moving before my eyes or twinkling as they moved toward my side and seemed like pushy but gorgeous faces looking up at me.

Line 10: They seemed like floating hands touching me.

Lines 11–16: The experience made me feel as if I were dancing and seemed to send me up to the sky with the stars and the moon.

Lines 17–18: Dear girl, how crazy I felt when I heard you.

Lines 18–23: How I cried when I heard your sweet voice on the phone, seeming to overcome the laws of time and nature.

Literary Analysis: Imagery, p. 166

Sample imagery for "Grandma Ling": Sight—deep hole; aqua paper-covered door; *Sound*—I heard her slippered foot softly measure the tatami floor with even step; *Touch*—not strong enough to dig that hole; stretched her arms; I could hug her; *Smell*—none; *Taste*—none

Sample imagery for "Drum Song": Sight—flat round feet of four claws each; red head; a line of mountains with blankets on their hips; *Sound*—a shake of gourds; *Touch*—go slow, so steady; lift your red head; a shake of gourds; *Smell*—none; *Taste*—none

Sample imagery for "Your Little Voice": Sight—wee skipping high-heeled flames; twinkling; pale important stars;

Sound—little voice over the wires came leaping; shouting of merry flowers; *Touch*—jostling of merry flowers; floating hands were laid upon me; whirled and tossed; delicious dancing; *Smell*—none; *Taste*—delicious dancing

Vocabulary Builder, p. 167

A. 1. T; 2. T; 3. F
B. 1. B; 2. A; 3. B
C. 1. B; 2. A; 3. C

Enrichment: The Telegraph and the Telephone, p. 170

A. 1. It allowed communications over great distances in a short time.
2. It lets the communicating parties hear each other in real time; it also lets many people use the wires at the same time.
3. Some people probably were delighted by them.
4. the speaker's excitement on hearing a beloved on the phone
B. Answers will vary.

Poetry Collections: John Updike, N. Scott Momaday, Alice Walker; Amy Ling, Wendy Rose, E. E. Cummings

Build Language Skills: Vocabulary, p. 171
Word Origins and Related Words

A. 1. You will not be able to cope with changing times if you are not able to change somewhat yourself.
2. The musical version would have songs and probably also dancing.
3. You need to be able to change the prong so that it fits the socket.
4. A person who visits new places needs to be able to make changes that help him or her fit in to the new location.
B. 1. restate; 2. convey; 3. reflect; 4. emphasize; 5. adapt

Build Language Skills: Grammar, p. 172
Infinitives and Infinitive Phrases

A. 1. to read poetry aloud; noun, serves as direct object (of *like*).
2. to recite poetry with a strong rhythm; adverb, modifies *easiest*
3. to do a poetry reading; adjective, modifies *assignment*
4. to set the poem to music; noun, serves as subject
5. to rehearse twice; adverb, modifies *able*
B. Sample Answers
1. I really want to get more exercise.
2. It is fun to go for long walks in good weather.
3. My cousin gave me tips to improve my stamina.

Poetry Collection: Amy Ling, Wendy Rose, E. E. Cummings

Selection Test A, p. 173
Critical Reading

1. ANS: B	DIF: Easy	OBJ: Comprehension
2. ANS: C	DIF: Easy	OBJ: Interpretation
3. ANS: A	DIF: Easy	OBJ: Literary Analysis
4. ANS: A	DIF: Easy	OBJ: Reading
5. ANS: D	DIF: Easy	OBJ: Comprehension
6. ANS: D	DIF: Easy	OBJ: Literary Analysis
7. ANS: B	DIF: Easy	OBJ: Reading
8. ANS: A	DIF: Easy	OBJ: Interpretation
9. ANS: D	DIF: Easy	OBJ: Comprehension
10. ANS: B	DIF: Easy	OBJ: Interpretation
11. ANS: A	DIF: Easy	OBJ: Reading
12. ANS: B	DIF: Easy	OBJ: Literary Analysis

Vocabulary and Grammar

13. ANS: A	DIF: Easy	OBJ: Vocabulary
14. ANS: C	DIF: Easy	OBJ: Vocabulary
15. ANS: D	DIF: Easy	OBJ: Grammar

Essay

16. Students will probably write four sentences or short paragraphs, one for each stanza of the poem. They should restate the basic content of each stanza, using simpler language and sentence structures—for example, using "tree" for "vertical earth / of tree bark and / branch." They should add words that are implied but not stated, such as "your whiskers dance *from the* bush to *the* burrow."
Difficulty: *Easy*
Objective: *Essay*
17. Students who discuss "Grandma Ling" should recognize that the speaker loves her grandmother and feels connected to her even though they cannot use language to communicate. Those who discuss "Your Little Voice" should recognize that the speaker is probably addressing a beloved and is amazed and delighted by the telephone's ability to carry the voice over the wires.
Difficulty: *Easy*
Objective: *Essay*

Selection Test B, p. 176
Critical Reading

1. ANS: B	DIF: Average	OBJ: Comprehension
2. ANS: C	DIF: Average	OBJ: Reading
3. ANS: D	DIF: Average	OBJ: Interpretation

4. ANS: B	DIF: Challenging	OBJ: Literary Analysis
5. ANS: A	DIF: Challenging	OBJ: Literary Analysis
6. ANS: A	DIF: Average	OBJ: Interpretation
7. ANS: C	DIF: Average	OBJ: Reading
8. ANS: D	DIF: Challenging	OBJ: Literary Analysis
9. ANS: A	DIF: Average	OBJ: Interpretation
10. ANS: B	DIF: Average	OBJ: Interpretation
11. ANS: D	DIF: Challenging	OBJ: Literary Analysis
12. ANS: D	DIF: Average	OBJ: Literary Analysis
13. ANS: B	DIF: Average	OBJ: Reading

Vocabulary and Grammar

14. ANS: B	DIF: Average	OBJ: Vocabulary
15. ANS: A	DIF: Average	OBJ: Vocabulary
16. ANS: A	DIF: Average	OBJ: Grammar
17. ANS: D	DIF: Average	OBJ: Grammar

Essay

18. Students should recognize the positive view of nature presented in the poem and the central idea that all animals, including human beings, are part of nature and follow nature's rhythm in order to survive and prosper. They should cite details from the first three stanzas that show the actions of the turtle, the woodpecker, and the snowhare, respectively, and should then point out the similarity of human beings implied by making the final stanza parallel to the other three.

Difficulty: *Average*

Objective: *Essay*

19. Students should note that both poems use strong images and should cite examples. They should recognize that both poems use images to convey a positive attitude toward their subject—Grandma Ling in one case, the person addressed and the telephone in the other. "Grandma Ling" is more direct in conveying its speaker's emotions and attitude, while "Your Little Voice" relies on images that require more interpretation by the reader.

Difficulty: *Challenging*

Objective: *Essay*

Poetry by Robert Frost and Walt Whitman

Vocabulary Warm-up Exercises, p. 180

A. 1. flung
2. grim
3. fearful
4. trodden
5. swaying
6. victor

B. Sample Answers

1. T. People often send bunches of flower, or *bouquets*, to loved ones.
2. T. If a bird *trills* loud enough, it could wake you if were asleep at five in the morning.
3. F. A desert has no trees, so there can be no *undergrowth*, or bushes and plants growing underneath them.
4. F. *Mournful* music would make you sad or sadder.
5. T. If your eleven o'clock curfew started today, hence, you should be home before eleven.
6. F. Both children have a *claim* on your attention.

Reading Warm-up A, p. 181

Sample Answers

1. (harsh, gloomy); After the hurricane, the scenes of the beach looked *grim*.
2. The snow had been coming down for hours, and now the winds had reached blizzard speed.; Last summer, we escaped a *fearful* tornado when we were visiting family in Iowa.
3. (wrapped); A glass bowl that was *flung* would break into pieces.
4. (walked); Doreen walked along the shoulder of the road through snow that no one else had *trampled*.
5. (the wind); The little girl laughed as she sat on the *swaying* swing.
6. saved the most travelers stranded in the blizzard; I was a *victor* last season when our softball team won all our games.

Reading Warm-up B, p. 182

Sample Answers

1. (the country, death); My friends and softball practice both have a *claim* on my afternoons.
2. death, funeral; An event where crowds would be joyous or happy—the opposite of *mournful*—is a Fourth of July parade.
3. (beneath towering trees); Some things you might find in the *undergrowth* are shrubs, reeds, flowers, weeds, and grass.
4. spring flowers; People might bring *bouquets* to someone's house when they are invited to dinner.
5. (bugle, notes, tune); A bird *trills* when it sings its song.
6. (time); However, it would be a long time *from this point* before that healing would begin.

Literary Analysis: Comparing Types of Description, p. 183

Sample Answers

2. grassy and wanted wear = the less popular route through life

3. Captain = Lincoln; trip = Civil War; ship = United States; rack = hard times; prize = peace and union

4. My Captain . . . my father—Lincoln; does not answer; no pulse = death

Vocabulary Builder, p. 184

A. Sample Answers

1. synonym—divided; antonym—converged; sentence— The road I was traveling on diverged and I was not sure which way to go.

2. synonym—rejoicing; antonym—mourning; sentence—Exulting over my *A* on the final exam, I reminded myself how smart it was of me to study hard.

B. 1. B; 2. C

Selection Test A, p. 186

Critical Reading

1. ANS: A	DIF: Easy	OBJ: Comprehension
2. ANS: B	DIF: Easy	OBJ: Interpretation
3. ANS: C	DIF: Easy	OBJ: Comprehension
4. ANS: D	DIF: Easy	OBJ: Interpretation
5. ANS: B	DIF: Easy	OBJ: Literary Analysis
6. ANS: D	DIF: Easy	OBJ: Literary Analysis
7. ANS: C	DIF: Easy	OBJ: Literary Analysis
8. ANS: D	DIF: Easy	OBJ: Comprehension
9. ANS: C	DIF: Easy	OBJ: Comprehension
10. ANS: A	DIF: Easy	OBJ: Literary Analysis
11. ANS: B	DIF: Easy	OBJ: Interpretation
12. ANS: A	DIF: Easy	OBJ: Interpretation
13. ANS: A	DIF: Easy	OBJ: Literary Analysis

Vocabulary

14. ANS: A	DIF: Easy	OBJ: Vocabulary
15. ANS: D	DIF: Easy	OBJ: Vocabulary

Essay

16. Literal meaning is the actual, everyday meaning of words. The literal meaning in "The Road Not Taken" is a person reflecting on the road he took when the roads diverged in the woods. The person chose to take the road that was least traveled. The literal meaning in "O Captain! My Captain!" is the death of a ship's captain after he brought the ship safely back from a dangerous journey. The speaker of this poem is mourning the death of his beloved Captain.

Difficulty: *Easy*

Objective: *Essay*

17. The figurative meaning of an image relies on figures of speech and the symbolic nature of language. In "The Road Not Taken" the two roads symbolize making important decisions, the traveler is the person making the decision, and the road less traveled represents his choice. In "O Captain! My Captain!" the Captain is Abraham Lincoln, the ship is the United States, the voyage is the Civil War, and the port is peace after the war.

Difficulty: *Easy*

Objective: *Essay*

Selection Test B, p. 189

Critical Reading

1. ANS: B	DIF: Average	OBJ: Literary Analysis
2. ANS: D	DIF: Average	OBJ: Literary Analysis
3. ANS: A	DIF: Average	OBJ: Comprehension
4. ANS: D	DIF: Average	OBJ: Interpretation
5. ANS: C	DIF: Average	OBJ: Interpretation
6. ANS: C	DIF: Average	OBJ: Literary Analysis
7. ANS: C	DIF: Average	OBJ: Comprehension
8. ANS: D	DIF: Average	OBJ: Literary Analysis
9. ANS: A	DIF: Average	OBJ: Literary Analysis
10. ANS: B	DIF: Challenging	OBJ: Interpretation
11. ANS: B	DIF: Challenging	OBJ: Comprehension
12. ANS: A	DIF: Average	OBJ: Interpretation
13. ANS: C	DIF: Challenging	OBJ: Literary Analysis

Vocabulary

14. ANS: B	DIF: Average	OBJ: Vocabulary
15. ANS: C	DIF: Average	OBJ: Vocabulary
16. ANS: A	DIF: Average	OBJ: Vocabulary

Essay

17. The speaker in "The Road Not Taken" tells of a decision that is represented by two roads dividing in the woods. Students may say that the speaker in "The Road Not Taken" may feel curiosity but not regret about the path he did not choose. The speaker in "O Captain! My Captain!" writes a eulogy comparing Lincoln to the captain of a ship. The speaker saw Lincoln as a great leader who preserved the union.

Difficulty: *Average*

Objective: *Essay*

18. Analogy is a type of figurative description that compares two or more things that are similar in some ways but otherwise unalike. In "The Road Not Taken," Frost creates an analogy between choosing between two roads in a wood and making important decisions in the course of one's life. The traveler is a person with a decision to make, the roads are the choices, and the less traveled path is the less conventional path that the speaker chose. In "O Captain! My Captain!" Whitman uses analogy to mourn the death of President Lincoln. Lincoln is the captain of a ship, the ship is America, the voyage is the Civil War, and the port is the peace that comes after war. Both authors create believable literal pictures that successfully lead to the deeper meanings found in each poem.

Difficulty: *Average*
Objective: *Essay*

Writing Workshop—Unit 4, Part 2

Comparison-and-Contrast Essay: Integrating Grammar Skills, p. 193

A 1. prepositional phrase
   2. noun
   3. prepositional phrase
   4. adjective
B. Answers may vary.
   1. In the tomb, was the mummy of King Tutankhamen.
   2. Preserved by Egypt's dry climate, the body was in excellent condition.
   3. Wearing a mask of solid gold, King Tut looked magnificent!
   4. In King Tut's tomb, archaeologists found objects to study.

Spelling Workshop—Unit 4

Words With Prefixes and Suffixes, p. 194

A 1. correspondence; 2. irresponsible; 3. impatient; 4. questionable; 5. performance; 6. cooperate; 7. existence; 8. reversible

B Sample Answer
   1. Some irresponsible characters claim to be related to a wealthy relative who is deceased. When the will is read there is no mention of their existence and they receive no inheritance.
   2. An impatient person often will not cooperate when a lengthy waiting period is required. He may demand that the waiting period be reversible and feel that the amount of time's questionable.

3. The perishable fruit arrived on time due to the performance of the shipping company. Any correspondence about the shipment will be sent to the owners of the company.

Unit 4, Part 2 Answers

Benchmark Test 8, p. 197

MULTIPLE CHOICE

1. ANS: C
2. ANS: B
3. ANS: A
4. ANS: D
5. ANS: B
6. ANS: C
7. ANS: A
8. ANS: C
9. ANS: A
10. ANS: B
11. ANS: C
12. ANS: B
13. ANS: D
14. ANS: C
15. ANS: A
16. ANS: D
17. ANS: A
18. ANS: B
19. ANS: A
20. ANS: A
21. ANS: B
22. ANS: C
23. ANS: A
24. ANS: B
25. ANS: C
26. ANS: C
27. ANS: B
28. ANS: C
29. ANS: B
30. ANS: A

ESSAY

31. Students' first lines should clearly show whether the poem is to be a lyric or a narrative poem. The first line for a lyric poem should create an impression of the river

by describing at least two details about it; the first line for a narrative poem should describe the setting and a main character.

32. Students should identify one example each of specific words and imagery from one of the poems in this test. They should clearly state whether they think the poet uses these effectively in the poem and should give supporting reasons for their opinions.

33. Students should list details that clearly address the writing prompt. They should include at least two similarities and two differences for each mode of travel. The similarities might include that both modes of travel can be exciting and that both afford interesting perspectives; differences might include that travel by car is slower and less convenient than travel by plane and that travel by car affords a better sense of the changing country than does travel by plane.

CURRICULUM